A SPIRIT THAT IMPELS

A SPIRIT THAT IMPELS

Play, Creativity, and Psychoanalysis

Edited by

M. Gerard Fromm

KARNAC

First published in 2014 by
Karnac Books Ltd
118 Finchley Road, London NW3 5HT

British Library Cataloguing in Publication Data

A C.I.P. for this book is available from the British Library

ISBN 978 1 78049 158 5

Edited, designed and produced by The Studio Publishing Services Ltd
www.publishingservicesuk.co.uk
e-mail: studio@publishingservicesuk.co.uk

www.karnacbooks.com

CONTENTS

To Edouard, Kevin, Mark, Michael, Paula and Sandy
To Paula, Anna, and Leo
To Joan and Erik

ACKNOWLEDGEMENTS

Many of the chapters that follow have been previously published in slightly revised form elsewhere. I am grateful to the publishers for their kind permission to collect them in this volume.

Chapter One, by Christopher Bollas, was previously published under the same title in *The Mystery of Things* (1999, pp. 167–180). It is being reprinted here with the permission of Taylor and Francis Books UK.

Chapters Two and Three, by Carol Gilligan and me respectively, were originally published under the same titles in *Hawthorne Revisited* (2004, pp. 83–91 and 99–112). David Scribner edited this volume for the Lenox Library Association, University Press of New England: Hanover, NH.

Chapter Four, by John Muller, was originally published under the same title in *The Psychoanalytic Quarterly*, LXXVII: 569–596, 2008, John Wiley and Sons.

Chapter Six, by Marilyn Charles and Karen Tellis, was originally published under the same title in *American Journal of Psychoanalysis*, 2009, *69*: 238–262, reprinted by permission from Macmillan Publishers, published by Palgrave Macmillan.

Chapter Seven was originally published under the same title in *The Facilitating Environment: Clinical Application of Winnicott's Theory*, which I edited with Bruce L. Smith, PhD, in 1989 (pp. 279–314), reprinted here by permission of International Universities Press.

Chapter Eight, by Ellen Handler Spitz, was originally published under the same title in *American Imago, 67*(1): 101–115, 2010, The Johns Hopkins University Press.

Chapter Nine was originally published under the same title in my book, *Taking the Transference, Reaching toward Dreams: Clinical Studies in the Intermediate Area,* 2012 (pp. 102–122), reprinted here by permission of Karnac.

Chapter Ten, by Joshua Wolf Shenk, was originally published in *Slate Magazine* and will also be featured in his forthcoming book, *Powers of Two: Finding the Essence of Innovation in Creative Pairs,* published by Houghton Mifflin Harcourt. It is reprinted here by permission of the author and his editor.

Chapter Twelve was originally published under the same title in *The Journal of Aesthetic Education*, University of Illinois Press, Winter, 2013, reprinted here by permission.

As the reader will see, this volume owes its inspiration to the many artists, scholars, clinicians, and seminar members who have made the Erikson Institute's annual Creativity Seminar a thrilling experience of engagement and learning. I am particularly indebted to the teachers and students in the Austen Riggs Center's Activities Department, whose passion for their creative work has an incandescent effect on all we do in this therapeutic community. I also want to thank Dr Nick Holliday for his imaginative contributions to the early Creativity Seminars, for his moving presentation in honour of our late colleague, Dr Yasmin Roberts, and for his sharing an image from his own artwork for the cover of this book.

Once again, I am very grateful to Lee Watroba, Program Manager of the Erikson Institute, for her enthusiastic and always reliable support for this project and for managing me with such a light and caring touch. And finally—once again and ever—I am very grateful to Maryjane Fromm, who knows how to create spaces of such beauty but also of such warmth and liveability. Her spirit impels probably less than it should, but it always inspires.

Christopher Bollas is a member of the British Psychoanalytical Society. He was Director of Education at the Austen Riggs Center in the mid 1980s and has been Professor of English at the University of Massachusetts and Visiting Professor of Psychoanalysis at the University of Rome (1978–1998). He is the author of many books, including *The Shadow of the Object*, and *The Mystery of Things*. His most recent publication is *Catch Them Before They Fall: The Psychoanalysis of Breakdown*. He is currently writing a book on schizophrenia.

Marilyn Charles is a staff psychologist at the Austen Riggs Center and a psychoanalyst in private practice. A training and consulting analyst at the Michigan Psychoanalytic Council and the Chicago Center for Psychoanalysis, she is a Contributing Editor of *Psychoanalysis, Culture, and Society*. She is incoming President of the APA Division of Psychoanalysis (39), Co-Chair of the Association for the Psychoanalysis of Culture and Society (APCS), and Co-Chair of the Division 39 Early Career Committee. She is also an artist and poet, and the author of four books, including *Patterns: Building Blocks of Experience*, and the forthcoming *The Stories We Live: Life, Literature, and Psychoanalysis*.

Christopher Fowler is Associate Director of Clinical Research at The Menninger Clinic and formerly the Director of Research at the Austen Riggs Center. As a clinical psychologist and researcher, Dr Fowler has lectured extensively in the USA and has many publications in the areas of personality disorders, suicide, and psychotherapy outcomes. He is a nationally recognised psychological assessment researcher and currently serves as a consulting editor for *Psychotherapy* and *The Bulletin of the Menninger Clinic*.

M. Gerard Fromm directed the Erikson Institute for Education and Research at the Austen Riggs Center for many years, where he is currently Senior Consultant. He teaches at a number of psychoanalytic institutes and is on the faculties of the Massachusetts Institute for Psychoanalysis and the Yale Child Study Center. He is the editor of *The Facilitating Environment: Clinical Applications of Winnicott's Theory* (with Bruce L. Smith, PhD) and *Lost in Transmission: Studies of Trauma across the Generations*. His most recent book, *Taking the Transference, Reaching toward Dreams*, reports on his clinical work at the Center.

Carol Gilligan is currently University Professor of Applied Psychology and the Humanities at the New York University. She taught for many years at Harvard where she held the university's first chair in gender studies. She is best known for her ground-breaking book, *In a Different Voice: Psychological Theory and Women's Development*. Her subsequent books include *The Birth of Pleasure: A New Map of Love*, and *Kyra: A Novel*. She is currently working with her son, Jonathan Gilligan, on *Pearl*, an opera adaptation of *The Scarlet Letter*. A founding member of the Erikson Institute Council of Scholars, she is a leading theorist of the relational dimension of human development.

John Muller is the former Director of Training at the Austen Riggs Center. He is the author of *Beyond the Psychoanalytic Dyad: Developmental Semiotics in Freud, Peirce, and Lacan*, co-author (with W. J. Richardson) of *Lacan and Language: A Reader's Guide to Ecrits*, co-editor (with W. J. Richardson) of *The Purloined Poe: Lacan, Derrida, and Psychoanalytic Reading*, and (with J. Brent) of *Peirce, Semiotics, and Psychoanalysis*. He is a founding member of the Lacanian Clinical Forum and the Berkshire Psychoanalytic Institute, and was the Erikson Scholar at Riggs in 1992–1993.

Joshua Wolf Shenk is an author, essayist, curator, and former Erikson Scholar based in Los Angeles. His book, *Lincoln's Melancholy*, was a *New York Times* Notable Book and a winner of prizes from the Lincoln Institute, the National Alliance for the Mentally Ill, and Mental Health America. *Powers of Two*, an exploration of creative pairs, will be published by Houghton Mifflin Harcourt in February 2014. His essays, articles, and reviews have been published in *The Atlantic*, *Harper's*, *The Economist*, *The New York Times*, and *The New Yorker*. The former director of the Rose O'Neill Literary House and a member of the general counsel of The Moth, he also curates the Arts in Mind series on the arts, creativity, and mental health in New York City.

Ellen Handler Spitz is the author of six books, each of which brings psychological perspectives to bear on the arts and/or on children's aesthetic lives. She is a regular contributor to *The New Republic* and to *Artcritical*. A Fellow of the New York Institute for the Humanities, she was trained as a special research candidate at the Columbia University Center for Psychoanalytic Training and Research. Dr Spitz has held fellowships at the Erikson Institute, the Clark Art Institute, the Getty, the Center for Advanced Study at Stanford, and the Radcliffe (Bunting) Institute, Harvard, among others. Currently, she holds the Honors College Professorship of Visual Arts at the University of Maryland (UMBC).

Karen Telis is an attorney and adjunct professorial lecturer in the Department of Justice, Law, and Society in the School of Public Affairs, American University, Washington, DC, where she has three times been awarded outstanding professor in an adjunct position. Long interested in art history, she served with distinction as French Docent at the National Gallery of Art. Her research on Picasso's painting of the Saltimbanques theme led to an important discovery about his life in his early Paris years, which she fictionalised into a novel. Living in Provence for nearly ten years led to a passion for Van Gogh and his landscapes, which she shares with her sister, Marilyn Charles.

Rochleigh Wholfe has performed on some of the most celebrated stages in the country, including Lincoln Center. Her Chautauqua performance, "My name is Harriet", was presented at the Smithsonian Institute, among other places. She participated in the National Urban

League's 1st Invitational Black Fine Arts Show, founded the first Women's Gallery in St Louis, Missouri, and founded and served as President of the Women's Caucus For Art in the Pioneer Valley, Massachusetts. Founder and Executive Director of her own company, Lotus of the Nile: Art for Conscious Living, her work is in many private collections nationwide. Her first art book, *From the Heart of the Soul: The Intuitive Work of a Visionary Artist*, was recently published.

Introduction

M. Gerard Fromm

Some time ago, a young woman struggling with psychosis approached the open door of her therapist's office for her first session. As she got to the threshold, she stopped and stepped back warily. After a few seconds, she approached again, and again retreated. She studied her therapist from a distance, and on her third approach, he said, "Jump!" She did, and thus her therapy began (Bollas, personal communication).

Erikson reminds us that "of all the formulations of play, the briefest and the best is to be found in Plato's *Laws*". Plato saw "the model of true playfulness in the need of all young creatures, animal and human *to leap*". "To truly leap," Erikson continues,

> you must learn how to use the ground as a springboard, and how to land resiliently and safely. It means to test the leeway allowed by given limits; to outdo and yet not escape gravity . . . (W)herever playfulness prevails, there is always a surprising element. (1977, p. 17)

Erikson should know something about play since he found his life's vocation in Anna Freud's and Dorothy Burlingham's nursery school, a school for the children of the people who had come to Vienna for analysis with Freud. For ten years, the Erikson Institute's annual Creativity Seminar has taken place within shouting—almost jumping—distance of the little red schoolhouse where Erikson's wife, Joan, started a nursery school programme as part of the Austen Riggs Center's Activities Department. The school is staffed by a Montessori-trained teacher, to whom interested patients apprentice themselves as assistant teachers for the dozen or so local three- to five-year-olds who attend every day.

Back across the garden, the Creativity Seminar is held in the conference room where the clinical staff of the Center meets daily to review its work with those patients and the many others who come from all over the country for an unusual but promising treatment programme. It is, indeed, unusual in today's world: intensive psychotherapy in a completely open and voluntary setting. Quite troubled patients are free to come and go from the moment of admission, because they have agreed to take responsibility for themselves, their safety, and their daily lives. To help them with this task, a trained staff joins patients in a therapeutic community in which the patients elect their leadership and both groups share authority for managing daily life.

But there is an important leap beyond managing daily life: creating it, and one venue for that is the Activities Department. Joan Erikson's inventiveness and conviction many years ago led her not only to begin the nursery school programme, but also to imagine a broad programme of creative activities in which artists and craftspersons invite patients into a student or apprenticeship role and set aside the task of interpretation or treatment in favour of deep engagement with one's inner potential—the spirit that impels, so to speak—and whatever raw materials one is drawn to.

This programme was, and still is, the inspiration for the Creativity Seminar, and in turn, the seminar is the inspiration for this volume. Wordsworth's lines from "Tintern Abbey"—which Christopher Bollas quotes in Chapter One and from which we take the title of this book—capture the essence of both: "In the mind of man – / a motion and a spirit that impels / All thinking things, all objects of all thought, / And rolls through all things" (1798, p. 22). The seminar's primary task is learning about the creative process. It is structured as a series of informal presentations or dialogues, alternating between artists opening up their own creative process, scholars taking us into an artist's life and work, and clinicians examining this process through the lens of their work with patients. It is a *working seminar*, which means that the presenters do not have answers to the seminar's questions, except perhaps for themselves; rather, learning comes about through active participation, through everyone's effort to learn together and through attention to the actual experience of the creative process as it is described, felt, and sometimes experimented with in the seminar itself.

Within this primary task, each seminar has a keynote theme, which now forms the structure of this book. The experience of these seminars has been astonishing. There is a cumulative impact from hearing artists describe, and take members into, their creative process. It is invariably real, moving, and utterly fascinating. In one unforgettable exercise, Tina Packer, founder and artistic director of Shakespeare and Co., picked two volunteers from the membership, sat them facing each other—so close that their knees interlocked—and, with her hands on their shoulders, took them into drama by simply asking each one to repeat after her. "Mother" to the man. *"Mother."* "Mother." *"Mother."* "Mother, thou . . ." And in three minutes of riveting, deepening repetitions, one word at a time, *"Mother, thou hast offended."* Then it was Gertrude's turn!

Unlike Hamlet, whose play was a vehicle through which the king's guilt might be revealed, the play of the Creativity Seminar does not "catch the conscience" off guard; rather, it catches the ego off guard. The artists, simply through their genuine efforts to open up their personal creative process, *speak into* the listener, bypassing intellectualisation and critical judgement, and setting up a resonance in members that they *must* contend with. So, they speak back: to the artists, to each other, and to themselves.

And then, they speak collectively in a closing plenary. One person stood up and said that she had been writing poetry for the past few days, and "I've never written a word of poetry before in my life, and I don't know what's happening to me." A spirit that impels can bring anxiety! Another found himself remembering a very upsetting early childhood moment and spontaneously reinterpreting his behaviour with more self-empathy in the light of an artist's work on her own grief. Another person said that he had heard and known that life and creativity were interwoven, "but I encountered it *physically* here. I feel foolish for having tried to accumulate knowledge when this other dimension is so important." At the end of one plenary, a person who had been relatively quiet because English was her second language spoke of the seminar as a "gift from nature" and spontaneously quoted Lao Tzu: "We hammer wood for a house, but it is the inner space that makes it liveable." "I can feel that some internal work is going on," she said.

The seminar becomes an *experiential* event—for the artists, too; one artist said that she had never opened up the connections between her art and her life in the way she had in her dialogue, and she was extremely grateful for what *she* had learnt. This kind of interaction, resonating with the unconscious, generates an experience much more than the sum of its parts. One year, a member's dream about a silver truck coming at her and her lying down in the road so that it—and then the two silver trucks that followed it—would pass over her led us to recognise in the plenary that this was the third and final day of the seminar, and it was time for the members to come out from under it and tell us and themselves how they were doing and what they were learning.

Because it is a summer seminar, which takes place in the Berkshires, there is an amazing array of cultural activities around us and sometimes an explicit link between the seminar and a major event: one year Shakespeare and Co.'s performance of *Hamlet* and another year the Tanglewood opening night performance of Mahler's *8th Symphony*. And the number of artists available to participate is also a great gift: Kate Maguire and Eric Hill of the Berkshire Theater Festival, Rolf Smedvig of the Empire Brass Quintet, the poet Sharon Olds, artists Jo Ann Rothschild and Jarvis Rockwell, opera singers Marquita Lister and Maureen O'Flynn, conductor Stefan Asbury, composers Joan Tower and Michael Gandolfi, dancer Leah Kreutzer Barber, playwrights Lyle Kessler and Mark St Germain, actors Margaret Ladd and Sam Waterston, and many others.

And, of course, Tina Packer, who, like Erikson, regularly brings us back to the Greeks and reminds us that it is to them that we owe the concept of drama as "play"—drama as an exercise of "deep play", as the communal playing out for all of us of the deepest dynamics of human emotion in order that we may leave the theatre not only emotionally spent, but profoundly informed about our humanity—and not infrequently profoundly cautioned as well. Among many other things, Greek drama teaches us that we have met the enemy, and he or she is us!

In Hamlet's play within a play, the king is surprised indeed. To his great chagrin, he sees, on the stage before him, *himself*. Next to Oedipus, Hamlet is Freud's favourite dramatic subject, and, not so surprisingly, he found in Hamlet the drama of Oedipus "in a reflected light" (1928b, p. 189). By that, he meant that

> Hamlet is able to do anything – except take vengeance on the man who did away with his father . . . the man who shows him the repressed wishes of his own childhood realized. Thus, the loathing which should drive him on to revenge is replaced in him by self-reproaches . . . which remind him that he himself is literally no better than the sinner whom he is to punish. (1900a, p. 265)

Freud also notes the context of Shakespeare's life as he was writing Hamlet: immediately following the death of his father, which itself occurred not long after the death of his son, Hamnet. Freud thus brings trauma—and ghosts—into a consideration of this work. The psychoanalyst Jacques Lacan points out that Hamlet's father is poisoned *through the ear* (Gallagher, 2002), and it is through the ear that words—words like the king's, which demand to be taken as the last word—are heard. Words, which should guarantee our relationship to the truth, can also poison it. But Hamlet listens to ghosts as well as to the king's words, and the gathering tension—in one ear and in the other, so to speak—explodes into his cataclysmic effort to restore an order of truth. Erikson thought it essential that the family, "in one of its exemplary forms", help the child with a critical boundary—the distinction between play and "irreversible purpose" (Erikson, 1961, p. 156). Hamlet's play explodes into irreversible purpose, in order that we take in the truths of what's being played out in front of us, so that it not become irreversible purpose in our own lives.

But, of course, there is more to Hamlet than psychoanalysts have dreamed of. Perhaps because drama so deeply inspired Freud, he brought the notion of play into psychoanalysis in his classic paper, "Remembering, repeating and working through" (1914g), in which he makes the startling statement,

> We render the compulsion to repeat harmless, and indeed useful, by giving it the right to assert itself in a definite field. We admit it into the transference as a *playground* in which it is allowed to expand . . . and in which it is expected to display to us everything . . . that is hidden in the patient's mind. (p. 134)

Displaying what was hidden was Hamlet's motive, as it was also Freud's. For both, the medium of revelation was a form of play. How harmless this process is, however, is up for discussion. Later psychoanalytic theorists such as the paediatrician, Donald Winnicott, and the former nursery school teacher, Erik Erikson, elaborated Freud's idea of this "intermediate region" into a broader understanding of play, more in terms of a person's coming into being than their coming out from hiding. For Winnicott (1971), play is the area of primary creativity. But, rather than my elaborating on his theoretical understanding of play, perhaps a bit of drama from his consulting room will suffice.

Joyce McDougall (personal communication) reports a vignette from her days as a psychoanalytic student, during which she and another trainee had the opportunity to visit Winnicott's clinic. Winnicott maintained his paediatric appointment at Paddington Green Hospital for forty years, where, over that time, he met with thousands of infants, mothers, children, fathers, and grandparents for one- or two-session consultations in what he called his "psychiatric snack bar". On this occasion, Winnicott ushered McDougall and her colleague, along with a young mother and her three-year-old son, into his worn, cramped, and scattered playroom. He sat on the floor playing with the child, while also talking with the mother, who was sitting on the couch. She told Winnicott that her ordinarily sweet little boy had suddenly become quite ill-tempered and obstreperous. Worst of all, toilet training was completely set back, and the lad was now worrisomely constipated. The father in this working-class household spent long hours at two jobs, and the boy's mother was at her wits' end.

Back and forth Winnicott went, playing with the little boy and chatting with his mother, as the trainees milled about. McDougall professed to have no idea what was going on; it seemed like chaos to her. Then Winnicott turned to the mother and said, "So how long have you been pregnant?" "What!" she said, "I haven't even told my husband yet!" "Well, *he* knows," Winnicott said, nodding toward the boy. "Go home and talk to him about it, and come back and see me in two weeks." McDougall was astonished. She later learnt that, when the young mother returned, she told Winnicott joyfully that she had had that talk with her son and not only was he great fun again, but "Dr Winnicott, he shits and shits and shits!"

Such is the power of play to communicate the truly essential, and such is the power of communication to create play in the system, even the gastrointestinal system! Winnicott, in his cryptic, elfish way, once described psychotherapy as taking place in "the overlap" between "two people playing together" (1971, p. 38). Whatever he meant by that, it is also the way the Creativity Seminar works. To our great surprise, the Creativity Seminar itself became such an experience for its presenters and members, and it is our hope that this volume both captures some of that engagement as well as stimulates it in the reader.

The central questions of this book are: how do we understand the creative process, what might psychoanalysis contribute to that understanding, what opens up within psychoanalysis by engaging with the subject of creativity, and what perhaps special relation does play have to both? These questions are addressed in the chapters that follow, each based on seminar presentations by scholars, artists, and psychoanalysts. Looking at creativity through a psychoanalytic lens, and, very importantly, *vice versa*, the authors examine great works (*The Scarlet Letter*, Mahler's *Eighth Symphony* and *The Miracle Worker*) as well as great artists (Van Gogh and Lennon/McCartney) for what we might learn about the creative process itself. Deepening this conversation are a number of clinical studies and other reflections on the creative process—in sickness and in health, so to speak. A central theme is that of "deep play", the level at which the spirit "rolls through" and the artist is unconsciously playing out, for all of us, the deepest dynamics of human experience.

References

Erikson, E. (1961). The roots of virtue. In: J. Huxley (Ed.), *The Humanist Frame* (pp. 145–165). New York: Harper.

Erikson, E. (1977). *Toys and Reasons*. New York: Norton.

Freud, S. (1900a). *The Interpretation of Dreams*. S.E., 4. London: Hogarth.

Freud, S. (1914g). Remembering, repeating and working-through, *S. E. 12*: 145–156. London: Hogarth.

Freud, S. (1928b). Dostoevsky and parricide. *S.E., 21*: 175–196. London: Hogarth.

Gallagher, C. (2002). *The Seminar of Jacques Lacan VI: Desire and its Interpretation* (1958–1959). London: Karnac.

Winnicott, D. W. (1971). *Playing and Reality*. New York: Basic Books.

Wordsworth, W. (1798). Lines composed a few miles above Tintern Abbey. In: *Lyrical Ballads, With a Few Other Poems* (pp. 21–24). London: J. & A. Arch.

On (not) being able to paint: the 2003 Creativity Seminar

I n 1950, under the pseudonym Joanna Field, the British psycho-analyst Marion Milner, published one of her several autobio-graphical books. *On Not Being Able to Paint* (1957) focused on the personal experience and serious difficulties encountered by its author in her effort to become a painter. It is a moving, articulate memoir, which lays out for us the human subject in the process of finding her subjectivity, a process of both excitement and peril. Milner, whose theoretical work both stimulated and elaborated Winnicott's ground-breaking studies of early childhood development, introduced from her own experience ideas central to her eventual understanding of creativity and the psychoanalytic process—concepts such as reverie, illusion, and medium.

In that same year, Erik Erikson wrote (in *Childhood and Society*, 1950) that play was "the royal road to the understanding of the . . . ego's efforts at synthesis" (p. 209) and "the most natural self-healing measure childhood affords" (p. 222). A year or so later, he helped his wife establish the activities programme at the Austen Riggs Center, a small psychoanalytically orientated treatment centre, through which the patient's struggle toward creativity inevitably illuminated the personal obstacles to that inner leeway or play in the system Erikson considered essential to health. In linking play to "self-cure" (p. 209) and in inventing an activities programme where artists and craftsmen become intimate teachers to patients-as-students, the Eriksons brought together the creative process and the treatment process.

In Chapter One, Christopher Bollas, one of today's leading theorists at the interface between clinical work and creative life, takes up this interplay. He uses André Breton's experiments in surrealism and his method of the "disinterested *play* of thought" (1934, p. 412, my italics) as a springboard to explore Freud's discovery of free association. He argues that, even though Freud underplayed this discovery in the service of treatment and of his allegiance to science, he had, in fact, discovered the beating heart—the spirit that impels—of the creative, and the self-curative, process. Freely associating between artistic creativity, dream life, and the analytic situation, Bollas describes a transformational—even "transubstantial"—process: "the free associative medium . . . [as] a new medium for self expression. Entering analysis a person will never be the same again".

References

Breton, A. (1934). What is Surrealism? In: H. B. Chipp (Ed.), *Theories of Modern Art* (pp. 410–417). Berkeley, CA: University of California Press.

Erikson, E. (1950). *Childhood and Society.* New York: W. W. Norton.

Milner, M. (1957). *On Not Being Able to Paint.* New York: International Universities Press.

CHAPTER ONE

Creativity and psychoanalysis

Christopher Bollas

I n "What is surrealism?" (1934), André Breton recalled how he "practised occasionally on the sick" (p. 412) during the war, using Freud's "methods of investigation", as he experimented in written monologue by throwing out ideas on paper, followed by critical examination. He invited Philippe Soupault to do this with him and soon they were writing automatically and comparing results. Although, of course, their contents varied, Breton noted that

> there were similar faults of construction, the same hesitant manner, and also, in both cases, an illusion of extraordinary verve, much emotion, and a considerable assortment of images of a quality such as we should never have been able to obtain in the normal way of writing, a very special sense of the picturesque, and, here and there, a few pieces of out-and-out buffoonery. (1934, p. 412)

The writings proved "strange", invested with a "very high degree of *immediate absurdity*" (p. 412). It was out of this experiment with Freud's method that Breton founded surrealism and, when he asked himself to define it, he wrote that it was "pure psychic automatism", which, through the spoken or written word, or some other means of expression, would reveal "the real process of thought" (p. 412). The associations created by the surrealist act created a "superior reality", more purely because they came from the unconscious, otherwise known in the forms of the dream and "the disinterested play of thought" (p. 412).

Breton's manifesto was a passionate attack on a trend in civilisation. Bullied by "absolute rationalism", mankind "under collar of civilisation, under the pretext of progress, all that rightly or wrongly may be regarded as fantasy or superstition has been banished from the mind, all uncustomary searching after truth has been proscribed" (p. 413). "All credit for these discoveries must go to Freud", he wrote, concluding, "the imagination is perhaps on the point of reclaiming its rights" (p. 414).

Freud's method of free association launched one of the more intense, if programmatic, periods in Western fine art, and Breton was not alone among those influenced by this way of imagining. In the novel, poetry, and music, Freud's stance was liberating, suggestive, and morphogenically concordant with a certain type of emergent representational freedom.

I doubt it was puzzling to artists that Freud shied away from their own particular transformations of his method. Even a casual reader would have noted his repeated effort to affiliate his discoveries with the scientific world and his odd habit of claiming that one day all his theories would be explained biologically. Readers of *Civilisation and its Discontents* (1930a) would also have noted that in his analysis of Western culture, he stressed the exchange of pleasure for civility, part of the psychical change brought about by development of the superego.

Whatever one thinks of the surrealist celebration of Freud, it is of interest that Breton and his colleagues brought to the foreground what Freud marginalised in his writings. If civilisation was a triumph of the conscience in a war with the instincts and the pleasure principle, Freud subverted this reality—perhaps what Breton meant by "absolute reality"—by inventing the free associative process.

To some extent, Freud took his method for granted, and as with many assumptions, it escaped further consideration and development. Like an astronomer who, having marvelled at the discovery of a telescope, subsequently gets lost in what he sees, he was naturally more interested in what he found through his method than in the method itself. We might see something of the same tension in much modern music, literature, and painting: a conflict between examination of the method that is one's craft and concentration on what can be manifested through the process. We can paint and figure without having to scrutinise the type of thought that is painting. We can compose a melody without having to think about what a musical idea is. Or we can write a poem and not have to examine the poetic process.

Indeed, this tension gives rise to certain intellectual wars, with some artists decrying the representation of the process of creativity and celebrating the figurative outcome of the creation, and others expressing clear irritation with the mimetic simplicity of a figure. Perhaps we all recognise the essentials of this debate: each side in this conflict loses meaning if its opposite is eradicated. Indeed, we know that writers, musicians, or painters who profess impatience with the deconstructivists—those artists whose figures are breaking down or cracked to begin with—are also intensely interested in the process that generates their creativity.

It is not too difficult to understand at least one of the sources of this impatience. If one is too self-conscious, or too self-examining, it might interfere with one's creativity. Perhaps the surrealist movement failed to realise its wish to employ the unconscious because an anxious self-awareness in their undertaking resulted in an overly stylised art. Indeed, this extreme in self observation—or representation of the character of the mind—led Dali to his celebrated "paranoiac-critical method", which elaborated the irrational character of mental contents in order to further illuminate the structure of the irrational. Paranoia, he wrote, was the "delirium of interpretation bearing a systematic structure" and he defined "paranoiac-critical activity" as a "spontaneous method of 'irrational knowledge', based on the critical and systematic objectification of delirious associations and interpretations" (quoted in Breton, 1934, p. 416). The surrealists experimented with the primary process in earnest: Max Ernst used hypnagogic illusions to provide material for his collages, Miró went hungry to inspire hallucinations, coming from what he thought of as the form of the object, but they did so in a curious combat of absolute unconsciousness and absolute consciousness, rather like a meeting of absolutes negating one another.

Perhaps abstract expressionism became the vital compromise. For, in the works of de Kooning, to take just one example, one can see how a technique, once sufficiently divorced from the figurative, allows for a certain type of unconscious influence that can be observed but not readily comprehended. Even as the process of painting becomes, to some, the aim of painting, heralding what could become a disturbingly intrusive self-observation, the result is mysterious. Even as the patterns typify and identify the works as the product of one artist, they open the project as a question none the less. What is this? What is one looking at? From which perspective?

De Kooning knew paints. He knew how to keep the paint on the canvas alive until the last possible moment, ready for its eradication and substitution with another colour, another shape. For every vision there was a revision, and revisions of the revisions. The cumulative visual effect is of time and space suspended in a moment, congealed into one representation. If this leads us to think of Freud's mystic writing-pad as a metaphor of the unconscious, realised in these paintings as layer upon layer of the many strokes of the brush, it also suggests Freud's metaphor of life itself, the self as the city of Rome in all its stages—Etruscan, Empire, Medieval, Renaissance—visible in the same gaze and superimposed on one another. Such is the story of any self. In the works of de Kooning, one gazes upon an object that, in its revisional intensity, reflects the dense overdetermination of psychic life. We witness it—indeed, for some, we are bewilderingly moved by it— guided less by Western conventions of narrative and figuration than by objectification of us, not as body or social being, but as unconscious movement or intelligent emotion.

"Art is a method of opening up areas of feeling rather than merely an illustration of an object", writes Bacon (1953, p. 620). Our words— feelings, affects, moods—are not adequate signifiers, as Bacon means much more through "feeling" than is conjured by this word. He adds, "A picture should be a re-creation of an event rather than an illustration of an object; but there is no tension in the picture unless there is struggle with the object" (p. 620). Emotion (from "*movere*"), or moving experience, is an inner event and might get us closer to what we try to signify by affect or feeling. We seem to be set in motion either by internal stimuli (such as a memory, or a wish, or a mysterious idea) or external stimuli (such as meeting someone, or reading a book).

Complex states of mind, emotions arise out of the vagaries of life, thick meetings between inner interests and circumstance. "The way I work", said Bacon, "is accidental . . . How can I re-create an accident? [Another accident] would never be quite the same" (p. 622). So, too, with an emotional experience. Bacon continues, "This is the thing that can only probably happen in oil paint, because it is so subtle that one tone, one piece of paint, that moves one thing into another completely changes the implications of the image" (p. 622). Many would agree that no two emotional states are alike, that each emotion changes the contents on the internal canvas.

It is possible to see, therefore, how some painters—following the surrealists—managed to identify (consciously or not) with the project that was Freud's. Indeed, it is more than possible that abstract expressionism actually has succeeded where surrealism failed, extending our understanding of the creative process that was tapped by free association, presenting us with a different type of Rome: a history of the differing emotional experiences of the painter, congealed into one single image, one that materialises psychic life in the form world of painting.

Dream theory, which includes the dream day, the dream event, its breakdown into other scenes upon association, and the discovery and interpretation of tissues of thought, is a particular theory of creativity. Examining this might enable us to see how—if at all—what takes place in analysis shadows some of the more radical representational expressions in the worlds of poetry, painting, and music.

Freud, however, was stubbornly opposed to consideration of the dream work as art-like. Wary of over-enthusiastic adoption by aestheticians, whom he feared would appropriate psychoanalysis, he openly ridiculed any vestige of the aesthetic in the dream. He worried that the transcendental aims of the aesthete would bypass the body's raw urges—the instincts—which held no aesthetic ambitions of their own, eviscerating the drive from the *gestalt*. Indeed, he thought that the aim of all instincts was to extinguish excitation, though he could find few examples to support this view. Stravinsky might have agreed with him, "All music", he wrote, "is nothing more than a succession of impulses that converge towards a definite point of repose" (1942, p. 35).

Perhaps, if Freud had constructed his theory of the dream after Kandinsky, Pound, Stravinsky, and Schoenberg, he would have thought differently, for their works have a lyrical raw passion, asserting the pleasure of the aesthetic that gives rise to new expressive forms. Perhaps he would have seen that the total dream process is very likely the cornerstone of the creative, a movement of the "to be represented" towards the fulfilment of this desire.

Those psychic intensities that are the ordinary inspirational events of everyday life are largely accidental, so what is their psychic status before they are dreamed? They would be, I suggest, internal mental structures (the little Rome of the day being designed but not yet dreamed), energised over-determinations moving towards some form of elaboration. In *Being a Character* (1992), I used the term "psychic genera" (p. 66) to identify an unconscious complex that uses its own gravity to draw to it previously unrelated mental phenomena. The gathering of these psychic gravities would be unconscious, but perhaps sensed as a mood arising out of a previous experience. The continuous presence of these psychic phenomena in the self often provides us with the feeling of being guided by a shaping spirit. What Wordsworth wrote in "Tintern Abbey"—"in the mind of man – / a motion and a spirit that impels / All thinking things, all objects of all thought, / And rolls through all things" (1798, p. 22)—is strikingly similar to the way artists describe the creative process.

Stravinsky believed emotion that passes as inspiration is a sign of the presence of something being worked upon by the artist in the moment. "Is it not clear", he writes, "that this emotion is merely a reaction on the part of the creator grappling with that unknown entity which is still only the object of his creating and which is to become a work of art?" (1942, p. 50). The inspired state of mind in the artist, he suggests, is a sign of an internal generative object emerging toward consciousness:

> This foretaste of the creative act accompanies the intuitive grasp of an unknown entity already possessed but not yet intelligible, an entity that will not take definite shape except by the action of a constantly vigilant technique. (p. 51)

The dreamer-to-be carries around unthought known foretastes of their dream during the day, not only elaborating disseminations from past dreams, but seeking objects that will move them further along the paths of dream life.

For the most part, Freud ignored the daily role of unconscious observation, the collecting, scrutinising, and selecting of psychical objects, an imbalance that Ehrenzweig redressed in his theory of "unconscious scanning" (1967, p. 5). We might also say that each person will, of course, have a long and exceedingly complex history of dream experiences, which, over time, will establish a kind of inner unconscious network that scans the world, collecting, scrutinising, and separating out those elements that are of interest. The dreamt looks for its dream objects in subsequent lived experience.

The dream is a puzzling illumination of one's unconscious interests, a manifestation of intangible interests seeking presentation. This transformation of the unthought known into consciousness becomes a kind of sphinx—a compound object—wrought from the intercourse of the self's psychic life and the aleatory movement of evocative objects. It is the moment when the collective impact of the day, bound into complexes of memory and desire, presents itself.

Freud's dictate that the dreamer should free associate to the dream meant that whatever integrity the dream seemed to have as an event in its own right was illusory, as associations fragmented it into shards, eventually disclosing tissues of thought that could be knitted into an interpretation. The unconscious latent thought of a dream could be found after free association created enough material to reveal the connecting links.

Depending on one's point of view, this is where Freud either limited or empowered psychoanalysis. For some, including many artists, Freud's reduction of this extraordinary process to a single latent idea was anticlimactic. Just as he declined to credit the work of the unconscious ego in the assimilation of psychically significant moments during the day, now he played down the fecund power of free associations. Freud was not interested in the dream as a paradigm of the creative. His more restricted aim was to gain access to the unconscious meanings of the patient's symptoms through free association to dreams. He did, however, allude to the impossibility of fully interpreting any dream, even though the extraordinary range of his own dream associations seems a pleasure in itself, equal to the delight of interpretation. Furthermore, it seems likely that he would have agreed that, once set in motion, free associations not only reveal hidden tissues of thought, but become a network of thought that will continue into the next day, and, together with other surviving networks, will collect, sort, dream, and disseminate future emotional moments.

It may be a measure of Freud's genius that this discovery, which would have been sufficient for many people, was only the first of many. For me, however, this is his greatest accomplishment. In a few years of work with his patients—affected by their rejections of his techniques—he settles on free association, and in that moment Western culture is changed forever. Many artists, like Joyce, were wary of affiliating themselves with Freud, yet grasped the psychoanalytic revolution, arguably more immediately and perhaps more extensively than did those in the psychoanalytical movement.

What was so radical?

To find the truth determining one's peculiar, inevitably conflicted states of mind, one discards the energy to know how and why and instead simply reports what happens to be on one's mind in the presence of the analyst. Of course, there would be resistances to this request, although paradoxically enough a resistance often pointed directly to the ideas that were being held back, but we would have to say that an entire civilisation would find itself in resistance to something so up-ending.

Yet, it is alluring, even when it brings up unwanted ideas. It is speech as true self, the verbal equivalent of Winnicott's "squiggle", or the moment when, according to Lacan, the subject discovers his own voice, revealed through slips of the tongue and curious wordings.

"It is through the unhampered play of its functions", writes Stravinsky, "that a work is revealed and justified", and, in the pure state, he adds, "music is free speculation" (1942, p. 49). Free association is also a speculation, a visionary moment in which the self derives from the prior day a hint of its future.

What does psychoanalysis bring to creativity? Freud unconsciously comprehended the process that was not simply at the heart of the creative, but was the creative process—a process involving two people where only one in privacy has been before. Narrating their day, their dream, their associations, analysands create themselves in the presence of the analyst. They might try to "figure" themselves, but the associative eventually breaks down these figures, and from the broken lines, discordant harmonies, and *caesurae* the psychic creations assert themselves.

The dream materialises the day's psychic reality through a transformation of form. It takes psychic intensities, held inside and sensed, and puts them into the form of a dream. This could be partly why people are not simply puzzled by their dreams, but, curiously, rather proud of them. We are not only impressed by their content, but, because they are transubstantiations, intangible psychic reality briefly visualised, we are slightly in awe of the process. "The basis of musical creation", writes Stravinsky, "is a preliminary feeling out, a will moving first in an abstract realm with the object of giving shape to something concrete" (1942, p. 27). But the musical idea moving about in Stravinsky's mind will change upon moving into "sound and time", the material of music.

This brings us to the oddity of creativity. When the painter paints, or the musician composes, or the writer writes, they transfer psychic reality to another realm. They transubstantiate that reality, the object no longer simply expressing self, but re-forming it. This might be considered a type of projection—a putting of the self into an object— but it is also a transubstantial change, where psychic reality leaves its home in the mind and moves into a different intelligence. Commenting on a recent work, Richter said: "that was an expression of my personal state of mind, and it hints at a method of translating my changed way of thinking into reality" (1995, p. 60).

The term "transubstantial object" allows me to think of the intrinsic integrity of the form into which one moves one's sensibility in order to create: into musical thinking, prose thinking, painting thinking. These processes could be viewed in part as transformational objects in that each procedure will alter one's internal life according to the laws of its own form. However, a transubstantial object also emphasises the "body" of the transforming object that receives, alters, and represents the sensibility of the subject who enters its terms and now lives within it.

An artist does not go easily into this altered state of unconsciousness. They feel the boundary between ordinary psychic life and the artistic workspace as one that is always difficult to cross, and sometimes unbearably so. Even as they become accustomed to entering this other realm, they are acutely aware of leaving themselves behind, thrown into a different form of life.

This challenge is not without precedent, as, at least once, we have been presented with the challenge of language, whether to enter it and to be transformed by it, or to refuse speech. For Lacan (1977), to enter language is to accept a deep change in the human sense of form, from the sensorial imagined order (of an apparently unified self) to wording the self into a new form of being. Art forms offer further challenges to the self and, as with language, what emerges from one seems not to be of one's own making, but guided by the form of an other.

Writers, painters, and composers often comment on the unknown, yet felt, inner structure gathering a specific work and its outcome.

"Often when I sit . . . and turn on my computer or my typewriter and write the first sentence, I don't know what I'm going to write about because it has not yet made the trip from the belly to the mind", writes Isabel Allende (in Epel, 1994, pp. 7–24).

> It is somewhere hidden in a very sombre and secret place where I don't have any access yet. It is something that I've been feeling but which has no shape, no name, no tone, and no voice. So I write the first sentence—which usually is the first sentence of the book . . . By the time I've finished the first draft I know what the book is about. But not before. (p. 8)

Art not only embodies this shapeless something, it transforms it into a different realm altogether. "A thing is brought forth which we didn't know we had in us", writes Milosz (1979, p. 3). Wallace Stevens writes,

> While there is nothing automatic about [a] poem, nevertheless it has an automatic aspect in the sense that it is what I wanted it to be without knowing before it was written what I wanted it to be, even though I knew before it was written what I wanted to do. (1979, pp. 50–51)

"If each of us is a biological mechanism, each poet is a poetic mechanism" (p. 51), he continues, to which we might add that the mechanism of transformation from the unthought known object that is the poem to be to the poetic object is derived from the aesthetic process that goes under the name of poetry. In the same way, that order of thinking that is painting, or composing, is the structure of transformation that transubstantiates internal objects from the deep solitude of an internal world into altered external actuality. "The poet at work is an expectation", writes Valéry in "A poet's notebook". "He is a transition within a man" (1979, p. 171).

This transition is not representational. It is presentational. What the poet writes, or the painter paints, or the composer composes has not existed before.

Something of this same transubstantiation occurs in an analysis. The patient has in mind a dream, or an event of the previous day, or a thought about the analyst, and as they speak their thoughts they experience their alteration through speech. Thinking something and speaking it are differing forms of representation, but speaking in a freely associative manner inaugurates a transubstantial shift, as the self senses a move from what has heretofore been the common ground of self-experience—thinking and talking—to a new form for being. As with the paints splashing on the canvas, or the musical ideas forming notes on the page, the free associating analysand not only creates himself in another place, but instantiates himself in the logic of an aesthetic that differs from purely internal experience or conversation.

Is it possible that this ending of a person's idiom as a self, and new beginning as a different form, is part of the pleasure of creativity? Of course, the leap into a different skin might be in order to evacuate the self into the object, rather than elaborate inner life. Often enough, the new form articulates psychic reality in ways not possible through customary modes of expression.

This raises a further question. What do the differing artistic realms offer as transubstantial objects? If I paint my ideas rather than put them to musical sound, I not only select a different form, I also find a different unconscious aesthetic. My ideas will materialise transformed, according to the characteristic of the representational form's unconscious structure. Perhaps we are all evolving towards some day in the far future when each of us will have developed sufficient skills as a poet, artist, musician, and mathematician—among others—to live in different forms, each of which must, of necessity, process us very differently, and, of course, reflect us in aesthetically distinguished manners. Creativity, then, could be viewed as a development in civilisation, not necessarily in terms of the evolution of art or poetry, for example, but as multiple expressions of psychic reality, which, in time, would be more intelligently served by crafting it in music, paint, or poetry.

Works of artistic imagination are form objects, samples of individual idiom made available to the other. Each form object demonstrates the compositional intelligence of its creator and its aesthetic structure suggests to its subsequent appreciators a peculiarly evocative integrity. Although the reader, listener, or viewer will always receive a form object according to the idiom of the self's receptive intelligence, each form object evokes a formal response.

This helps me understand the reassurance I experience on seeing the works of an artist whom I admire. If I travel to a new museum and find a de Kooning, I feel delight and reassurance. These are works I feel I know. But what do I know? The transubstantial object certainly allows for the possibility that my aesthetic grasp of the other is linked with the aesthetic category of the object. That is, these works evoke the experiencing me that exists in and through the medium of paint. It brings something out in me, or, to put it in the vernacular, it "speaks to me". I could not, however, put what it "says" or what I "hear" into words. Some individuals are irked by the critical examination of their work, not only because they might be distressed with the judgement, but also, it seems to me, because they have entered a different realm, which is not the written word, even if their realm is prose fiction or poetry, which uses the word as its medium.

In a psychically literal sense, we are moved by the work of art, processed by its form. Even if we only glance at one painting, hear a few bars of music, or read a few lines of a poem, we shall have been gathered by the aesthetic of the other, remarkably preserved in the after-effects of their life forms of their idiom left behind.

"If I alter any reader's consciousness, it will be because I have constructed a consciousness of which others may wish to become aware, or even, for a short time, share", writes Gass (1996, p. 47). But, as Gass knows only too well, the consciousness constructed by the novel is not the same as ordinary consciousness, although each writer uses that medium to express aspects of his own idiom.

Is it accurate to say that the artistic object only reflects the self, even if we qualify this by assuming that the artist also expresses contemporary culture and artistic tradition? As the transubstantial object differs in form from the self, it bears the self, yet becomes a new body for that being. "The music of prose", writes Gass, "elementary as it is, limited as it is in its effects, is nonetheless far from frivolous decoration; it embodies Being; consequently, it is essential that the body be in eloquent shape" (1996, p. 326). The "object" through which we create—painting, prose, music—has its own processional integrity, its own laws, and when we enter it to express our idea within its terms, we shall be altered by the object. "For the last two years I have been making a series of paintings with 'je t'aime' written across them", writes Robert Motherwell. "I never thought much about it, but I am sure in part it is some kind of emphasis or *existing in* what is thought" (in Caws, 1996, p. 18). Existing in a thrown thought, projected into a different aesthetic realm, and objectified in a different and challenging way: transubstantial projective objectification.

The same principle operates when the analysand enters analysis. There are familiar elements (a vestige of social life, ordinary talk, a unit of time, etc.), but the free associative medium, although borrowing its integrity from inner speech and inner association, becomes a new medium for self-expression. Entering analysis, a person will never be the same again. He will have found a new object for self-transformation and there is nothing like it, just as there is nothing like painting, nothing like poetry, and nothing like music.

"Art belongs to the *unconscious*!" wrote Kandinsky to Schoenberg.

> One must express *oneself*! Express oneself *directly*! Not one's taste, or one's upbringing, or one's intelligence, knowledge or skill. Not all these *acquired* characteristics, but that which is *inborn, instinctive*. And all form-making, all *conscious* form-making, is connected with some kind of mathematics, or geometry . . . But only unconscious form-making, which sets up the equation "form = outward shape", really creates forms. (Schoenberg & Kandinsky, 1984, p. 23)

Perhaps that inner object that is the work to be finds its most direct expression in the geometry or mathematics—that is, the specific intelligence—of the medium of the creativity rather than in the object. The work that Allende says is "in her belly" only emerges through writing, and one of the features of any person's creativity is the selection of the particular form through which to express the creative idea.

"In one way only can form be discussed in an objective sense" (p. 87), writes Bloch in *Essays on the Philosophy of Music* (1985). He adds,

> This is where the formal, constructional, objectifying element is not a medium but itself an objective component, as is especially the case with stage effects, with rhythm and especially with the different types of counterpoint that determine the shaping subjects as categories of their innate being. (p. 87)

This determination of the shaping subject—the logic of form—is an expression of the innate being of the subject, now moved from inner experience to the property of musical expression. He continues,

> here the shaping subject has truly entered into a 'form' as its deeper aggregate condition, a 'form' accordingly representing the lower,

> quasi-epistemological, metaphysically skeletonic part of the object
> arrangement itself. (pp. 87–88)

Musical form, we may add, is not simply a medium, it is an objectification of that intelligence that is shaping its idea, and the structure of inspiration reveals itself in the object arrangement, that is, in musical form.

Creative life usually involves a drawing in of the self, perhaps because all the self's inner resources are devoted to the creative act. Freud also recognised this need in the formation of psychoanalysis, as patient and analyst retreat from the stimuli of the world. A withdrawal in order to crystallise the work harks back to the age before social responsiveness, predating even the primary mediating presence of language. Each of us has been part of this drawing in of being, first when we are inside the mother's body, and then held by her concentration for many weeks after our birth, what Winnicott termed "primary maternal preoccupation" (Winnicott, 1956, p. 300). In psychoanalysis, the recumbent position, the absence of visual socialisation, the presence of an auditory intimate, and the absence of an agenda recreate the mood of the earliest states of consciousness. Free associative thinking may begin as a type of chat, just as the artist's sketch is a way of beginning, but eventually analysand and artist respond to what is being called for. For the patient, it means a deepening of the associations, in the artist/analyst as well, a generative loosing of the self into the work.

In our beginnings, held inside the mother's body, then immersed in her psychic and somatic textures, we are enfolded beings. Bion (1962) believed that analysis allowed for an alteration in the analyst's being, as he dreamt the patient's material, transforming the patient's communications into his dream objects. This craft certainly derives from a maternal process and gives birth to inspired ideas and interpretations. In the composer, writer, or creative artist, a similar reverie is established, although, after years of practising this retreat, creative people enter it alone, manage it by themselves, and take the object-to-be as a type of other.

Retreat into this realm taps and develops the skill of unconscious creativity, driven by the core of one's being. Psychoanalysis transforms unconscious complexes—symptomatic, pathologic, transferential—into consciousness, but it also enhances the self's unconscious capability. Bion reckoned that psychoanalytic training was an education in intuition.

The kind of thinking required in psychoanalytic work evokes those objects of conflict that are a part of our existence. No one represented conflicts with early objects as well as Klein (1975). In her mind, each self is engaged in a ceaseless remembering of the earliest encounter with the object, enacting them in all subsequent relations. The type of thinking evoked by psychoanalysis, or the concentration of the creative artist, calls forth the passions of love and hate, the objects of each, and the self's violent evasions of the consequence of being. Thus, free association might intend to be objective and dispassionate, but, as the associations move deeper into the self, they will convey the self's experience of its objects, a burden that saturates the freely associated thought with meaning. For these ideas not only bear their symbolic structure, as Lacan (1977) emphasised, they are also like independent characters in a developing opera of sorts. The classical way of listening allows the logic that is sequence to arise out of the material, taking into account those ruptures or shallows that indicate resistance, those emphases created by parapraxal moments, and those disseminations occasioned by polysemous words. The object-relational way of listening to the same material transforms the sequence of ideas into characters—treated as parts of the self or parts of the object—who constitute the theatre of transference. Each way of listening finds a different type of conflict operating in a different realm. In literature, it might be the difference between the conflict revealed in the idiom of the writing and the conflict demonstrated in the enactments between characters. In painting, it might be the difference between the logic of the developing ideas—thought constituting itself in the intelligence of the step-by-step move of the brush—and the theatre of established figures of the painter's world once again engaging themselves on the canvas.

In "the use of an object" (1971), Winnicott argued that spontaneity could only develop out of a principle of ruthlessness. In order to use an object, the self must be free to destroy it. It is the mother who sanctions this in the first place; indeed, she is to be the initial object of such destruction. After a period of relating in which the infant's love and hate are mingled through a sense of concern for her, the infant gradually feels more secure in his or her ability to use the mother, not confusing such wear and tear with damage.

Perhaps something of the same principle underlies Freud's injunction to the dreamer to break up the body of the dream through free association. The feelings and self-states brought into the dream as an experience are stored as is; breaking them up through free association will not erase memory of the dream experience. Indeed, the security of the dream as a thing in itself allows for its destruction, and use as an object of inspiration.

Whether one considers the dream or the mother as object, both the Freudian principle and Winnicott's idea amount to a breaking-up of the figure. Freud breaks up the figures of the dream and Winnicott breaks up the mother, and from each emerges a dynamically fragmented universe of potential meanings. These psychological theories were developing over a period of sixty years when something of the very same principle was being celebrated in fine art, music, and prose. Following the impressionist breaking of representational figuration, we find in cubism, surrealism, and abstract expressionism a moment in the artist's development when the figure breaks up. It might shatter into the cubist, futurist, surrealist, or abstract. Furthermore, this dissemination of the object was often signified by the figure of a woman, painted again and again, who begins to break up.

Many critics, looking at Picasso's or de Kooning's paintings of a woman, argue that she is being destroyed in a misogynist attack on the female. These criticisms miss the context of this breaking-up. It usually occurs just before the fragmentation of the sublime other into a bizarre refiguration, or a shattered object, often abstracted into a thick movement of colour and shape. I suggest that what we see here mirrors what Freud and Winnicott wrote about the breaking-up of the figurative. Breaking the woman becomes the breaking of the mother's body, momentarily losing the need for figuration, but employing her as a project for the realisation of self. She is now the process of painting, an immanent presence, de-objectified and reformed as the guardian intelligence of the form of painting.

Certain abstract works of art, like certain modern novels (of Joyce, Faulkner, for example) disfigure customary representation in order to present the work of creativity within the form itself, playing with the elements of form, implicitly recognising the desire in the recipient to see something of the magic of form at work.

Psychoanalysis can show a similar lack of respect for the sanctity of the figurative. In the struggle to engage the invisible, the analyst (like the artist) breaks the figure: not to find out what is inside but to realise the immaterial intelligence of form that is authorised in the name of the mother. If the infant is to come into true self-relating, says Winnicott, then he or she must be free to invent the mother and self. For patients to use analysis, they must be free to invent many an analyst in the transference and to destroy the integrity of the person of the analyst in order to express themselves. The analyst, up to a point, accepts this use.

Painters, composers, and writers who take liberty in destroying the figures of our life none the less rely upon the integrity of the figure even as they destroy it. Like psychoanalysts, they recognise the paradox of this freedom. It could not occur without a sense of privilege deriving from the figure, the mother who gave birth, but who shall be "destroyed" as she is used. Taking liberties, as it were, is not sublime. As a self creates many an other out of the primary figure, what is gained in freedom of expression is lost in terms of personal security. In time, the waves of representation suggest too many possible figures, and eventually the primary mother is beyond reach. Abstract expressionists might well have pined for the simplicity of the figure, just as the self, beset by creation of so many multiple representations of the primary object, grieves the mother lost to us all.

A Picasso or de Kooning might well return in mind to the woman, armed with the ambivalence that comes from the freedom to destroy. How, it might be posed, can the mother allow us to destroy her? Refinding her, even in the altered form, then, may be a relief in the midst of what will be renewed efforts of destruction.

We are separated from the mother, the father, the family, and, arguably, from our culture by the fecund complexity of psychic life. No figure shall survive intact. Our thoughts—in visions and revisions—will revise all figures so frequently that only the principle of figure shall remain. Free association releases this complexity in a bound space further narrowed by the reluctance of the patient to fully embrace it, and by the analyst who seeks his interpretations. Creative work in dance, poetry, drama, prose fiction, music, painting, and sculpture also involves tacit devolutions of the figure as revisioning creates multiple figures, overlying one another.

If we cannot have singular objects to embrace for consolation's sake, we do have the body of separate forms, into which and through which we alter and articulate our being. This is the great promise of any art form. It is, often enough, the reality of the psychoanalytical method.

References

Bacon, F. (1953). *Catalogue*. London: Tate Gallery.

Bion, W. R. (1962). *Learning from Experience*. New York: Basic Books.

Bloch, E. (1974). *Essays on the Philosophy of Music*. London: Cambridge University Press, 1985.

Bollas, C. (1992). Psychic genera. In: *Being a Character* (pp. 66–100). London: Routledge.

Breton, A. (1934). What is Surrealism? In: H. B. Chipp (Ed.), *Theories of Modern Art* (pp. 410–417). Berkeley, CA: University of California Press.

Caws, M. (1996). *What Art Holds*. New York: Columbia University Press.

Ehrenzweig, A. (1967). *The Hidden Order of Art*. Berkeley, CA: University of California Press, 1971.

Epel, N. (Ed.) (1994). *Writers Dreaming*. New York: Vintage Books.

Freud, S. (1930a). *Civilization and its Discontents*. S.E. 21. London: Hogarth.

Gass, W. (1996). *Finding a Form*. New York: Knopf.

Klein, M. (1975). *The Psycho-Analysis of Children*. London: Free Press.

Lacan, J. (1977). *Écrits: A Selection*. New York: W. W. Norton.

Milosz, C. (1979). Ars poetica? In: R. Gibbons (Ed.), *The Poet's Work* (pp. 3–4). Chicago, IL: University of Chicago Press.

Richter, G. (1995). *The Daily Practice of Painting*. Cambridge, MA: MIT Press.

Schoenberg, A., & Kandinsky, W. (1984). *Arnold Schoenberg, Wassily Kandinsky: Letters, Pictures, Documents*. London: Faber and Faber.

Stevens, W. (1979). The irrational element in poetry. In: R. Gibbons (Ed.), *The Poet's Work* (pp. 48–58). Chicago, IL: University of Chicago Press.

Stravinsky, I. (1942). *Poetics of Music*. Cambridge, MA: Harvard University Press.

Valéry, P. (1979). A poet's notebook. In: R. Gibbons, *The Poet's Work* (pp. 170–183). Chicago, IL: University of Chicago Press.

Winnicott, D. W. (1956). Primary maternal preoccupation. In: *Through Paediatrics to Psycho-Analysis* (pp. 300–305). New York: Basic Books, 1958.

Winnicott, D. W. (1971). The use of an object and relating through identification. In: *Playing and Reality* (pp. 86–94). New York: Basic Books.

Wordsworth, W. (1798). Lines composed a few miles above Tintern Abbey. In: *Lyrical Ballads, With a Few Other Poems* (pp. 21–24). London: J. & A. Arch.

The Scarlet Letter — the artist and analyst as outsiders: the 2004 Creativity Seminar

T he people who come to Austen Riggs for treatment tend to have multiple and longstanding difficulties, covering the full range of serious human troubles. They come because other treatment programmes have not worked well for them. They are, to some extent, "outsiders", not only because they struggle to function in the world, but also because, to psychiatry, they have generally been considered "treatment-resistant".

They also come because the unusual treatment programme at Riggs seems promising to them. It is, indeed, unusual in today's world: a formerly "insider" programme in the heyday of psycho-analysis that has increasingly found itself an "outsider" amid current treatments. Well past the edge of Hawthorne's wilderness, patients at Riggs engage in intensive individual psychotherapy while joining a completely open therapeutic community in which they share author-ity with the staff for managing daily life, and for engaging the issues of judgement, norms, passions, projection, and meaning so embedded in the drama of *The Scarlet Letter*.

Taking up the role of citizen in this therapeutic community devel-ops a range of strengths in our patients and limits their potential drift into the more non-therapeutic aspects of the patient role. But communities, as we see in *The Scarlet Letter*, are not necessarily an unmitigated blessing; they might offer a sense of belonging at the expense of playing out social tensions and narrow beliefs in damagingly projective and constricting ways. Suffice it to say that our work with patients has led us to the conviction that their struggle toward their own creative process and toward the social conditions for its development are central to their growth.

2004 was the 200th anniversary of Nathaniel Hawthorne's birth, and the Creativity Seminar was one of a number of events celebrating and revisiting our first great American novelist. In 1850, this quintessential New Englander wrote *The Scarlet Letter*, the densely symbolic tale of love and sexual transgression in the context of colonial Puritanism. Hester Prynne is marked for her sin with a scarlet "A". Never actually called an *adulteress* in the novel, she is instead referred to as an *artist* because of her beautiful embroidery. And, while her lover's nemesis is described darkly as a kind of *analyst* (fifty years before Freud), it is Hester who offers true understanding and counsel to suffering individuals. She can do this in part because she has been placed "outside" her community. She is the "other", and from this position she can meet the "otherness" in those who come to her and can offer them her "sympathetic knowledge".

Hawthorne's masterpiece provides us with a point of departure in examining the place from which the artist creates and the analyst listens. Freud once made a provocative comment about a connection between the two: writing to a minister who was attempting to practise this new treatment, Freud (1910) commented, "Your analysis suffers from the . . . weakness of virtue. It is the work of an over-decent man who feels himself obliged to be discreet". Freud saw this as

> incompatible with . . . psychoanalysis. One has to . . . transcend the rules, sacrifice oneself, betray, and behave like the artist who buys paints with his wife's household money, or burns the furniture to warm the room for his model. Without some such criminality there is no real achievement. (p. 38)

The analyst, Freud seems to be saying, needs to become an "outsider" in order to contact the "outsider" in the patient, to form a new community of two before there can be any hope of the patient's rejoining another community. Freud links the analyst with the artist and suggests that passionate commitment to the work sets one apart from social concerns, even if this necessary work may also occur on behalf of society. The two chapters that follow take up Hawthorne's allegory and Freud's challenge. Carol Gilligan finds a "moonlight visibility" in Hawthorne's tale, a perspective outside the apparently rational order of that day—and this one as well—from which she takes profound inspiration for the establishment of relationships between men and women "on a surer ground of mutual happiness". I then consider the doctor–patient relationship within the story, as well as a number of critical developmental issues. Questions for psychoanalysis emerge from these explorations and for the deep and powerful connection between Hawthorne and his mother.

Reference

Freud, S. (1910). Letter to Oskar Pfister. In: H. Meng & E. Freud (Eds.), *Psychoanalysis and Faith: The Letters of Sigmund Freud and Oskar Pfister* (pp. 38–40). New York: Basic Books, 1963.

CHAPTER TWO

A moonlight visibility: turning
The Scarlet Letter into a play

Carol Gilligan

"Moonlight, in a familiar room, falling so white upon the
carpet, and showing all its figures so distinctly, – making every
object so minutely visible, yet so unlike a morning or noontide
visibility . . ."

(Hawthorne, 1898, pp. 45–46)

I t was the death of his mother that impelled Hawthorne to write
The Scarlet Letter. As a child, he had seen his mother scorned by
his father's family after his father, a sea captain, died in Surinam
when Nathaniel was four. Raised by his mother, who took him and his
sisters and went back to live with her family, Hawthorne was brought
up in a household of women. Following his graduation from Bowdoin
College, he lived for twelve years in his mother's house, teaching himself to write. But it was only with *The Scarlet Letter* that he managed to
still a critical, censorious voice inside him, reflecting subsequently in
his journal, "I think I have never overcome my own adamant in any
other instance" (1870, p. 301).

Hawthorne calls *The Scarlet Letter* a romance, a blending of the
actual and the imaginary. It also has the character of a dream, its

manifest content concealing its latent meanings. Setting his story in seventeenth century Boston, Hawthorne draws on historical figures, the Reverend John Wilson, Governor Bellingham, and Mistress Hibbins, who was burned as a witch, to establish "an iron framework of reasoning" (1898, p. 193), a powerful alliance of church and state where "religion and law were almost identical" (p. 62), a patriarchal world where women were divided into "goodwives" (p. 63) and witches. Within this framework, he places the triangle of Hester Prynne, her lover Arthur Dimmesdale, and her husband—the man who calls himself Roger Chillingworth. At its centre, Pearl, the luminous child whose existence reveals her mother's "lawless passion" (p. 197), becomes the voice of emotional truth in a world where such truths cannot be spoken.

Seen in a morning or noontide light, Hester has committed the crime and sin of adultery. The magistrates, moved by compassion, thinking that her husband, missing for two years, is probably at the bottom of the sea and seeing that she was young and fair and doubtless was strongly tempted, have waived the penalty of death, ruling instead that she wear a scarlet "A" as a badge of shame. Arthur Dimmesdale, the pious young Reverend who has "done a wild thing" (p. 163), the favourite son of the Puritan fathers, appears in the eyes of the Puritans as Christ-like in his embrace of suffering, while Chillingworth appears as a fiend in seeking to worm his way into the minister's heart. Within this Christian world-view, Pearl is seen as a wild and unruly child.

In naming Hester's lover and husband Dimmesdale and Chillingworth, Hawthorne invites us to consider how two men, described as unusually sensitive and perceptive, come to inhabit these identities. Chillingworth was "a wise and just man" (p. 207), devoting his life to "the advancement of human welfare" (p. 206). Held captive by the Indians, he learnt from them the healing powers of nature, and, bringing these skills into the Puritan settlement, he became a skilled physician. Dimmesdale was revered by his congregation, a man singled out for his intelligence, but, as a noontide perception gives way to a moonlight visibility, Hester defines a radical shift in perception.

Dimmesdale's embrace of suffering becomes an evasion, a betrayal of love, ironically in the name of the Heavenly Father. Chillingworth, however fiend-like in his pursuit of Dimmesdale, is also the one who says that Hester should not be standing alone on the scaffold, who attends to the screaming infant, providing a remedy that calms her and one for her mother as well; in the end, he becomes like a father to Pearl in a way that was previously unimagined, leaving her all his money and property, which were considerable, thus freeing her to lead her own life. And Hester, seeking and gaining Chillingworth's release from her promise to conceal his identity, turns the Puritan world-view on its head. "My sin," she says, "was to enter into this marriage when I felt no love. And his crime was to persuade me to fancy myself happy by his side, at a time when my heart knew no better" (pp. 209–210).

A morality play has given way to a psychological drama, and it was this drama I sought to stage when Tina Packer of Shakespeare & Company invited me to transpose Hawthorne's romance into a play. In overcoming his adamant, Hawthorne did what Virginia Woolf would do in "Killing the angel in the house" (1974, p. 241). He silenced an internalised voice that had kept him from saying what he saw. The challenges I faced in writing the play lay in dramatising the radical shifts in perception and revealing the emotional subtext that drives the characters and their actions.

A stands for adultery, but it also comes to mean "able" (p. 192), as Hester is seen as more of a woman than the "goodwives" (p. 63) of Puritanism:

> Such helpfulness was found in her—so much power to do, and power to sympathize—that many people refused to interpret the scarlet A by its original signification. They said it meant Able; so strong was Hester Prynne, with a woman's strength. (p. 192)

Living outside the framework of Puritanism, Hester sees the frame. "Is the world then so narrow?" (p. 234), she asks the anguished Dimmesdale, a man whose "genuine impulse" (p. 171) was to adore the truth, yet who was living a lie. "Doth the universe lie within the compass of yonder town, which only a little time ago was but a leaf-strewn desert?" (p. 235).

It was an age in which

> the human intellect, newly emancipated, had taken a more active and a wider range than for many centuries before. Men of the sword had overthrown nobles and kings. Men bolder than these had overthrown and rearranged—not actually, but within the sphere of theory . . . the

whole system of ancient prejudice, wherewith was linked much of ancient principle. (p. 196)

As Hester roams the forest on the edge of the settlement, her mind runs free, "cast(ing) away the fragments of a broken chain" (p. 196). Charged by Providence with raising a daughter, she questions the ancient prejudices and principles that govern the relationship between man and woman, dividing her from Dimmesdale and Dimmesdale from himself, restricting her ability to cultivate in her daughter "the germ and blossom of womanhood" (p. 197), and restraining women from assuming "what would seem to be a fair and suitable position" (p. 197) in the new society.

Colour defines the contrast between Hester and the goodwives: she is radiant, her hair dark and abundant, the scarlet letter embroidered brilliantly in red and gold thread; they are grey and pale. Hester sees that "the whole race of womanhood" and "the very nature of the opposite sex, or its long hereditary habit which has become like nature" (p. 198) are, in reality, part of a "system of society" (p. 197) that, built up in one way, could be "torn down and built up anew" (p. 97). Such speculation, the narrator tells us, would have been held by our forefathers to be "a deadlier crime than that stigmatized by the scarlet letter" (p. 196). Freeing her sexuality, Hester released herself from the constraints of Puritanism; from this vantage point, she sees "the foundations of the Puritan establishment" (p. 197) as a human construction, neither divinely ordained nor natural.

The Scarlet Letter was written in 1850, at the height of abolitionist feminism. Hawthorne had married Sophia Peabody, whose older sister, Elizabeth, was among its leading activists. While Hawthorne, at least in his noontide presentation, was neither an abolitionist nor a feminist, the word "patriarchy" runs through "The Custom House", the introductory sketch he appends to his romance: "patriarchal body of veterans" (p. 16); "the father of the Custom House—the patriarch" (p. 22); "this patriarchal personage . . . [who] was, in truth, a rare phenomenon; so perfect, in one point of view, so shallow, so delusive, so impalpable, such an absolute nonentity in every other" (pp. 23–24). The word returns when Dimmesdale ("the minister in a maze") considers telling the truth: "patriarchal privilege" (p. 259); "the sanctified old patriarchal deacon" (p. 259). It is clear what is at stake. And Hester protects Dimmesdale's position, not only at her own expense, but also at the expense of her relationship with her daughter, the luminous Pearl.

Pearl's "remarkable precocity and acuteness" (p. 214) encourage Hester to see her as someone whom she could entrust "with as much of her mother's sorrows as could be imparted, without irreverence either to the parent or the child" (p. 214). And yet, when Pearl's searching questions open the way to such a relationship, Hester holds back. She sees emerging in Pearl's strong emotions and character the

> sterling attributes [of a] noble woman . . . the steadfast principles of an unflinching courage—an uncontrollable will,—a sturdy pride, which might be disciplined into self-respect,—and a bitter scorn of many things which, when examined, might be found to have the taint of falsehood in them. (p. 214)

Yet, paradoxically, to keep Pearl with her, she must distance herself from her and educate her daughter to live within the bounds of a Puritanical order.

The music of the Puritans—the certain harmonies and serene majesty of their hymns—offered a way to evoke the experience and allure of living within an all-encompassing worldview. Struggling to find a sufficient counterweight, I was drawn by Hester's conflict, familiar through my research with women, and also to the voice of Pearl that rang true to my experience in working with girls. I fleshed out the relationship between Hester and Pearl to show their playfulness and joy with one another and built the first act around the tension between emotional truth and "an iron framework of reasoning" (p. 193), a tension that culminates in a series of lies. Dimmesdale lies to Chillingworth, Chillingworth lies to Dimmesdale, and Hester lies to Pearl, who becomes hysterical.

"Mother," Pearl asks, "what does the scarlet letter mean? . . . Mother!—Mother!—Why does the minister keep his hand over his heart?" (p. 216). She has made the connection nobody was supposed to see. "What shall I say?" Hester asks herself (p. 215). She says,

> Silly Pearl, what questions are these? There are many things in this world that a child must not ask about. What know I of the minister's heart? And as for the scarlet letter, I wear it for the sake of its gold thread! (pp. 215–216)

She cannot tell Pearl what Pearl intuitively knows, cannot allow her to know it for fear that the child will be taken away from her: "Hold thy tongue, naughty child!" she says, "Do not tease me; else I shall shut thee into the dark closet!" (p. 216). Act I ends with Pearl throwing herself on the floor and screaming.

In the second act, I depart from Hawthorne's text to show what he only alludes to: the love between Hester and Dimmesdale, Dimmesdale's Election Day sermon that electrifies the congregation, and Pearl as a young woman living in Italy—the parts of the story the narrator excludes in summarising it as "a tale of human frailty and sorrow" (p. 61).

Hester is introduced at the beginning of the novel as a sensual and spirited young woman, tall, "with a figure of perfect elegance, on a large scale" (p. 66); the scarlet A that she embroiders "so fantastically" (p. 67) illuminates her, "taking her out of the ordinary relations with humanity, and enclosing her in a sphere by herself" (p. 67). By the end of the novel, she is the woman to whom other women come for comfort and counsel in love, "demanding why they were so wretched, and what the remedy?" (p. 311). She assures them of her

> firm belief that at some brighter period, when the world has grown ripe for it, in Heaven's own time, a new truth would be revealed in order to establish the whole relation between man and woman on a surer ground of mutual happiness. (p. 311)

For a time, she imagined that she might be the prophetess of this revelation, bringing the truth that would establish a new order of living, but she "had long since recognized the impossibility" (p. 311).

Hawthorne's insight into Hester's predicament is brilliant. With the economy of the single letter "A", he captures how the very passion that enables a woman to free herself from the iron framework of patriarchy also disables her by causing her to be seen, in the eyes of the Puritans, as an impure woman, a woman who has been adulterated. "A" means adultery, "A" means able, "A" means angel and apostle; the novel floats all these possibilities and then draws its sombre conclusion: "The angel and apostle of the coming revelation must be a woman, indeed" (p. 312), but she must be lofty and pure as well as beautiful and wise, not through "dusky grief" (p. 312), but through the ethereal joy of sacred love. The very possibility turns out to be impossible, at least within the world of the novel. But while Hester cannot free her lover, the aptly named Dimmesdale, she does succeed in freeing her daughter, who, by the end of the novel, is living in Italy.

I wrote the love scene in the forest to show the passion between Dimmesdale and Hester when they rekindle their love and plan to leave the Puritan settlement. With Tina Packer, who directed the play, I puzzled over the question Dimmesdale asks once he grasps the possibility of embracing joy: "Why did we not find it sooner?" (p. 214). Since Hester's husband was presumed to be dead and Dimmesdale was unmarried, why had they not left, why did they not marry? Dimmesdale's character posed the most difficult challenge for us, and also for the actors, who struggled to find him sympathetic. Tina and I wrestled with the question of how to understand his internal struggle, how to dramatise his conflict, or even how to ask the question.

I wrote Dimmesdale's Election Day sermon in response to this challenge. In the forest when Dimmesdale encounters Hester—their first time alone in seven years—his manhood returns and his body is restored to health. Standing in "a flood of sunshine" (p. 237), they see their love as having "a consecration of its own" (p. 232). Returning home, Dimmesdale flings the sermon he prepared into the fire and writes another with the same "impulsive flow of thought and emo-tion" (p. 268) that Hawthorne experienced in writing *The Scarlet Letter*. I saw Dimmesdale's epiphany as a radical insight into Christianity that dissolved the tension between his ministry and his manhood: if God is love, how can love be sin?

I imagined he would buttress this perception with Scripture, citing the Gospel of John: "He that dwelleth in love, dwelleth in God, and God in him" (1 John 4:16, the Bible, 1769). In confessing his sin, he would seek to take his congregation with him, reminding them that when Christ said, "He that is without sin, let him cast the first stone at her" (John 8:7, the Bible, 1769), he was speaking of a woman taken in adultery. It was Pearl, the little child, who had sought to lead him to this place, urging him to turn a moonlight visibility into a noontide vision by standing with Hester, and with her not only at night or in the forest, but in the marketplace in the full light of day. But it is a vision that he cannot sustain.

At the end of Act II, as the light fades on the dying minister, Hester rises and leaves him, taking off her Puritan cap and joining Pearl, who stands at the front of the stage. The music shifts from the Puritan hymn, "O bless the Lord my soul," to the contemporary, "Uncommon ritual" as Hester removes Pearl's Puritan costume and a young woman wearing a simple but elegant black dress appears in the place of the girl.

I wrote an epilogue for Pearl. "We left," she says, "my mother and I, shortly after my father's death." She grew up in England and went to live in Italy when Hester returned to Boston, "hiding her bright hair under a Puritan cap, donning her old gray dress, and yes, the scarlet letter". Hester's counsel to the Puritan women in the novel becomes her benediction for her daughter in the play; stating her conviction that a new truth will ground the relation between man and woman not in sorrow, but in happiness, Hester kisses Pearl and leaves.

A swing comes down where the platform of the pillory stood, and, as Pearl begins to swing, a young man enters, dressed in Italian slacks and an open shirt. He stands behind her, pushing her higher. They laugh, and when she gets off the swing, they embrace.

"We have a daughter," Pearl says, "a wild and unruly Sophia. Today is her birthday." Like Pearl in the play, she is seven years old.

Hawthorne sees into the structure of patriarchy with a clarity that few modern writers have attained. He sees its effects on sensitive men, rendering one dim and the other chilling, and also on relations between mothers and daughters, restraining a mother from affirming her daughter's perceptions or telling her what she knows about men and love. How astonishingly modern this 1850 novel is; as I write, a woman in Nigeria, accused of adultery, is in danger of being stoned to death in accordance with the law of Sharia. An alliance of church and state is solidifying in many parts of the world, encouraging militant fundamentalism and supported by "an iron framework of reasoning" (p. 193).

The voice of what Hawthorne, in a seemingly contemporary vocabulary, refers to as the "inner man" (p. 258) or "profounder self" (p. 259) is the voice that exposes the iron framework, revealing its hypocrisies and its lies. But the shift in framework confuses the ability to distinguish the real from the imagined: "No man, for any considerable period, can wear one face to himself, and another to the multitude, without finally getting bewildered as to which may be the true" (p. 256). Hawthorne presents conflicting accounts of what happened that day on the scaffold when Dimmesdale exposed the place over his heart where he had kept his hand. Some said they had seen the scarlet letter identical to Hester's imprinted on his flesh. Others denied there was any mark whatever. The official version was that the minister, "by yielding up his breath in the arms of that fallen woman" (p. 306), had made of his death a parable, conveying "the mournful and mighty lesson, that, in the view of Infinite Purity, we are sinners all alike" (p. 306). The reader is left to choose among these many theories.

I choose to go with Hester, to resist the allure of the *pietà*, to follow the inspiration of Jason Fitzgerald, who designed the sound for the Shakespeare & Company production in modulating the strains of the Puritan hymn into the brighter sounds of "Uncommon ritual". In the forest, when Hester undoes the clasp that fastened the scarlet letter and throws it among the withered leaves, she experiences an "exquisite relief. She had not known the weight, until she felt the freedom!" (p. 241). When she removes the cap that confined her hair, "her sex, her youth, and the whole richness of her beauty, came back from what men call the irrevocable past" (p. 242). Love "had been aroused" (p. 242) from a death-like slumber. Unclouding Dimmesdale's vision by revealing the possibility of leaving "these iron men and their opinions" (p. 235), Hester challenges him to give up the name of Arthur Dimmesdale and to make himself a brighter one.

I read *The Scarlet Letter* as a letter written by Hawthorne to his mother after her death, expressing what he could not say to her—or perhaps even know—while she was living. In the character of Hester Prynne, he reveals his insight into her situation; in Pearl he captures a child's perception and also the pressures on the child not to see or say what is true. In Dimmesdale and Chillingworth, he exposes the vulnerabilities of men whose artistic sensibilities are dulled or frozen by the strictures of a patriarchal order. His moonlit romance thus becomes an epitaph of sorts, a benediction for his mother, and also perhaps an act of self-forgiveness for the extent to which he had stood apart. It carries the recognition, or, perhaps, the wish, that the very nature of man, or what, through "long hereditary habit" (p. 198), had come to seem like human nature, could be essentially modified, that woman could assume a fair and suitable position in a reconstructed society, and that relationships between man and woman could be established on "a surer ground of mutual happiness" (p. 311).

References

Hawthorne, N. (1870). *Passages from the English Note Books of Nathaniel Hawthorne*. Boston, MA: Fields, Osgood.

Hawthorne, N. (1898). *The Scarlet Letter*. New York: Doubleday & McClure.

The Holy Bible, King James Version (1769). Oxford Edition. New York: Oxford Edition.

Woolf, V. (1974). *The Death of the Moth and Other Essays*. San Diego: Harcourt Brace Jovanovich.

CHAPTER THREE

Dimmesdale's ailment, Hawthorne's insight

M. Gerard Fromm

"Every dream has at least one point at which it is unfathomable; a central point, as it were, connecting it with the unknown." With this epigraph, James Mellow begins his award-winning biography, *Nathaniel Hawthorne in His Times* (1980). The words are Freud's, from *The Interpretation of Dreams* (1900a). Mellow ends his biography with Melville's belief, as conveyed by Julian Hawthorne, "that Hawthorne had all his life concealed some great secret, which would, were it known, explain all the mysteries of his career" (p. 589).

Hawthorne's life and work abound in mystery. He was an attractive but elusive person: a combination of reserve, coolness, gentility, and unexpected attentiveness that could transfix the other person in a middle distance of interest, loyalty, and unsatisfied desire. After his death, his wife, Sophia, said that he "veiled himself from himself. I never dared gaze at him . . . It seemed an invasion into a holy place . . . [H]e was . . . to me a divine Mystery . . ." (Miller, 1991, p. 9).

The mysteries of *The Scarlet Letter* are themselves many and a major source of the novel's power. It is at once a romance, a tragedy, and an allegory, dense with symbolism and themes that can be read historically, biblically, even clinically. From that latter angle, a number of questions invite examination. How did Hawthorne know about psychosomatic illness—Dimmesdale's ailment—fifty years before Freud? How might we think about his startling descriptions of the treatment relationship and of child development? Does a clinical perspective on his life history contribute anything to an understanding of the text?

*   *   *

Arthur Dimmesdale is suffering; he is pale, emaciated, melancholic, and progressively weakened by pain. His will to live is fading. He is eventually treated by the physician, Roger Chillingworth, with whom Hawthorne sets up that basic tension between faith and science pervading Western culture since the fourteenth century. "In [a doctor's] researches into the human frame, it may be that the higher . . . faculties of such men were materialized, and . . . lost the spiritual view of existence amid the intricacies of that wondrous mechanism . . ." (1990, p. 119). On the other hand,

> (t)here was a fascination for the minister in the company of the man of science, in whom he recognized an intellectual cultivation . . . together with a range and freedom of ideas, that he would have vainly looked for among the members of his own profession. (p. 123)

Dimmesdale's faith, "supporting, while it confined him", met in Chillingworth "a window . . . admitting a freer atmosphere into the close and stifled study, where his life was wasting away . . ." (p. 123).

To be a doctor implies healing, but "to doctor" can mean to adulterate—to make impure by the mixing in of foreign or inferior elements. The American Psychological Association would certainly have affixed a scarlet A upon Dr Chillingworth for his breach of professional ethics, because he adulterated his therapeutic role with another role, that of wronged husband, and he allowed a murderous countertransference to mix with an initially therapeutic attitude. For Dimmesdale, on the other hand, Chillingworth's doctoring not only risks the revelation of his sin, it risks transforming the higher order of spirit into faithless materiality, a form of reverse alchemy. If Chillingworth were actually offering therapeutic understanding, would that absolve Dimmesdale of moral responsibility?

Adulteration or corruption—and both the hope for, and fear of, transformation—is a central theme of *The Scarlet Letter*, represented in

Chillingworth's doctoring and Dimmesdale's ministry, and enacted, though never named as adultery, in Hester's drama. Hawthorne had just experienced his own humiliating struggle with corruption in two ways: first, he had just been dismissed from his position in the Salem Customs House on politically motivated allegations of relatively standard, but politically based, unfair practices; more basically, he hated the fact that, in order to support his art, he had had to compromise himself by coming into the marketplace at all (the setting in which Hester is first humiliated) and involve himself—"an inoffensive man of letters"—with the customs of "thick-skulled and no-hearted" men (Egan, 1995, p. 5).

In the tension between Chillingworth and Dimmesdale, Hawthorne dramatises the potential for worldly knowledge to adulterate the spirit. Therapeutic help and the possibility of freedom are corrupting seductions to the genuinely guilty person. The novel can be read as an allegory about an original sin (whatever happened between Hester and Arthur preceded our knowing them) and the loss of Eden in a grasping for knowledge, carnal and otherwise. It is also relentlessly, if anxiously, a psychological *tour de force*, and the emerging science of psychology can be found both between and within its lines. Etymologically, psychology is the study of the soul, and one could argue that the mixing of these two terms (study and soul) represents, at least potentially, exactly the kind of adulterous danger our fictional doctor and patient dramatise.

*   *   *

Chillingworth, and, therefore, Hawthorne, knew something about psychosomatic illness and about the treatment stance eventually described by psychoanalysis. "(N)ot only the disease interested the physician, but he was strongly moved to look into the character and qualities of the patient . . ." "Wherever there is a heart and an intellect, the diseases of the physical frame are tinged with peculiarities of these." In Dimmesdale, "thought and imagination were so active, and sensibility so intense, that the bodily infirmity would be likely to have its groundwork there". The doctor "strove to go deep into the patient's bosom, delving among its principles, prying into his recollections, and probing everything with a cautious touch . . ." (Hawthorne, 1990, pp. 123–124).

Erik Erikson once advised his trainees that "you need a history and you need a theory, then you must forget them both and let each session stand for itself" (personal communication). Chillingworth wanted to know his patient's history. He had theories about the unconscious interaction between mind and body. He knew about a therapeutic stance of neutrality and empathy, which might allow the unconscious to speak.

> If (the investigator) possess native sagacity, and a nameless something more, — let us call it intuition; if he show no intrusive egotism, nor disagreeably prominent characteristics of his own; if he have the power . . . to bring his mind into such affinity with his patient's, that this last shall unawares have spoken what he imagines himself only to have thought; if such revelations be received without tumult, and acknowledged not so often by an uttered sympathy, as by silence, an inarticulate breath, and here and there a word, to indicate that all is understood . . . then . . . will the soul of the sufferer . . . flow forth . . . (Hawthorne, 1990, p. 124)

Belief in the soul–body connection constituted the historical foundation for the treatment of mental disorders. Disease was, for centuries, regarded as God's punishment for sin, exorcism was used in cases of possession, and the later procedure, called the "cure of souls", understood mysterious physical symptoms to be the result of a "pathogenic secret" (usually a sexual one) and confession to be its cure (Ellenberger, 1970). *The Scarlet Letter* takes its place within that latter tradition.

Freud stepped into and decisively advanced the scientification of this confessional tradition. *Studies in Hysteria* (1895d) argued that the symptoms of the hysteric stemmed from a pathological secret, kept secret even from herself through the work of unconscious repression. Hypnosis, then the quasi-sleep technique of free association—with the patient in a recumbent position and the analyst not intruding into the patient's field of vision—were the methods of accessing the patient's mental life and developing the material for the interpretation of what the patient was ambivalently trying to tell both of them.

Hawthorne's knowledge of, and wariness about, the clinical psychology of his day were evidenced in his distress over Sophia's interest in mesmerism. From early childhood, Sophia had suffered from numerous physical ailments; her mother never expected her to marry.

She became interested in the possibility of a cure for her headaches through hypnosis (also called "magnetic sleep"). Hawthorne responded with an uncharacteristic and panicky declaration:

> I am unwilling that a power should be exercised on thee, of which we know neither the origin or the consequence. . . . Supposing that the power arises from the transfusion of one spirit into another, it seems to me that the sacredness of the individual is violated by it; there would be an intrusion into the holy of holies . . . [My] view . . . is caused by no want of faith in mysteries; but from a deep reverence of the soul, and of the mysteries which it knows within itself. (Mellow, 1980, p. 190).

Like the doctor and patient in his novel, Hawthorne linked bodily suffering and spiritual vulnerability.

*   *   *

Hawthorne's insight into hysterical trouble long preceded Freud's, and, clearly, the maladies and the psychology of his day were sources of this knowledge. Another was his own life. Hawthorne's father died on a sea voyage to South America when the little boy was four. His mother (who, a bit like Hester, suffered the disgrace of having borne her first child only seven months after her marriage) became reclusive, depressed, and weakened, living out a withdrawn, though perhaps controlling, form of mourning for the rest of her life. In Sophia's ailments and weaknesses, Hawthorne found the perfect transferential life partner. He is said to have been transfixed at the first sight of her, after years of relative withdrawal in his mother's house.

He, too, was no stranger to emotionally based ailments. Not only did he suffer periods of depression, but, at age nine, following an injury to his foot, he seemed to unconsciously prolong his debilitation for over two years, using it to avoid school, to secure a place in his adopted home (his grandfather's), and to elicit a female servant's carrying him about, a form of physical affection pointedly denied to her children by his mother. The circumstances precipitating his ailment are suggestive (Miller, 1991, p. 48); his grandmother had just collapsed into acute grief at the near simultaneous death by stroke of her husband and the loss at sea of her son. Hawthorne might well have reacted to these events with the painful memory of his own father's death at sea, and an unconscious demand to be held might have protested the subsequent loss of his mother to depression. Hawthorne, thus, did not only know *about* the body's suffering with emotional trouble, he knew it first-hand in himself and, very likely, through identification with his mother.

*   *   *

In 1637, Hester's historical namesake, the English Puritan, William Prynne, criticised the abuses of power of church officials and, for his crime, was branded on his cheeks with an S and an L (for Seditious Libeller) (Hawthorne, 1990, pp. vii–viii). Prynne claimed that the letters stood for Stigmata Laudis; thus, he transformed official judgement through his own interpretation, claiming a sign connecting him, in praise, with God. Dimmesdale's A, in a climactic scene, can also be seen as a stigmata, an ecstatic union-in-suffering with the object of his love and his transgression. Like St Francis, given over completely, including physically, to suffering with Christ, Dimmesdale reveals that he is *with*, in a most basic and identificatory sense, Hester. Thus, he returns her transformational reassurance to him that "Thou shalt not go alone" (1990, p. 198).

The revelation of the scarlet letter on the flesh of Dimmesdale's chest is called the "operation of his spirit upon his body" (p. 258). Explanations of this phenomenon included Dimmesdale's penitential self-mutilation, Chillingworth's vengeful mix of medications, and "the effect of the ever active tooth of remorse, gnawing from the inmost heart outwardly . . ." (p. 258). In revealing it, Dimmesdale finally and publicly joins Hester, bringing her A-as-signifier together with Arthur as the signified. What Dimmesdale anticipates only as a shameful and damning admission turns out also to be an ecstatic reunion.

A consideration of identification illuminates not so much *what* Hawthorne knew about psychosomatic illness, but *how* he knew it. *The Scarlet Letter* powerfully suggests an answer to this question. "(T)he scarlet letter had endowed (Hester) with a new sense . . . it gave her a *sympathetic knowledge* of the hidden sin in other hearts" (p. 86, my italics). It was "her passport into regions where other women dared not tread" (p. 199). Chillingworth, too, has "a sympathy that will make (him) conscious" (p. 75), though he exploits it for revenge, and Hester's daughter, Pearl, functions on purely instinctive intuition, without "a grief that should . . . humanize and make her capable of sympathy" (p. 184). Dimmesdale, though he has "never gone through an experience" that would "lead him beyond . . . received laws" (p. 200), has the capacity for sympathetic knowledge even if he disavows it to his own peril. In learning of Chillingworth's betrayal, Dimmesdale says, "I did know it! Was not the secret told me in the natural recoil of my heart. . . . Why did I not understand?" (p. 194).

The answer to that question has to do with Hawthorne's romanticist mistrust of the Enlightenment exaltation of reason and with the way that illness absorbs the psyche, leading even the paranoid to fail to realise that somebody might be out to get him:

> [I]t was impossible to assign a reason for such distrust and abhorrence, so Mr. Dimmesdale, conscious that the poison of one morbid spot was infecting his heart's entire substance, attributed all his presentiments to no other cause. (p. 140)

For Hawthorne, reason deceives. In contrast, "the sympathy of Nature" (p. 203) resonates with Hester's and Arthur's love, and "the great heart" of the people, facing Hester, Arthur, and Pearl on the scaffold, "overflow(ed) with tearful sympathy, as knowing that some deep life-matter—which, if full of sin, was full of anguish and repentance likewise—was now to be laid open to them" (p. 254).

Hawthorne always counters the polarisation of good and evil—the localisation, projection into, and extrusion of the representation of evil being the primary effort of seemingly rational, puritanical authority— with a more complex, human, and multivalent attitude: sin *and* anguish, "fellow-sinner *and* fellow sufferer" (p. 67). Sympathetic knowledge crosses the boundary between one person and another, and adulterates absolute judgements with the human likelihood that to truly know is to love.

* * *

If Chillingworth bears similarities, in his more benign form, to a psychoanalytically orientated psychiatrist, Hester draws on her capacity for sympathetic knowledge to become an exceptional therapist herself.

> [A]s Hester had no selfish ends . . . people brought all their sorrows and perplexities, and besought her counsel, as one who had herself gone through a mighty trouble. Women, more especially,—in the continually recurring trials of wounded, wasted, wronged, misplaced, or erring and sinful passion,—or with the dreary burden of a heart unyielded, because unvalued and unsought—came to Hester's cottage, demanding why they were so wretched, and what the remedy! Hester comforted and counseled them, as best she might. (p. 263)

Hawthorne, like his three major characters, had the therapeutic gift of "heart-knowledge" (p. 260). Dimmesdale's superiority over the rest of the church fathers has to do with his ability to speak in "the heart's native language" (p. 142). Whether Hawthorne's gift, like Dimmesdale's, was nurtured by "the prick and anguish of his daily life" (p. 141) is an interesting question, and one cannot help but wonder about its origins. The depth of his understanding of women and the notion of sympathetic knowledge itself would suggest that it lies in his early relationship with his mother.

On Independence Day 1804, Nathaniel Hawthorne was born in a house on Union Street in Salem, Massachusetts. Descended from a line of public officials who tortured young women condemned as witches and later from a line of seafaring captains, Hawthorne grew up in a household of lonely, reclusive women. (In 1785, about 11% of the population of Salem were widows (Miller, 1991, p. 11). Salem paid for its commercial success by the loss of its men at sea.) There is no data about his early relationship with his mother. We do know that Hawthorne hated to be parted from her, even though she was a reserved and not very gratifying person. He even once expressed the wish that he had been born a girl so that he would not have to be separated from her. He also seemed to feel that she would have great difficulty in being separated from him; he was extremely frightened to tell her that he was marrying (at the age of thirty-eight), as was Sophia about making this announcement to her mother.

Most strikingly, Hawthorne reacted to his mother's death with, first of all, what his wife called a "brain fever" (Miller, 1991, p. 273) and then with the feverish writing of *The Scarlet Letter* over a period of six months. Hawthorne described his experience at her deathbed in his journal:

> I love my mother; but there has been, ever since my boyhood, a sort of coldness of intercourse between us, such as is apt to come between

persons of strong feelings, if they are not managed rightly. I did not expect to be much moved at the time . . . though I knew that I should deeply remember and regret her . . . I found tears slowly gathering in my eyes . . . for a few moments, I shook with sobs. For a long time, I knelt there, holding her hand; and surely it is the darkest hour I ever lived. (Mellow, 1980, p. 297)

Hawthorne's mother's death released him into a rare breakdown into grief, and it also released his capacity to write. We might remember here Dimmesdale's other, if minor, ailment: "his thoughts had ceased to gush" (Hawthorne, 1990, p. 223) in his preparation of his Election Sermon. After his encounter with Hester in the forest, "he wrote with such an impulsive flow of thought and emotion, that he fancied himself inspired" (p. 225). Emotional reconciliation had cured a writer's block. Perhaps his mother's death had overwhelmed Hawthorne with (and freed him to express) the "strong feelings" he alluded to as dangerous "if not rightly managed". Hester listened to the Election Sermon (the date for which was determined by the Day of Resurrection) "with such intentness, and sympathized so intimately, that the sermon had throughout a meaning for her, entirely apart from its indistinguishable words" (p. 243). As, perhaps, had Hawthorne's intimacy with his mother at her death: "(s)he knew me", even if she "could only murmur a few indistinct words" (Mellow, 1980, p. 297).

*   *   *

In Freud's comment about the unfathomable place in every dream, the German word translated as the "central point" is *nabel*, the navel, the mark of the former bodily union between infant and mother. Hawthorne's capacity for identification, for sympathetic knowledge, must have come about through early, intimate, wordless connection with his mother. It might also have been the basis for his anxiety that there could indeed be "the transfusion of one spirit into another", as though the boundaries between mother and son might be permeable and one could actually become lost in the other.

The Scarlet Letter has been interpreted persuasively within the psychoanalytic theory of the family romance (Kennedy-Andrews, 1999): the oedipal drama of the wronged and vengeful father figure, the rivalrous and sexually guilty son, and the woman over whom they struggle. It is a rich framework for meaning making in the novel and in Hawthorne's life. A son left by his father to his mother at age four can indeed feel a kind of guilty victory, along with a fear of a vengeful return. Melville was not the only person to wonder about Hawthorne's dark secrets, and Hawthorne's comment at his mother's deathbed invites us to wonder *what* "strong feelings".

On the other hand, it could be argued that the boundary usually set by the father's forceful presence was, for Hawthorne, set obscurely and insecurely by his absence and substantiated in his mother's apparently life-long depression. Something about her was unreachable, even if it never let go. Like Pearl relating to the scarlet letter rather than to her mother, Hawthorne as a little boy might have encountered his mother's depression as something coming between them, a pain-filled mystery to be solved, provoking longings, anger, guilt, and desperate, if unconscious, curative efforts. Hester is referred to once as the "fallen mother" (1990, p. 117), and, during his vigil, Dimmesdale sees "his mother, turning her face away . . . methinks she might yet have thrown a pitying glance towards her son!" (p. 145). In the climactic revelation scene, Dimmesdale staggers toward Hester like "the wavering effort of an infant, with its mother's arms in view . . ." (p. 251). Hester physically supports Dimmesdale as he ascends the scaffold, an image of a mother finally holding the boy who cannot walk.

It is, however, in the story of Pearl and Hester that the mother–child relationship is most explicitly represented by Hawthorne. Like Hawthorne, Pearl is fatherless; Pearl even declares herself to "have no Heavenly Father" (p. 98). (Chillingworth sees "no law, nor reverence for authority" in Pearl, but Dimmesdale sees "the freedom of a broken law" (p. 134).) Pearl's innate gift is for a primitive kind of identification, especially mimicry; she is instinctively attuned to Dimmesdale's reflexive putting his hand to his heart, and she *knows*, though she cannot know that she knows, that it relates to the letter on her mother's breast.

> Children have . . . a sympathy in the agitations of those connected with them . . . especially, a sense of any trouble; Pearl . . . betrayed, by the very dance of her spirits, the emotions which none could detect in the marble passiveness of Hester's brow. (p. 228)

This is sympathetic knowledge in its natural, undeveloped, lived-out form.

Pearl both seeks and resists the discovery of the third party to her relationship with her mother. She studies Dimmesdale relentlessly, enquires of him, and asks for his recognition. On the other hand, the task of deciphering the scarlet letter and, of course, of understanding her mother is *hers*, her "appointed mission" (p. 180). In the critical brook-side scene, Hester reconciles with Dimmesdale. Pearl, on the other side of the brook, that is, with a new boundary between herself and her mother, is felt by Hester as "estranged" from her, "out of the sphere in which she and her mother dwelt together, and . . . now vainly seeking to return to it" (p. 208). But the truth of this had to do not with Pearl's wandering, but with Hester's having "admitted" another person, Dimmesdale, "within the circle of the mother's feelings" (p. 208). Pearl "hardly knew where she was" (p. 208).

Hester realises that "Pearl misses something she has always seen me wear [the scarlet letter which Hester has finally cast off]. Children will not abide any . . . change in the accustomed aspect of things" (p. 210), says Hester, and, indeed, during this drama, Pearl looks again and again at her mirror image in the brook, as though to say that what is reflected back from her mother must be exactly the image Pearl has always known, with nothing new having come between them. When Hester takes back the scarlet letter, Pearl declares, "Now thou art my mother . . . And I am thy little Pearl" (p. 211).

But it is Pearl's fate to be "humanize(d)" by grief. The kiss from Dimmesdale she refused in the forest—the mark of her father—she embraces on the scaffold. "A spell was broken. The great scene of grief . . . had developed all her sympathies; and as her tears fell upon her father's cheek, they were the pledge that she would grow up amid human joy and sorrow . . ." (p. 256). Pearl's demand (and her *appointed* mission) to be everything to her mother (in Freudian terms, an oedipal insistence, from one party or the other, to admit no Third) relents and accepts with both "joy and sorrow" the Other with whom her mother has all along been in relationship. The psychoanalyst Lacan describes this as the movement from the Imaginary Order, in which only the gratifyingly mirroring twosome exists, to the Symbolic Order, which limits desire in both parties but frees a child to "grow up amid human(s)" (1977).

The drama of *The Scarlet Letter* is, on the one hand, about separation overcome (between Arthur and Hester) and, on the other, about separation established (between Hester and Pearl). The child is, however reluctantly, freed by the mediating return of the father. Perhaps the story of Pearl, Hester, and Arthur suggests a slightly different version of the oedipal triangle for Hawthorne: that at his mother's deathbed, he is released from the futile effort to cure her in order to be cured by her, and released to feel *for* her rather than simply *with* her. Perhaps Hawthorne's mother's death meant to him that she had at last joined his dead father, and that her sobbing, loving son had finally understood her lifelong absence and made his peace with it. Hawthorne had achieved the grief that had eluded him and his mother for so long. Melancholia had become mourning.

*   *   *

Hawthorne's creative gift lies in his ability to move his readers *into* his characters through identification with their most basic human emotions. This always brings about "Another View" (Hawthorne, 1990, p. 159) of them, beyond the initial or official one. And there is always a remainder of mystery. The power of official authority to determine meaning—the A *must* signify Adultery; Hester is *not* an individual, but a type, a symbol (1990, p. xx)—is continually subverted by the author's capacity to move us into sympathetic knowledge. The human subject always eludes external, fixed signification, and she does so because we feel her feelings and identify them in ourselves.

Hester's A comes to stand for Able in the townspeople's eyes (an ironic, punning reversal of the scarlet letter's being earlier referred to as the mark of Cain). It could just as easily stand for Angel, which is Dimmesdale's word for her, or for the Artist who embroiders. Like Hester, Hawthorne, too, is an embroiderer—of tales (p. xxxvi); his A might stand for Author (a word homophonically embedded in his name, and very close in sound to the name Arthur). Hawthorne's becoming an author, in the male world he was expected to inhabit, was an ongoing stressful act of taking authority for his life and an assertion of the gift of sympathetic knowledge he had developed in identification with a woman. In *The Scarlet Letter*, the most important A might have to do with the triumph of personal and moral Authority over institutionalised authoritarianism. A Freudian oedipal victory would have had to do with the son's *power* to defeat his father (or the official fathers of the story); oedipal resolution has to do with the surrendering of power in favour of a longer-term project of taking *authority* over one's life. This is a process of both identifying with *and* separating from parental figures, a process involving love, repudiation, and grief.

* * *

Finally, there is Ann. "(A)t the threshold" of the story and of the prison door is "a wild rose-bush", offering its "fragrance and fragile beauty . . . that the deep heart of Nature could pity and be kind . . ." "(I)t had sprung up under the footsteps of the sainted Ann Hutchinson" (Hawthorne, 1990, p. 48), a historical figure and leader of the Antinomians, who believed that "the law is fulfilled in love" (p. 274) and that God spoke directly to the justified soul, without the necessary mediation of the official (male) ministry. Governor Winthrop, upon whose death the townspeople interpret the A in the sky as referring to his Angelic status, once angrily declared to Ann Hutchinson: "We are your judges, not you ours . . ." (Harding, 1990, p. xvii).

Banished from the soil of Boston in 1638, Ann nevertheless gives birth to a rose bush in Hawthorne's tale. This notion of fertile, female soil contrasts with Dimmesdale's worries that grass would never grow on his grave, and with the description of Chillingworth as potentially "sink(ing) into the earth, leaving a barren and blasted spot" (p. 175). Hawthorne himself had had a dream, years before, of lying down to sleep and awakening to find the earth completely burned beneath him (Mellow, 1980, p. 308). But there is "an absolute circle of radiance" (1990, p. 90) on the floor around Pearl and "a magic circle" (p. 234) around Hester. Hawthorne seems to be highlighting the generativity and emotional integrity of women in contrast to the sterilising officiousness and guilty compromises of men, including himself.

Ann Hutchinson's drama of judgement is also Hester's. Pearl is the blossom of both. Pearl "cr[ies] for a red rose" (p. 107); she is even named "Red Rose" (p. 110) by one of the ministers. Soon after his mother's death and his writing *The Scarlet Letter*, Hawthorne and Sophia had one more child. Rose grew up to become a nun ministering to cancer patients. She took the name Mother Alphonsa, which, of course, derives from alpha, the Greek letter A. For Hester, Pearl is "the scarlet letter endowed with life" (p. 102). Can we discern in the story of Rose—in her life's work, in her assumed name—the playing out of an unconscious sympathetic knowledge between herself and her father, and her carrying forward, as though his naming her had "endowed" it "with life", the "appointed mission" of transforming an A?

References

Egan, K. Jr. (1995). The adulteress in the market-place: Hawthorne and *The Scarlet Letter*. *Studies in the Novel*, 27: 5.

Ellenberger, H. F. (1970). *The Discovery of the Unconscious*. New York: Basic Books.

Freud, S. (1895d). *Studies on Hysteria. S.E.*, 2. London: Hogarth.

Freud, S. (1900a). *The Interpretation of Dreams. S.E*, 4–5. London: Hogarth.

Harding, B. (1990). Introduction to *Nathaniel Hawthorne, The Scarlet Letter*. Oxford: Oxford University Press.

Hawthorne, N. (1990). *The Scarlet Letter*. Oxford: Oxford University Press.

Kennedy-Andrews, E. (Ed.) (1999). *Nathaniel Hawthorne: The Scarlet Letter*. New York: Columbia University Press.

Lacan, J. (1977). *Ecrits*. New York: W. W. Norton.

Mellow, J. R. (1980). *Nathaniel Hawthorne in His Times*. Baltimore, MD: Johns Hopkins University Press.

Miller, E. H. (1991). *Salem Is My Dwelling Place*. Iowa City: University of Iowa Press.

Mahler, Freud, and the symphony of a thousand: the 2005 Creativity Seminar

G ustav Mahler was born on 7 July 1860, in the small Moravian town of Kaliste. The 2005 Creativity Seminar began on his birthday. Stuart Feder, one of the presenters, writes that "the boy's affinity for music was apparent from the time when only singing could soothe him on the bumpy road to Ledec" (2004, p. 16) where his maternal grandparents lived. In their attic he was to discover an "enormous box" (p. 16) on which he played his first melodies. One imagines that this singing must also have been soothing to his mother, who lost her first child, Isador, to an accident the year before she gave birth to Gustav. Feder writes that "Mahler, like his ideal, Beethoven, was born in the shadow of death" (p. 14), "a replacement child" (p. 15).

We have learnt a great deal about the sense of mission felt by such children, especially if the surviving child is the eldest of his siblings. We have also learnt something about music through current infant research and everyday experience. Oral Hershiser, the former star pitcher for the Los Angeles Dodgers, was asked, during an interview, how he prepared for an especially important game. He said that he simply found himself humming a little tune as he warmed up, and it kept him calm. He had no idea what the tune was or where he had learnt it—until his mother phoned him. She happened to be watching the interview on television and was surprised by her son's story. This was the tune she had hummed to him constantly when he was a baby. So, the music of the human voice makes its mark early, and for some, like Mahler, becomes the medium through which the most powerful human emotions are expressed.

Mahler worked through more than one life crisis in his music, including the crisis of 5 July 1907, when his beloved elder daughter, Marie, named for his mother, died of scarlet fever and diphtheria. Devastated by this loss and the two other "hammer blows" (a phrase that comes from his description of his premonitory *6th Symphony*) (Feder, 2004, p. 124) of his forced resignation from the Vienna Court Opera and the diagnosis of his own heart murmur, Mahler gave exquisite form to grief in *Das Lied von der Erde* and his *9th Symphony.*

Ninety-five years ago, there was yet another blow; no gift or letter arrived from his wife, Alma, for Mahler's fiftieth birthday. Taking a rest cure for her own grief and unfulfilled ambitions — including ambitions to compose, which Mahler explicitly demanded she sacrifice for the sake of his music — Alma had begun an affair with the young architect, Walter Gropius. When Mahler learned of it, he broke down completely into a major and, at times, suicidal depression. He had just begun to pull himself together when he consulted Freud on 26 August 1910. They walked for four hours through the streets of Leiden, where, to use Winnicott's phrase from a different context, "something halfway between an analysis and a conversation broke out between" them (Winnicott, 1989, p. 508). Following their talk, Mahler gave Alma the only gift of jewellery he ever offered her, and, equally unprecedented, dedicated his monumental *8th Symphony* to her.

The première two weeks later was one of the major cultural events of the new century, a continuation of that late nineteenth-century explosion of European creative potency and pride that had led to the Eiffel Tower and, later, the *Titanic.* On 12 September 1910, 1,029 performers were assembled on stage to inaugurate the grand opening of the *Neue Musikfesthalle* in Munich. The *8th Symphony* was unlike anything ever heard before: a triumphant "gift of joy" Mahler called it, in two apparently disparate sections, the first, a setting of the ninth century Pentecostal hymn, "Veni Creator Spiritus", and the second, the final scene from Goethe's *Faust.* Mahler had brought together neobaroque music, sung in Latin, with romanticist music at its apex, sung in German, into his only fully choral symphony.

Composed four years earlier, during a time in their marriage when Mahler first realised Alma's growing unhappiness with his inattention, the *8th* can be seen as a grand effort at uniting apparent contradictions. Its themes include creative inspiration, the gift of being able to speak across differences, the Faustian bargain, the unifying power of love, and unearned redemption through the intercession of a wronged woman and the grace of a divine mother. It is as though the insight Freud helped Mahler articulate four years later—an insight stemming from Mahler's realisation that Alma's middle name was also Marie—had already intuited itself in this unique musical achievement. In the chapter that follows, John Muller explores the nature of sublimation as it relates to this magnificent work, which ends with the words, "The indescribable is here performed".

References

Feder, S. (2004). *Gustav Mahler: A Life in Crisis.* New Haven and London: Yale University Press.

Winnicott, D. W. (1989). James Strachey: Obituary. In: *Psychoanalytic Explorations*, Cambridge, MA: Harvard University Press.

Sublimation and *das Ding* in Mahler's Symphony No. 8

John Muller

When Gustav Mahler arrived at his summer retreat in June, 1906, he was, as usual, filled with doubt about whether he would be able to compose. He reports, however, being immediately "seized by the Spiritus creator" which "shook and lashed" him as he felt the music being "dictated" to him (quoted in de La Grange, 1999, p. 889; see also Mahler, 2004, p. 234, 357). Earlier that year, he had said of his difficulties, "There was the Court, there was the press, there was the audience, there was my family, and finally the enemy in my own breast . . . Often, it was terrible!" (de La Grange, p. 394). After he had finished the symphony in August 1906, he wrote,

> I have finished my Eighth Symphony. It is the grandest thing I have done yet, and so peculiar in content and form that it is really impossible to write anything about it. Try to imagine the whole universe beginning to ring and resound. These are no longer human voices, but planets and suns revolving. . . . It is a gift to the nation. All my previous symphonies are just preludes to this. In the other works everything is still subjective-tragic—this one is a great joy-bringer. (quoted in de La Grange, p. 926)

We can see in this creative transformation the work of sublimation. Sublimation, in my view, has a triadic structure in which the creative work as sign produces new effects in us that bring us in contact with a nameless presence.

Mahler's Eighth Symphony is the first symphony written primarily for the voice as an instrument; it uses two texts that direct the reader to a transcendent object. The first text, the ninth-century Latin hymn, "Veni Creator Spiritus", is a plea for grace; the second text, Part Two of Goethe's *Faust*, celebrates the redemption of Faust as well as his lover Gretchen and three penitential women (Mary Magdalene, the Samaritan woman in the Gospel of John, and Mary of Egypt). Both texts affirm the fragility of human beings and our inability to save ourselves by ourselves. Mahler uses these texts not only to point to a dimension we long for beyond our human reach, but he also performs the inadequacy of human language to bring us there by enveloping us with the human voice in sonority rather than in signification. The effect is to use the texts to create a verbal signifying direction, then an edge-of-signification threshold limit marked by complex contrapuntal polyphonies in which the words become dense, and then sheer sonorous resonance, and this is repeated over and over.

Sublimation in psychoanalysis

In surveying psychoanalytic theories of sublimation, I have suggested (Muller, 1999) that a wide range of psychological functioning is engaged in the act of creating through a sensible medium as well as in the effects produced by the object created. These modes of engagement reach across a broad range of mental states; I describe five types of sublimation, each related to a particular psychological organisation, along the lines of the hierarchical model proposed by Gedo and Goldberg (1973). I have labelled these as pre-subjective, subjective, dyadic, triadic, and post-subjective.

1.   The *pre-subjective* dissolution of boundaries in very disturbed patients requires some materiality as a medium to set markers in an otherwise dedifferentiated, nameless psychotic terrain. Since language no longer provides an anchoring and containing function for them, such patients carve on their flesh, paint with their

blood, find ways to use substitute objects: a patient who was suicidal one night stretched out his bed sheet on the floor and painted on it, and the next morning told me, "I hanged the pic-ture instead of myself." The premier statement of this condition is carved on a wooden sign that hangs over the entrance to the shop–studio at the Austen Riggs Center: "No one has ever writ-ten, painted, sculpted, modeled, built, or invented except literally to get out of hell—Antonin Artaud".

2.   A *subjective* focus on maintaining a sense of cohesion often takes the form of using others to regulate one's equilibrium; created works can serve as self-objects (Kohut, 1976) or as opportunities to repair internal objects damaged by one's felt aggression (Klein, 1929).

3.   *Dyadic* relations with created objects often mirror or replace inter-personal relationships; for example, Arnold Modell states that the "psychology of creativity" can be "modeled on the psychology of object relations" (1970, p. 224). In this kind of engagement with the created object, sublimation can assist with the work of mourning.

4.   *Triadic* psychological structures (id–ego–superego, drive–object–aim, self–other–ideals) form the basis of Freud's view of sublima-tion, as when he wrote, "Sublimation is a process that concerns object-libido and consists in the instinct's directing itself towards an aim other than, and remote from, that of sexual satisfaction" (1914, p. 94). In this mode of sublimation, drive gratification is achieved because repression is bypassed.

5.   *Post-subjective* engagement in sublimation goes beyond an ego-centric attempt toward self-expression, drive gratification, or use of others to mirror oneself, grants the personal limitations of one's mortality, and attempts a transformation of one's narcissism into an affirmation of a transcendent horizon. This function of subli-mation is directly at odds with a common contemporary summa-tion such as the following, which states that "the forms and structures of music embody the experience of human subjectiv-ity, and the analysis of music must focus on its function in the actualization, elaboration, and enhancement of self-experience" (Hagman, 2005, p. 98). The contributions of Lacan (1992) are useful in thinking about sublimation at the post-subjective level of engagement, and it is at this level of engagement, and not as a

form of self-expression, that I will be considering Mahler's *Eighth Symphony*.

The French psychoanalyst Jacques Lacan (1901–1981) emphasised the structuring effects of language on experience, on what he called the three registers of experience (Felman, 1987; Muller & Richardson, 1982). The Symbolic register organises experience through any sort of articulation, so that through systems of signs presented in language, ritual, institutions, and all forms of culture, we are suffused with models that map our lives. The Imaginary register consists of all the ways we are captivated by the sensuous aspects of objects, the imagery which fascinates and incites desire, the image we try to present of ourselves, the mirroring reflections that promote the ego's prestige. The register of the Real is what is left over, for what we call reality is a collage of the Symbolic and the Imaginary, while the Real is what lies beyond the epistemological frontier of names and images. The Real is undifferentiated, without gaps, associated with the dissolution of boundaries and the loss of distinction between subject and object. Sublimation approaches the Real, the nameless, through the presentation of what Lacan called *das Ding*, "the Thing".

For Lacan, sublimation does not provide a substitute object, a replacement for some lost object, but, rather, brings us contact with a nameless non-object. To borrow Freud's metaphor for his intervention with Mahler when they met for a four-hour session in 1910, sublimation is "as if you would dig a single shaft through a mysterious building" (quoted in Feder, 2004, p. 233; see also Jones, 1955, and Mitchell, 1958): sublimation sends a beam of light down into ourselves, exposing the structure of our desire in relation to the nameless. It is this nameless non-object that was addressed by Lacan, following Freud, as "the lost object" or *das Ding*, "the thing", that which is least individuated and determined and yet can still be spoken of in some way (Muller, 1987).

In his "Project for a scientific psychology" (1895), Freud attempts to describe the earliest relational matrix between an infant and his or her care-taker from which an iconic form of understanding develops; Freud writes,

> Thus the complex of a fellow-creature falls into two portions. One of these gives the impression of being a constant structure and remains as a self-contained *thing*; while the other can be *understood* by the

activity of memory – that is, can be traced back to information about the subject's own body. (1950a, p. 331)

This "cognised" aspect of the mother is graspable through an iconic identification, a mirroring experience, a likeness of perceived bodily signs, whereas the other "portion" remains "as a self-contained *thing*" (1950a, p. 331) ("als *Ding* beisammenbleibt", 1950b, p. 416) and cannot be understood, cannot be mirrored, is without likeness, and remains unknowable, "an unassimilable portion (the thing)", writes Freud (1950a, p. 366) ["einen unassimilierbaren Teil (das Ding)," 1950b, p. 445]. This unassimilable, unknowable, nameless "portion" of the mother becomes the basis for the lost object of desire.

In his later essay on negation, Freud (1925h) emphasises that *das Ding* refers to pre-subjective aspects of experience in which primitive attributions of "good" or "bad" are narcissistically made based on whether something is assimilated or spat out, and that this inchoative state precedes the subject–object distinction: "The antithesis between subjective and objective does not exist from the first", writes Freud (1925h, p. 237). Once the subject–object distinction is constituted, however, the unassimilated "portion" of experience is lost to understanding. This creates a void, a gap, in the experience of the objective, something remains opaque, strange, and unassimilable in the other, as well as on the side of the subject, since a "portion" of the subject's own pre-subjective experience is lost to understanding once the subject–object distinction takes hold. This loss is the foundation of human desire and of all forms of human enquiry. Hence, Freud can state that the "first and immediate aim, therefore, of reality-testing" is not to find an object but "to re-find" it (1925h, p. 237), because "a precondition for the setting up of reality-testing is that objects shall have been lost which once brought real satisfaction" (1925h, p. 238). The setting up ("die Einsetzung", 1948, p. 14) of reality testing, not necessarily its further development and operations, is motivated by the search for the lost and impossible object of desire, that which was "unassimilable" in the other and, likewise, unnameable in experience.

What makes this "object" lost and impossible? I take Freud's description of the transition from pre-subjective experience to the establishment of the "antithesis" between subject and object as referring to what Winnicott called "the place where it can be said that *continuity is giving place to contiguity*" (1967, p. 101), that is, where continuity gives way to separation, to the splitting effects of the intervention of language and signifying convention:

> What is lost in this transition from immediacy to mediated relations is maternal sonority as such, which is now necessarily taken as a *sign* of presence; what originally was sheer sonorous resonance is now quickly overshadowed by words expressed in a given tone of voice. The same shift affects mother's smell, touch, rhythm, color, taste, each of which, once they become signs of presence and of desire, lose their former immediacy and now become idiosyncratic traces of the lost object, that portion of the mother that remains unassimilable and *als Ding beisammenbleibt*—remains as a self-contained thing. (Muller, 1999, p. 118)

This is what I think Freud conveys when he writes to Fliess of "the prehistoric, unforgettable other": "Attacks of dizziness and fits of weeping—all these are aimed at *the Other*—but mostly at the prehistoric, unforgettable other who is never equaled by anyone later" (Masson, 1985, p. 213).

Lacan addressed this primordial field of the unforgettable lost object through the experience of what he called "that excluded interior" (1992, p. 101), referring to it as "the emptiness at the center of the real that is called the Thing" (p. 121). He gives a new name to what is lost in the subject as well as in the object, lost because of the subject–object opposition and the mediating intervention of signifying convention, referring to what is lost "as the central place, as the intimate exteriority or 'extimacy' that is the Thing" (1992, p. 139). Lacan here separates himself from those such as Loewald (1988), for whom sublimation "is a kind of reconciliation of the subject–object dichotomy" (p. 20), for, according to Loewald, it is "the original unity that is in the process of being restored, or something of it saved, in sublimation" (p. 13). For Lacan, sublimation does not restore such unity but, rather, brings us to the edge of a nameless void, for he writes that "in every form of sublimation, emptiness is determinative" (1992, p. 130). He gives examples of prehistoric cave paintings lining the inside of a void, the frescoes on the walls lining the cavities of temples and churches, the potter's jug which can be receptively empty only because it encloses a void: he repeats that "All art is characterized by a certain mode of organization around this emptiness" (1992, p. 130).

For Lacan there is no adequate object of desire, no possibility of becoming "whole", since our origin as human subjects is founded on a lack, a gap, a "something missing" that we can never replace.

In keeping with Freud, Lacan stressed that in the primordial field preceding the subject–object distinction, *das Ding* "was there from the beginning, that it was the first thing that separated itself from everything the subject began to name and articulate" (1992, p. 83). It is "the first outside" and "is to be found at the most as something missed. One doesn't find it, but only its pleasurable associations" (1992, p. 52). The place of *das Ding* is related to the place of the mother at the earliest edge of signification:

> I mean that the whole development at the level of the mother–child interpsychology—and that is badly expressed in the so-called categories of frustration, satisfaction, and dependence—is nothing more than an immense development of the essential character of the maternal thing, of the mother, insofar as she occupies the place of that thing, of *das Ding*. (1992, p. 67)

Why, then, is *das Ding* said to be the void at the centre of the subject?

> The reason is that *das Ding* is at the center only in the sense that it is excluded. That is to say, in reality *das Ding* has to be posited as exterior, as the prehistoric Other that it is impossible to forget—the Other whose primacy of position Freud affirms in the form of something *entfremdet*, something strange to me, although it is at the heart of me, something that on the level of the unconscious only a representation can represent. (1992, p. 71)

In sublimation, this representation has a specific function. Lacan, in giving "the most general formula" of sublimation, states that "it raises an object . . . to the dignity of the Thing" (1992, p. 112). He then gives the example of Jacques Prevert's linking together in a wall, hanging hundreds of empty match boxes, each of them enclosing the void, showing "the Thing that subsists in a match box", as an example of raising an object to the dignity of *das Ding*. In sublimation, therefore, we are given "the revelation of the Thing beyond the object" (1992, p. 114). We are given access to the lost, impossible object of desire through the back door, as it were, bypassing repression and the constraints of subject–object thinking.

In summary, in this post-subjective mode of engagement, sublimation does not present the desiring subject with an object of desire or need, but, rather, engages the very structure of desire itself by addressing desire's void through the revelation of *das Ding* beyond the art object, present in its absence through our own longing, expectation, hope, illusion, exquisite sadness, and ecstatic resonance.

Sublimation and das Ding in Symphony No. 8

Where do we see *das Ding* in Mahler's Symphony No. 8? Mahler's words, quoted earlier, bring together a number of Lacanian themes regarding sublimation. Mahler states his symphony is "so peculiar in content and form that it is really impossible to write anything about it", implying that in transcending the conventional signifying framework of the symphony, he has broached the nameless, the unwritable. When he asks the reader to try "to imagine the whole universe beginning to ring and resound", he takes us to the limit of ordinary signs and invokes the possibility of sheer sonority, prior to the subject–object distinction of our familiar framework in which signs stand for objects in some respect. The usual dimension of vocal signification has been altered: "These are no longer human voices, but planets and suns revolving". The human voice has here become transpersonal, evocative rather than denotative, located at the edge of signifying capacity, especially in passages of complex polyphony as well as in high-pitched, extended, open-vowelled solos. The voice here, as Mahler stated, is "the most beautiful instrument of all" (quoted in de La Grange, 1999, p. 933). The figure of "planets and suns revolving" articulates the symphony's structure and resonance with that of a cosmic scale of light and movement.

Mahler contrasts this symphony to all of his previous ones: in them "everything is still subjective–tragic", whereas the Symphony No. 8 "is a great joy-bringer". I read this to suggest that in the previous symphonies an element of self-expression, of mirroring of subjective states, has a dominant role, whereas in the present one a greater degree of transcendence of the purely personal has been achieved. As Feder (2004), in his recent psychobiography of Mahler, writes,

Autobiographical sources were symbolized in Mahler's music rather than blatantly represented in some literal fashion. Mahler was in this sense a master of sublimation, as deeply personal sources of musical content were divested of the particular and rendered universal. (p. 119)

Rather than conveying subjective aspects of gaining or losing an object of desire, the symphony seems to open up the structure of desire itself as an arc governed by an impossible longing, a longing whose nameless object sustains the very desire destined never to reach its human realisation.

Mahler's symphony has two parts: the first consists of a polyphonic elaboration of the Latin hymn, "Veni Creator Spritus"; the second part sets to music the ending of Goethe's *Faust*, Part Two, completed the year before Goethe died at the age of eighty-three. The two texts span a thousand years of European history and draw on the two languages that shaped the course of most European languages and culture. The Latin hymn was translated by Goethe (de La Grange, 1999, p. 892) in 1820; de La Grange states that "Mahler never ceased to read Goethe and was steeped in his thinking" (1999, p. 929). Goethe's text ends with a paean to "das Ewig-Weibliche"; "the Eternal-Womanly"; we can ask: how do we get from the Creator Spiritus to das Ewig-Weibliche?

Symphony No. 8, Part One: Veni Creator Spiritus

Lacan follows Freud in identifying the three fields of sublimation as science, religion, and art. Each takes its own position toward *das Ding*. Lacan states that science forecloses *das Ding* through a kind of negative hallucination, or unbelief, operating as if it did not exist and did not function as cause of desire. This allows it to ground its claim to pretended objectivity. Religion circles around *das Ding* in a kind of respectful displacement. Art represses *das Ding* by covering its place with a representation.

Mahler chose as his first text in the Eighth Symphony a venerable Latin religious hymn, the Veni Creator Spiritus, and we can attempt to see how it circles around *das Ding*. The hymn dates probably from the ninth century. Some scholars make a case for its being composed by Hrabanus Maurus, Abbot of the Benedictine monastery at Fulda, a student of Alcuin, and later the Archbishop of Mainz, who died in 856. In its oldest accepted version, dating from tenth-century manuscripts

(Wilmart, 1932), it has six four-line stanzas, with eight syllables per line. It begins with the second person singular imperative form of the verb "to come", "Veni", here more a petition or invitation than an imperative, addressed to the Spirit as Creator, and is a request for the visitation of grace. The first three stanzas offer descriptive terms for the Spirit being addressed, that is, the second person "You" of the imperative "Veni", and the second three stanzas state in what forms grace is being requested.

Here (with my literal translation) is the standard version of the text (Wilmart, 1932, pp. 41, 44; also in de La Grange, 1999, p. 894), which de La Grange states "is clearly the one Mahler had before him during his first week" at his summer retreat in June of 1906 (1999, p. 894, n. 30):

Veni creator spiritus,	Come creator spirit,
Mentes tuorum visita,	Visit your minds,
Imple superna gratia,	Fill with grace from above
Quae tu creasti pectora.	The hearts you created.
Qui paraclitus diceris,	You who are called consoler,
Donum Dei altissimi,	Gift of God most high/deep,
Fons vivus, ignis, caritas,	Living spring, fire, love,
Et spiritalis unctio.	And spiritual balm.
Tu septiformis munere,	You seven-formed in gift,
Dextrae Dei tu digitus,	You finger of God's right hand,
Tu rite promissum patris,	You of old promised by the Father
Sermone ditans guttura.	Enriching throats with speech.
Accende lumen sensibus,	Inflame with light the senses,
Infunde amorem cordibus,	Pour love into hearts,
Infirma nostri corporis	The infirmities of our body
Virtute firmans perpeti.	Fortify with lasting strength.
Hostem repellas longius	Drive the enemy far away
Pacemque dones protinus,	And grant continuous peace,
Ductore sic te praevio	With you leading the way
Vitemus omne noxium.	May we avoid all harm.
Per te sciamus, da, patrem	Through you may we know the Father
Noscamus atque filium,	And have familiarity with the Son,
Te utriusque spiritum	And you the spirit of each
Credamus omni tempore.	May we believe in all seasons.

The following two stanzas, included by Mahler, are considered later additions to the hymn:

Da gaudiorum praemia,	Grant the rewards of joy,
Da gratiarum munera,	Give the favours of graces,
Dissolve litis vincula,	Break the chains of wrangling,
Adstringe pacis foedera.	Make fast the ties of peace.
Gloria Patri Domino	Glory to the Lord Father
Natoque, qui a mortuis	And to the Son, who from the dead
(Deo sit Gloria	(Glory be to God
Et filio qui a mortuis)	And to the Son who from the dead)
Surrexit, ac Paraclito,	Rose, and to the Paraclete,
In saeculorum saecula.	Unto generations of generations.

The bracketed words in the last stanza, which is another but later Doxology, were added by Mahler; the seventh stanza, with its rhymed scheme a-a-a-a, although included in some old German manuscripts, was clearly written by another hand aiming at greater polish, in marked contrast to the direct simplicity of the six-stanza accepted version (see Wilmart, 1932, p. 41, n. 3). It was apparently this seventh stanza that was missing to Mahler as he was composing and observing the rigour of the sonata form of Part One (de La Grange, 1999, p. 893). When the text arrived by telegram, he was astonished at the perfect fit with the music:

> . . . he felt so elated, so moved about this that he told the story . . . and spoke of his "ecstatic joy" at the "miracle," the "mystery" which made the "words of the text coincide exactly with the bars already composed, and with the spirit and content of the composition". (de LaGrange, 1999, p. 428)

The Latin hymn's stated attributes of the "You" being addressed, with "You" being repeated in the Latin second person singular "Tu", like the use of "Du" in German, the intimate form of religious address, include the following:

> Creator of minds and hearts
> Source of grace
> Called Paraclitus (advocate, counsellor)
> Gift of God most deep/high

Living Source
Fire
Love
Spiritual balm
Seven-formed gift
Promised by the Father
Enriching throats with speech
Finger of God's right hand (as presented later, for example,
in Michelangelo's Sistine Chapel ceiling depicting the
creation of Adam).

These attributes are various attempts to give names to what is experienced as the nameless and wholly gratuitous source of life, grace, love, consolation, and speech. This source from the start is named as "Creator" of both our minds (*mentes*) and bodies (*pectora*, "breasts") and whose presence is requested through "grace" that comes from beyond (*superna*) as a gift of God who is beyond ("*altissimi*," "most high", as in the heavens, or "most deep", as in an abyss). We do not presume to know the Creator Spiritus as most beyond, but we can say, "You who are called Paraclitus", called or spoken of as the advocate, consoler or counsellor, somehow held in speech by language's ability to allude to and address what is not immediately given in experience as present. Yet, this power of speech, that which makes us most human in our ability to address the Other, itself derives from the Spirit who "enriches our throats with speech", transforming what is merely "guttural" into the very hymn we are now speaking. Living source, the warmth and light of fire, love, and the skin-to-skin contact of "unction" ("unctio" means a rubdown with oil), these suggest a maternal nourishing, including the transmission of the "mother tongue". The concrete imagery is warranted by our acknowledgement that, body and mind, we are created and remain dependent.

The term "septiformis", "seven-formed", refers to the traditional seven gifts of the Spirit, as initially formulated in the text of the prophet Isaiah (11: 1–2):

There shall come forth a shoot from the stump of Jesse and a branch shall grow out of his roots. And the Spirit of Yahweh shall rest upon him,

the spirit of wisdom and understanding,
the spirit of counsel and might,

the spirit of knowledge and piety,
and he shall be filled with the spirit of the fear of the Lord.

The Hebrew word here for spirit is *ruah*, a word that appears more than 350 times in the Hebrew Bible. One commentator writes,

> It is used in the first place to denote wind or a breath of air. Secondly, it is used for the force that vivifies the human being—the principle of life or breath and the seat of knowledge and feeling. Finally, it indicates the life of God himself, the force by which he acts and causes action, both at the physical and at the 'spiritual' level. (Congar, 1997, p. 3)

But the meaning of "spiritual" is, at best, ambiguous:

> What do we mean when we speak of 'spirit' and say that 'God is spirit'? Are we speaking Greek or Hebrew? If we are speaking Greek, we are saying that God is immaterial. If we are speaking Hebrew, we are saying that God is a storm and an irresistible force. This is why, when we speak of spirituality, a great deal is ambiguous. Does spirituality mean becoming immaterial or does it mean being animated by the Holy Spirit? (Danielou, 1971, quoted in Congar, 1997, p. 4)

The Greek risks abstraction of what in the Hebrew is experienced as more startling, more numinous, with the features that Otto, in *The Idea of the Holy*, named as "tremendum" and "fascinosum", the fearfully awesome and the gripping, features that are associated with the "Wholly Other" (Otto, 1926).

Mahler made modifications to the Latin text.

1.   He emphasised our body's infirmities, naming them first in stanza four and placing that stanza third, ahead of its usual position. The body's infirmities and the request for lasting strength constitute one of the major musical themes of the symphony.

2.   He substituted the word "pessimum", "most distressing", for "noxium", "harm", although some of the older manuscripts have this word. We can speculate about the possible resonance with the German word "Pessimismus" and the affects associated with it.

3.   He omitted the attributes, "promised by the Father" and "enriching throats with speech" in stanza three. The promise of the Spirit

in the Bible (e.g., Joel, 2, 28–29 and repeated in Acts 2,17) might have had complicated associations for Mahler, a Jew who became a Catholic convert, as required by his appointment as director of the Vienna Court Opera. This complexity was evident when Mahler "admitted that the Eighth was perhaps the Mass he would never be able to bring himself to write because he couldn't compose music to the Credo" (de La Grange, 1999, p. 929).

4.   The attribute of the Spirit, "enriching throats with speech", may have been omitted by Mahler because signifying speech was subordinated in the symphony to sonorous vocalisation. The sonority that so characterises Mahler's music disturbed many critics who attended the performances of his works (Painter, 1995), and there is a four thousand year tradition of warnings against the seductiveness of the singing human voice when it is disjoined from words (Dolar, 1996). Mahler's "original and wholly modern use of solo voices and chorus, with an unsurpassable mastery of sonority, colour, timbre, and acoustics, has not yet inspired a detailed study, but it merits one" (de La Grange, 1999, pp. 932–933).

The tone and rhythm of the opening music in which "Veni" is sung to the Spirit are consistent with joyful, even ecstatic, expectation while remaining an invitation for contact and an appeal for grace that reaches beyond our power to achieve by ourselves. The Creator Spirit is asked to come with grace into our minds and hearts because we are frail mortals who do not see, do not love, and will die of bodily infirmities or be killed by the enemy. Following the opening of "Veni", the main themes, organised by the musical frame, and in particular the vocal solos, include the following.

1.   *Imple superna gratia*: Fill with grace from above. This is the first vocal solo passage of the symphony; the subsequent polyphonic repetition of "gratia" washes over us like rain, generous, gratuitous, life-giving, reminiscent of the Credo in Bach's B-Minor Mass when the chorus repeats "in remissionem", "for the remission of sins". This theme of grace is echoed in the second movement by the repetition of the musical theme when Gretchen refers to Faust's spirit and says, "Er ahnet kaum das frische Leben", " He barely senses the new life", and also by the invocation of the

gracious Mater Gloriosa and the Ewig-Weibliche which draws us onward.

2. *Infirma nostri corporis*: The infirmities of our body. This musical section is one of the few passages when the symphony's tone spirals downward to become dark and foreboding, counterpoised by a contrasting violin solo, as fragile as an individual life. Mahler had a near-death experience with internal bleeding in 1901 (Feder, 2004). Following this medical crisis, he told Bruno Walter: "I possessed certainty, but I have lost it; and tomorrow I will possess it and lose it the day after" (quoted in de La Grange, 1999, p. 462). In 1907, one year following his composition of the Eighth Symphony, again at his summer retreat, his older daughter, aged five, died of diphtheria; he was then also told he had a grave heart condition. Three months before the symphony's first performance in 1910, he learnt that his wife, Alma, was having an affair. Within a year, Mahler was dead. Our fragility and ineluctable mortality are the clearest signs of our human inadequacy and establish our existence as always at the edge of the nameless abyss. When the chorus asks the Spirit to drive the enemy far away, we hear a dissonant shriek and an impassioned plea for peace. In the second movement, the "Infirma" musical theme is repeated in conjunction with the Angels' reference to "ein Erdenrest," an earthly residue, painful to bear, which clings to Faust's spirit.

3. *Accende lumen sensibus*: Inflame the senses with light. The tenor's yearning for "lumen, lumen" movingly underscores how insufficient we are and how dependent we are on grace. Mahler stages his only march of the symphony after this moving plea for light, as if to ironise, by repeating "sensibus", how ready we humans are to aggrandise our senses and be proud of it. This is referenced in the second movement by the plea "O Gott! . . . Erleuchte mein bedürftig Herz!", "O God! Light up my insufficient heart!" just before the redemption of Faust is announced.

The links between the first and second movements of the symphony are vastly more complex than this. Schoenberg wrote,

When one tries to grasp that these two sections of the Eighth Symphony are nothing other than one single extraordinarily long and broad idea, a single idea conceived, contemplated and mastered at a stroke, then one stands amazed at the power of a mind which, even when young, was fit for unbelievable things, and which here achieves the seemingly impossible. (quoted in de La Grange, 1999, p. 905)

Symphony Number 8, Part Two

The lines immediately preceding the closing chorus invite us to join the "higher spheres." Goethe's text reads as follows:

Mater Gloriosa [speaking to Gretchen about Faust]:

Komm! Hebe dich zu höhern Sphären!	Come! Lift yourself to higher spheres!
Wenn er dich ahnet, folgt er nach.	When he senses you, he follows after.

Chorus:

Komm! Komm!	Come! Come!

Doctor Marianus and Chorus:

Blicket auf zum Retterblick,	Look up to the redemptive gaze
Alle reuig Zarten,	All contrite frail beings,
Euch zu sel'gem Glück	That you may to blissful happiness
Dankend umzuarten!	Be gratefully translated!
Werde jeder bess're Sinn	May every better sense
Dir zum Dienst erbötig;	Become ready for service to you,
Jungfrau, Mutter, Königin,	Virgin, mother, queen,
Göttin, bleibe gnädig,	Goddess, stay gracious,
Bleibe gnädig!	Stay gracious!

"Gnade" is the German word for "grace." The "higher spheres" bring to mind Mahler's own comment about "planets and suns revolving" and resounding in his symphony. The text, in repeating "Komm!", rejoins the text of the Latin hymn, beginning with "Veni", "Come", inviting the Creator Spirit to come with grace into our minds and hearts. Here, however, the invitation comes *from* the Other, from the "Mater Gloriosa", whose gaze is redemptive to us frail creatures, for through it we can have access to the bliss she offers us as the impossible combination of virgin, mother, queen, and goddess, who is asked to stay gracious. Earlier she was addressed as "Du Gnaden-reiche! Du Ohnegleiche!", "You rich in grace! You unequalled!" And again, "Du Ohnegleiche, Du Strahlenreiche", "You unequalled, You richly radiating light". Here we have an invitation to/from the prehistoric unforgettable Other to join us frail mortals through grace and light.

The final lines of *Faust*, Part 2, which conclude the symphony, may be read (and heard) as the culminating affirmation of the presence in absence of *das Ding*, the nameless and indescribable lost and impossible object of desire which draws us on (my translation):

Alles Vergängliche	Everything transient
Ist nur ein Gleichnis;	Is but a parable;
Das Unzulängliche	That which falls short
Hier wird's Ereignis;	Here becomes event;
Das Unbeschreibliche	The indescribable
Hier ist's getan;	Is here performed;
Das Ewig-Weibliche	The Eternal-Womanly
Zieht uns hinan.	Draws us onward.

Human experience as transient and mortal is "only" a sign, a likeness, whose object, pointed to through analogy, is something else which is not yet named. The inadequacy of human experience, its inability to reach out on its own and attain the nameless is here declared to be "event", a visible occurrence. The nameless, that which cannot be written, is here performed, put into act, engaged, made Real. The nameless is the "Eternal-Womanly", Lacan's "la Chose maternelle", Freud's *das Ding*, which draws us on as the impossible object of desire, and which here, in this final passage of the symphony's performance, in its sonority, through sublimation, is present, but precisely as absent for human realisation, as the impossible non-object of human desire.

The music does everything it can here to show us this impossible object, and then it seems to do a bit more by using silence: there is a momentary pause (between sections 202 and 203) for both chorus and orchestra after "Ist nur ein Gleichnis", "Is only a parable", as if to direct us to the unnamed term of the analogy (see the score in Mahler, 1989, p. 246). The silence is like a gap that lets us "see" through the music to what the music "sees" and is trying to show us. The silence as inarticulate sets a limit to the music at this moment in so far as the silence, as silence, articulates precisely what cannot be named—*das Ding* beyond the music, or what, in terms of the music, is not. When the chorus repeats, with more insistence and force, "Alles Vergäng-liche ist nur ein—", "Everything transient is only a—", instead of hear-ing again the expected "Gleichnis", we are given a loud single percussive beat followed by the forte "Das Ewig—", "The Eternal—", in multiple repetition of the very vowels that open the Symphony, "Veni", "Come".

Conclusion

The Latin hymn is overtly a prayer for grace and an acknowledgement of the transcendence of the Holy Spirit; the end of Part Two of Mahler's symphony has been called a "hymn to the action of grace" (de La Grange, p. 912). Adorno thinks otherwise; writing of Part One, he tells us that

> the invocation is addressed, according to an objective sense of form, to the music itself. That the Spirit should come is a plea that the compo-sition should be inspired. By mistaking the consecrated wafer of the Spirit for itself, it confuses art and religion. (1971, p. 139)

I agree we should try not to confuse art and religion or anything else (e.g., politics) with religion, but one can still make the effort to see how they might be related. Adorno also states, referring to the Eighth Symphony as the "magnum opus",

> The magnum opus is the aborted, objectively impossible resuscitation of the cultic. It claims not only to be a totality in itself, but to create one in its sphere of influence. The dogmatic content from which it borrows its authority is neutralized in it to a cultural commodity. In reality it worships itself. [Its] Holy of Holies is empty. (p. 138)

Here, Adorno may be confusing commodity and art, or, rather, making such a Marxist analysis of late capitalism that we are enjoined from thinking that art and commodity might be distinct, even though we may buy and sell anything. He goes on to present with approval a remark of Hans Pfitzner (a composer who worked hard to ingratiate himself with Mahler through Alma—see Feder, 2004, p. 131): Adorno is here discussing

> . . . the ritual art-works of late capitalism. Their Holy of Holies is empty. Hans Pfitzner's jibe about the first movement, *Veni Creator Spiritus*: "But supposing He does not come," touches with the percipience of rancor on something valid. (1971, p. 138)

Adorno sees Mahler as double-crossed, or double-crossing us into believing that something is present when it is not. I would prefer to think Mahler is engaged in a double traverse, addressing what is beyond the known through the incantation "Veni" in Part One, and in Part Two, in the other direction, *we* are addressed, in Faust's place, "Komm! Komm!" by what lies beyond our subject–object field. The charge that this might be a lie is unwarranted in this context: it may be an illusion, for there is no other way to represent it except by another representation that, elaborated by musical genius, constitutes a massive illusion, intricately structured, detailed, and moving.

What I am calling the double traverse has to do with the semiotic impact of addressing and being addressed. Bakhtin (1981) claims that in any address, an ideal Other is framing the signifying field, guiding one's articulation toward clarity. I would say that any articulation, therefore, requires a kind of act of faith that the Other will comprehend my statement, for it is the Other's potential comprehension that I set before me as I begin to speak (or write). In a like manner, the possibility of being addressed by an Other depends in part on my willingness to believe that the Other is capable of addressing me and that I am capable of listening and responding. If I dismiss the possibility of being addressed, I will most probably miss the address, should one be made to me. This double traverse, in which the addressor becomes somehow the addressee, suits George Steiner's view of all great art:

> The archaic torso in Rilke's famous poem says to us: "change your life." So do any poem, play, painting, musical composition worth meeting. The voice of intelligible form, of the needs of direct address from which such form springs, asks: "what do you feel, what do you think of the possibilities of life, of the alternative shapes of being which are implicit in your experience of me, in our encounter?" (1989, pp. 142–143)

That the Holy of Holies might be empty is but another way of saying that sublimation brings us to the edge of an abyss, the extimacy which is called *das Ding*, the unnameable in experience and the void that marks the arc of human desire. When music can bring us to this edge we weep, we are flooded with longing, we find most other things around us, for the moment at least, unsatisfying. Adorno appears to sense this when he writes,

> Mahler's music holds fast to Utopia in the memory traces from child-hood, which appear as if it were only for their sake that it would be worth living. But no less authentic for him is the consciousness that this happiness is lost, and only in being lost becomes the happiness it itself never was. (1971, p. 145)

I would say the experience of the lost, impossible object of desire in sublimation brings not happiness, but a kind of resonance with one's human condition, that the experience of finding absence in this way is precisely what art gives us. We look and find nothing, no-thing, what Peirce called but another name for God, what Heidegger called *das Nichts*. We are cognitively entrained by the subject–object structuring of experience to go from object to object in our associations, to go from something to something, so that we expect to find something in the Holy of Holies. When we find nothing, we conclude God does not exist. God might not exist, but to conclude this from finding no-thing simply attests to our own limitations. What is of interest is how we find the no-thing, and how we are addressed by it, especially in a work of art.

Das Ewig-Weibliche as *das Ding*, the lost, impossible object of ecstatic desire, impossible to attain on this earth, reconciles the opposition between Adorno's viewpoint, that the Holy-of-Holies is empty (1971, p. 138), with Mahler's tragic experience, the void of extimacy. I cannot give you the object, Mahler seems to be saying, but I will bring you to the edge of the unnameable and bring you the joy of sublimation, and say with Goethe, the unnameable is here performed.

References

Adorno, T. (1971). *Mahler: A Musical Physiognomy*, E. Jephcott (Trans.). Chicago, IL: University of Chicago Press, 1992.

Bakhtin, M. (1981). *The Dialogic Imagination: Four Essays by M. M.* Bakhtin, M. Holquist & C. Emerson (Trans.). Austin, TX: University of Texas.

Congar, Y. (1997). *I Believe in the Holy Spirit*, D. Smith (Trans.). New York: Crossroad.

De La Grange, H. (1999). *Gustav Mahler, Volume 3, Vienna: Triumph and Disillusion*. Oxford: Oxford University Press.

Dolar, M. (1996). The object voice. In: R. Salecl & S. Zizek (Eds.), *Gaze and Voice as Love Objects* (pp. 7–31). Durham, NC: Duke University Press.

Feder, S. (2004). *Gustav Mahler: A Life in Crisis*. New Haven, CT: Yale University Press.

Felman, S. (1987). *Jacques Lacan and the Adventure of Insight: Psychoanalysis in Contemporary Culture*. Cambridge, MA: Harvard University Press.

Freud, S. (1914c). On narcissism: an introduction. *S.E., 14*: 73–102. London: Hogarth.

Freud, S. (1925h). Negation. *S.E., 19*: 235–239. London: Hogarth.

Freud, S. (1950a)[1895]. Project for a scientific psychology. *S.E., 1*: 295–398. London: Hogarth.

Freud, S. (1950b). *Aus den Anfangen der Psychoanalyse*. London: Imago.

Freud, S. (1954). *The Origins of Psycho-analysis: Letters to Wilhelm Fliess, Drafts and Notes: 1887–1902*, M. Bonaparte, A. Freud, & E. Kris, (Eds.), J. Strachey (Trans.). London: Imago.

Gedo, J., & Goldberg, A. (1973). *Models of the Mind: A Psychoanalytic Theory*. Chicago, IL: University of Chicago Press.

Hagman, G. (2005). The musician and the creative process. *Journal of the American Academy of Psychoanalysis and Dynamic Psychiatry, 33*(1): 97–117.

Jones, E. (1955). *The Life and Work of Sigmund Freud*, Volume 2. New York: Basic Books.

Klein, M. (1929). Infantile anxiety-situations reflected in a work of art and in the creative impulse. In: *Contributions to Psycho-Analysis, 1921–1945* (pp. 227–235). London: Hogarth Press, 1948.

Kohut, H. (1976). Creativeness, charisma, group psychology: reflections on the self-analysis of Freud. In: J. Gedo & G. Pollock (Eds.), *Freud: The Fusion of Science and Humanism* (pp. 379–425). New York: International Universities Press.

Lacan, J. (1992). *The Seminar of Jacques Lacan, Book VII: The Ethics of Psychoanalysis, 1959–1960*, J.-A. Miller (Ed.), D. Porter (Trans.). New York: Norton.

Loewald, H. (1988). *Sublimation: Inquiries into Theoretical Psychoanalysis*. New Haven, CT: Yale University Press.

Mahler, G. (1989). *Symphony No. 8 in Full Score*. New York: Dover.

Mahler, G. (2004). *Letters to his Wife*, H.-L. de LaGrange and G. Weiss (Eds.), A. Beaumont (Trans.). Ithaca, NY: Cornell University Press.

Masson, J. (Ed.) (1985). *The Complete Letters of Sigmund Freud to Wilhelm Fliess, 1887–1904*. Cambridge, MA: Harvard University Press.

Mitchell, D. (1958). Mahler and Freud. *Chord and Discord*, 2(8): 63–66.

Modell, A. (1970). The transitional object and the creative act. *Psychoanalytic Quarterly*, 39: 240–250.

Muller, J. (1987). Lacan's view of sublimation. *American Journal of Psychoanalysis*, 47(9): 315–323.

Muller, J. (1999). Modes and functions of sublimation. In: J. Winer (Ed.), *The Annual of Psychoanalysis*, Vol. XXVI/XXVII (pp. 103–125). Hillsdale, NJ: The Analytic Press.

Muller, J., & Richardson, W. (1982). *Lacan and Language: A Reader's Guide to Ecrits*. New York: International Universities Press.

Otto, R. (1926). *The Idea of the Holy*, J. W. Harvey (Trans.). Oxford: Oxford University Press.

Painter, K. (1995). The sensuality of timbre: responses to Mahler and modernity at the *Fin de siècle*. *19th-Century Music*, *XVIII*(3): 236–256.

Steiner, G. (1989). *Real Presences*. Chicago, IL: University of Chicago Press.

Wilmart, A. (1932). *Auteurs Spirituels et Textes Devots du Moyen Age Latin: Études d'Histoire Litteraire*. Paris: Études Augustiniennes, 1971.

Winnicott, D. W. (1967). The location of cultural experience. In: *Playing and Reality* (pp. 95–103). New York: Basic Books, 1971.

The play's the thing: the 2006 Creativity Seminar

T he 2006 Creativity Seminar gives this book one of its principal themes: play, which is central to both Erikson's and Winnicott's work. The chapter that follows takes up the theme of "deep play" within the transference with a very troubled patient. We began this volume with the story of the anxious, hesitant young woman who could not bring herself to cross the threshold into her therapist's office—until he said, "Jump!" What we come to understand in Christopher Fowler's harrowing and moving clinical account is that the work with some patients insists that the therapist jump, too.

We also noted in the Introduction Freud's comment that

> We render the compulsion to repeat harmless, and indeed useful, by giving it the right to assert itself in a definite field. We admit it into the transference as a *playground* in which it is allowed to expand . . . and in which it is expected to display to us everything . . . that is hidden in the patient's mind. (1914g, p. 134)

However, in the chapter that follows, the compulsion to repeat is anything but harmless, and forces us to remember again Erikson's critical distinction between play and "irreversible purpose" (Erikson,

1961, p. 156). This patient's life seemed lived on the razor's edge of that distinction, and threatened at every turn—especially turns involving separation—to cross over into irreversibility.

In this first fully clinical chapter, Christopher Fowler brings us into this drama—the family drama as it becomes intertwined with the treatment drama—and illustrates the therapeutic trajectory from actualised unconscious fantasy, deeply connected to traumatic experience, to the realisation of a hidden story, a therapeutic movement brought about through the medium of deep transference play. The patient's story, like Hamlet's, is full of family conflict, betrayal, vengeance, love, and loss, and, again, like Hamlet's, there is no shortage of blood.

References

Erikson, E. (1961). The roots of virtue. In: J. Huxley (Ed.), *The Humanist Frame* (pp. 145–165). New York: Harper.

Freud, S. (1914g). Remembering, repeating and working-through. *S.E., 12*: 145–156. London: Hogarth.

Stepping on to the transference stage: from actualised unconscious trauma to therapeutic play

J. Christopher Fowler

> Psychotherapy takes place in the overlap of two areas of playing, that of the patient and that of the therapist. Psychotherapy has to do with two people playing together. The corollary of this is that where playing is not possible, then the work done by the therapist is directed towards bringing the patient into a state of being able to play. (Winnicott, 1971, p. 38)

This evocative quote from paediatrician and psychoanalyst Donald Winnicott illuminates a core therapeutic challenge for therapists undertaking psychodynamic treatment of patients with severe character pathology. Sifting among the array of diagnoses, life stories, and chaotic backgrounds of patients, there appears a singular similarity: the problem of creating and maintaining a viable therapeutic alliance and space in which patient and therapist play out a symbolic drama, primarily through language and illusion, to resolve conflicts, and to symbolically put to rest the traumatic past by neutralising repetition compulsions.

Rather than using symbolic language, patients with severe character pathology frequently live out mental conflicts, pathogenic fantasies, and cyclical interpersonal patterns with the therapist without recognising the repetition or grasping emotional links to past experiences (Volkan, 2004, 2010; Volkan & Ast, 2001; Volkan & Fowler, 2009; Volkan, Ast, & Greer, 2002). In such cases, it becomes the therapists responsibility to help the patient shift from actualising to developing a capacity for therapeutic play in the form of a therapeutic story (Volkan, 1976, 2004) that can then come under conscious influence and lead to the creation of a new experience and a new internal representation or "new object" (Kernberg, 1975; Loewald, 1960; Volkan, 1976). Perhaps more so than any other psychoanalyst, Volkan has articulated the therapeutic principles and techniques necessary for bringing about this transformation (Volkan, 2010). As such, this chapter does not represent a new formulation or break new ground. Rather, it serves as an illustration of the technical challenges of shifting from actualised unconscious fantasies to symbolic play in a particularly harrowing case. More importantly, to my mind, it highlights the creative therapeutic play between two people engaged in a high stakes treatment.

Before turning to a case, it is necessary to briefly describe the form of actualisation of a traumatic experience that is more common among psychiatrically hospitalised patients with severe self-destructive tendencies. Unlike acting out/acting in (Fenichel, 1945), enactment (Jacobs, 1986), or revisiting the past with a pilgrimage (Volkan, 1979), the patient engages in risky, destructive, brinkmanship that evokes in the social partner the playing out of a role in an unfolding drama (Sandler, 1976). This does not appear to relate to the unanalysed past of the therapist as in the case of enactment, and neither is it a re-enactment of a past trauma. Rather, it is a particularly unpleasant form of projective identification (Klein, 1946) in which the patient's self-destructive behaviours induce in the therapist or social partner a set of feelings the patient finds unbearable. In short, the actualisation creates a *catastasis* — the dramatic climax of a play, preceding the catastrophe, in which the action is at its height.

A rare glimpse of an actualised unconscious fantasy (free from the theoretical trappings of a clinician) comes from a self-directed interview with Spalding Gray, the dazzling auteur of such memoirs as *Monster in a Box*, *Swimming to Cambodia*, and *Gray's Anatomy*. By most accounts, Gray was a deeply narcissistic, funny, and gloomy man obsessed with the conviction that he would kill himself. The extended extract picks up as Gray discusses playing a suicidal man:

At the time Steven Soderbergh cast me in that movie, I was having a lot of suicide fantasies. I was darkly convinced that at age 52, I would kill myself because my mother committed suicide at that age. I was fantasizing that she was waiting for me on the other side of the grave. Steven said I was his only choice for that role because he had read Impossible Vacation, which was about a man ruled by regret. I was taken by the fact that the character in the script had chosen cutting his wrists as the method of suicide, because that was one of my fantasies. So, this role was so powerful. To have my wrists made up for two hours, and five hours of setting up the blood—I was a witness to it for all this time, and I realized the old cliché of what a mess [suicide] is to leave for someone else to find—what a stupid, passive-aggressive, piggish thing to do to someone. After we finished the suicide scene, I walked back to the hotel with the make-up and dried blood. During this three-minute walk no one noticed except for this bum who ran from me. I got to the hotel and the people at the check out counter said, "Oh, gross," but that was it, because they knew I was in a film. I needed to have a reaction from someone. So I walked into the hotel drugstore and there was a woman about my mother's age when she committed suicide, filling out prescriptions. I held up my wrists and said, "Do you have anything for my wounds?" She said, "*My, God, what did you do?*" I answered I'd cut my wrists and she went into shock and said, "Well, we have Mercurochrome" and she frantically began to look for it. It was a vicious thing to do. I later realized that I was enacting a reversal of my mother's suicide. I had turned to my mother and said, "Look—what does it feel like to have your son commit suicide?" (*Los Angeles Times*, 1994)

This glimpse into a traumatic actualised fantasy, Gray's "suicidal" drama, speaks to the urgency to evoke in another an unbearable feeling, to exact revenge, and to rewrite his story in the living out of a long-held suicide fantasy. The pharmacist/mother's reaction— shocked, fumbling for words, and thrown off balance, is precisely the effect patients have on clinicians in such events. Unlike the pharmacist/mother, the therapist, holding the analytic frame as a guide, can open the way to a therapeutic story by taking up the assigned role, and, in time, help the patient transform the actualised fantasy into a therapeutic story with a different, less traumatic ending.

In the case of Spalding Gray, actualisation of his fantasy was not enough. Here is what is known about the events leading to his death. In June 2001, during a trip to Ireland, Gray's life fractured both physically and mentally when a small truck smashed into his car head-on. Gray suffered a head injury, a broken hip, and severed sciatic nerve. The result: a metal plate in his skull, a metal plate in his hip, a brace to hold up his drooping foot, all of which required extensive surgeries and rehabilitation. Once Gray learnt to walk, the suicide attempts began, culminating in Gray's suicide by drowning in the icy waters of the Upper Bay of the Hudson River (Williams, 2004). It was no coincidence that drowning was one way his mother had tried to commit suicide.

Spalding Gray's death stands in stark contrast to the urgency of his interaction with the pharmacist/mother. Gray's traumatic actualisation reminds us that patients are desperate to be understood and to escape their suffering. When patients engage in actualisation of a fantasy, the therapist must take up a role unconsciously assigned by the patient (Davoine & Gaudillière, 2004; Sandler, 1976; Volkan, 2004, 2010; Volkan & Ast, 2001; Volkan & Fowler, 2009; Volkan, Ast, & Greer, 2002) in order to move from traumatic actualisation to potential therapeutic play and the emergence of a therapeutic story. It is understandable why therapists are tempted to retreat to "risk management" strategies; however, premature efforts to manage the reality of risk (unless a realistic threat of physical harm or boundary transgression is imminent) might negate the patient's actions and interrupt the potential emergence of play.

When self-destructive behaviours do escalate, the communication of trauma to the therapist can become obscured and the frame of the psychoanalytic treatment can be lost in chronic crisis management. While inner life dominates the landscape in our consulting rooms, we must hold in mind the real dangers of suicidal behaviour. Narcissistic injuries, broken relationships, and loss can throw patients into deep despair and suicidal actions. The top priority is always patient safety, but this should not eclipse the search for meaning embedded in the actions. In the high-risk case discussed below, hospital staff provided much of the medical and social supports the therapist needed, so that a focus on meaning could be held in the psychotherapy. This example highlights the transition from actualisation to therapeutic story.

Prudence

Prudence is not her real name, yet the name fits her conservative southern manner, and deeply ingratiating interpersonal style.

Prudence is also the antithesis of this middle-aged divorcee—a bungee-jumping, skydiving, self-described thrill-seeking adrenalin junkie. To place her life in danger seemed to be the ultimate thrill, and once she had a near-death experience, she moved on to the next thrill. The one risk she never abandoned was attempting suicide. In the course of her life she had made many near-lethal suicide attempts interspersed among a chronic pattern of severe non-suicidal self-injury and anorexia. As a result, she spent much of her adult life moving between psychiatric hospitalisations and pursuing a career as a highly skilled real estate mogul and fanatical collector of a rare breed of horses.

During our initial consultation, Prudence informed me that her outpatient therapist sent her to the hospital because she had resumed deep cutting, carving through layers of muscle and severing nerves, requiring surgical repair. She repeatedly reopened the incisions in order to see the blood gush. In a desperate attempt to forestall the cutting, her surgeon placed a cast over her arm—she cut through the cast and down to the bone. She shared these gruesome details in a most cheerful manner. Her perfectly manicured hands created a jarring contrast to forearms and legs scarred from years of self-inflicted cutting. The paradox of her fierce destructiveness and cheerful demeanour created an eerie *dis-ease* in me. It was in this state of *dis-ease* that I agreed to work with Prudence, a veteran with decades of intensive psychiatric care.

She allowed me the courtesy of taking her life history, and took up the patient role, stating that she hoped to gain an understanding of why she had once again returned to cutting and starving as a means of dealing with stress. She shared the details of recent stressors including losing a bid on a prized stallion at auction. Prudence marked the onset of her cutting and starving to feeling unbearably envious of the young, attractive woman who "stole" her horse.

She noticed two things about her emotional life. First, there were periods of time when she felt nothing. These were terrifying moments, filled with fears of disintegration and sensations of falling forever. To escape these experiences, she would cut in order to see blood gush from her veins. In her mind, the red blood signalled she was alive, that she had feelings. She experienced immediate relief, would bandage her arm and go about her business without revealing what she had done. In the second state, emotions were a messy jumble, bleeding into one another without distinction. As I later learnt, she recognised this as fury but could not stake a claim on this particular emotion, because that would imply she had the right or privilege to be angry. It also signalled that she would be just like her mother and father, both of whom carried a public image of grace and self-control, but were dreadful alcoholics with hair-trigger tempers and little self-control.

Prudence's memory of her parents reflected the paradox of her emotional life and her public image. Memories of her father were split between the sweet, handsome, athletic father and the scary daddy who became bitter and hostile after a car accident left him paralysed. The daddy of the wheelchair evoked terrible memories of a drunken monster brandishing a shotgun and blowing a hole in the ceiling during a fight with her mother. Memories of mother shifted between the equivalent of a modern-day soccer mum and that of a southern Medea, threatening to kill her children during fits of rage. She and her siblings were fawned over during the good times, but were used as pawns in an ugly chess match between her parents when fights broke out. Among the stories she shared about her past was the following: "Mummy sent me in to tell Daddy that she had just taken an overdose and was dying. Daddy instructed me to tell Mummy, 'Good luck and farewell'".

Prudence and her siblings lived a life of privilege but were emotionally terrified by the chaos. Her brother, the eldest and the family namesake, became a drug addict, while her older sister developed obsessional rituals and settled into a quiet life as a rigid character. As the youngest child, she was left to create an identity out of the aristocratic social façade and violently chaotic home life. In time, she became a fearsome character capable of damaging her body without mercy or pain, and without fear of the consequence. It was this person I encountered in my office.

During the first three months of the treatment, she shifted from being cautious and emotionally distant to forming an idealising paternal transference, viewing me as a kind Southern gentleman. She claimed to feel soothed by my voice and "kind eyes", but her overt compliance and ingratiating style alerted me to a silent fear of a scary daddy. Efforts to develop a therapeutic space for dreams, fantasy, and associations were initially met with resistance in the form of further starving, but the cutting ceased. Within a few months her weight stabilised and she appeared to deepen her therapeutic engagement.

During the third month of treatment, I left for a ten-day vacation. When I returned, Prudence guiltily shared a dream in which we were skinny-dipping together in her mother's pool. She developed fantasies that I shared her passions and declared that I looked just like the love of her life—her favourite horse. Throughout the week, she flirted in the sessions, telling me, "You're easy on the eyes, doctor." I smiled politely, but said little, suspecting that the erotic material represented a form of "reaching up" (Blos, 1979) in an attempt to avoid feelings related to our recent separation.

The following Monday, she developed a potent resistance against feelings of desire, weakness, and frailty, by speaking of vindictive fantasies of destroying herself as others watched helplessly. I imagined these omnipotent fantasies were connected to our separation, as well as to her parents' seeming hatefulness toward each other and to her childhood impotence, which she seemed to have defended herself against by a grandiose self-destructiveness. I worked to help her understand the meaning of her fantasies and wondered aloud if her wish for revenge was related to my vacation. She politely ignored my efforts at a linking interpretation. In the remaining sessions of the week, I worked to understand and empathise with her feelings, but refrained from further premature intellectual interpretations of her fantasies, allowing the budding negative transference to emerge (Volkan & Fowler, 2009).

The negative transference escalated rapidly in a chillingly destructive drama; in the final minutes of her Friday session—before a weekend separation—she revealed a long-held secret: "Before coming to the hospital I smuggled a scalpel in my suitcase. I keep it hidden in my lingerie drawer." Her tone was confessional, but simultaneously subtly threatening. I silently reflected on the fact that for the past several sessions she had been producing vindictive fantasies of making her parents suffer. Now I perceived the slightest curl of her lips as she uttered "lingerie drawer". Sensing the seriousness of the moment, I silently fretted over details: "Why is she telling me this in the last two minutes of the session?" I then became preoccupied by a conference I was directing that weekend, felt a sudden pang of annoyance, and momentarily lost my therapeutic focus. With time running out, I regained my composure and surprised myself by responding almost exclusively to her furtive smile. Mirroring her anxiety and paradoxical excitement, I responded, "Something's gotta give!"

Technically, although I did not realise it consciously at the time, the intervention was an effort at *marked mirroring*, a technique advocated by Bateman and Fonagy (2004) in the treatment of borderline psychopathology in which the therapist expresses similar but differentiated affective experience from the patient. In the thirty seconds it took to escort Prudence to the door, I puzzled over why I did not explicitly insist she turn in the scalpel. My tone signalled my appreciation for the gravity of her secret, and my recalling our earlier encounters over her self-destructive behaviours reassured me that she understood that she was now responsible for terminating her destructive plans. Then, as she left the office, I found myself musing over the lyrics of a Frank Sinatra song:

> When an irresistible force such as you
> Meets an old immovable object like me
> You can bet just as sure as you live
> Somethin's gotta give.

"Something's gotta give" conveyed my insistence that she get us out of this dangerous spot, but I noticed it simultaneously evoked images of a playful, sexually tinged tussle. I then became preoccupied by another thought; she told me she was keeping the scalpel in her lingerie drawer. The series of associations that followed included the scalpel as restorative phallus for her feelings of weakness, the sexualised element that she had conveyed through her ecstatic experiences associated with cutting, and the fact that Frank Sinatra was of her parents' generation. As I closed the door, I wondered if the erotic material from earlier sessions was not simply a matter of reaching up, but a prelude to a different emerging paternal transference.

Later that afternoon, I found an envelope in my mailbox addressed to "Dr Fowler", with an odd, dark-red smudge on the corner. When I held it up to the light, I saw the word, *SCALPEL*. The package signalled that she had both resumed cutting and surrendered the scalpel. My sense of dis-ease returned as I struggled to imagine what my insistence — or perhaps my non-insistence — might have activated. Later that day, I learnt that she informed the nursing staff of her resumed cutting.

In preparation for our Monday session, I placed the unopened envelope containing the scalpel on the ottoman in front of her chair because I wanted to convey that her actions outside the therapy session were, in fact, between us. When she saw the envelope, a flash of rage quickly gave way to apologies. Prudence asked if I was giving the scalpel back to her. I remained silent. She wondered if I brought it in in order for us to talk about it. I said, "Yes." She then expressed guilt for keeping this secret from me, and for the first time in her five-month treatment, she looked genuinely scared. She stared at the envelope and said, "It could hurt me." I sat quietly. Her associations turned to omnipotent stories of what she called "cheating death". Before the hour was up, she asked me if I would keep the scalpel for her. I agreed. She left.

The next day, she expressed relief that I had taken the scalpel, but wondered if I was frightened of her "destructive side". She then turned to thoughts of her mother and linked her new fear of herself to the destructive mother of her childhood. She believed that her mother had taken over part of her soul, and that she cuts in order to "bleed out the bad mother". She remained somewhat sceptical about my willingness to be with such a destructive force. My remarks to her highlighted her willingness to bring in this destructive mother-image, her upset earlier in the week about the forthcoming long holiday weekend, and her destructive vengeful fantasies that emerged in the context of my upcoming absence. Silently, I imagined that every Friday session might represent my leaving her alone with the destructive mother inside her, with whom she felt merged.

On the following Tuesday (after the long weekend), I learnt that she had seriously cut her left wrist, necessitating a lengthy emergency surgery. Had she hidden more scalpels? Had I missed some clues? How had I failed to grasp the imminent catastrophe?

Prudence returned to her session the next day hoping that a feasible treatment could be created in the open hospital setting despite her near-lethal destructive behaviour. She was once again quite contrite and in a state of panic. I was in quite a state myself; at the sight of her bandaged arm, my blood began to boil, but I sat silently waiting to see what bubbled up in the space between us. As I listened to her apologies, I noticed a strange sensation; I felt enormous tension in my body and noted that I was holding the arms of my chair very tightly. From the periphery of my awareness, I heard Prudence bargaining to keep her treatment; she was terrified that she had thrown away our relationship. Her tears and anxiety had a rehearsed quality, so my attention returned to sitting still. I noticed that my feet were firmly planted on the floor, my hands planted on the armrests, and I felt a paralysis setting in, which I rationalised as a side effect of my emotional state.

I was filled with "therapeutic interpretations", which had been rehearsed in my mind many times since I learned of her cutting. Now, however, they seemed detached and formulaic, so I waited and tried to listen to her and to my feelings. She surprised me when she attacked me for making her give up her scalpel. It made her feel weak that she so easily caved into my demands; the scalpel stood for her independence from her mother, from doctors, from everyone. The fierceness of her attack and the grandiosity of her counter-phobic stance caught me momentarily off guard, but I refrained from countering with "therapist words", words that might dilute the intensity of the moment and pull me from the odd bodily sensations I was experiencing. I remained silent and still, though with an intensity I was sure she was beginning to experience.

Prudence became increasingly anxious. In the midst of another salvo of apologies, she cried, "I'm sorry Daddy!" Suddenly, I was her father sitting in a wheelchair. I remained immobile, puzzling over her slip of the tongue. She began apologising to her father, begging not to be punished. In that moment, I was foisted into the role of the scary daddy of the wheelchair, and she was the little girl apologising for her misdeeds. I remained in role, mostly responding with "Hmm ... Hmm!" When time was up, she stood to leave the room. Wishing not to disturb the illusion, I remained seated. She closed the door behind her.

When she returned to my office for her next session, she glanced at the ceiling, which led me to think that I had not blown a hole in the roof (metaphorically or literally). She now began apologising for the crimes of her childhood and her adolescent rebellion. In sessions of emotionally wrenching apology, Prudence began to associate to her pre-accident daddy, the handsome, sweet father of her early childhood. By Friday, the deep regression faded as she returned to addressing me as her therapist. I said nothing about this shift but returned to standing up at the end of sessions.

During her Monday session, she recalled playing hobbyhorse on her daddy's knee. She suddenly realised that this good experience with her strong, handsome daddy had sparked her love affair with horses and riding. She then remembered her mother scolding her father for the hobbyhorse play. Prudence wondered aloud, "Had my mother seen the pleasure in my eyes and stopped it?" Prudence embarrassingly spoke of the genital sensations stimulated by bouncing on her father's knee, followed by the terrible feelings of guilt she had about any sexual experiences or fantasies about men. In the next session, she bravely continued to open up this previously unspoken area of personal experience. She told me of her worry that I disapproved of her flirting with me when she said, "You are easy on the eyes". She also began to talk about her mother's infidelities after her father's accident and her little girl fantasies that maybe her mother would let her have her daddy.

When the curtain closes on traumatic actualisation

Several months after the surgery and following another long holiday weekend, she had the fantasy of reopening the wound. I wondered aloud if she were letting me know she was angry with me. She continued with the fantasy: "I would rip the bandages away, tear open the skin, and blood would splatter on the walls just as it had during the surgery." She then imagined my shocked expression and laughed as she exclaimed, "I'll show you!" I said nothing as she lingered over such a delicious thought. But, although I said nothing, I felt a wave of exhaustion as I imagined her long years of grandiose destructive fantasies compensating for feelings of loss and weakness.

Perhaps she caught the expression on my face because in the next moment she was crying. Something had struck a deep chord of emotion, and for the first time Prudence began to face the cost this inner war had inflicted on her body and life. She wept for herself and for the brutality she had heaped upon her body. That night she dreamed of a small human trapped inside a grape; for her, this represented a nascent version of her self who needed to be cared for rather than used as a chess piece to exact revenge on me. The image also carried associations to wine—and to alcoholism—but also to the need for a skin. Over time, we followed the development of her capacity for self-empathy, but also held in focus her periodic impulse toward savage attacks on her vulnerability when others disappointed or abandoned her.

The following month, we expanded on this theme by exploring the historical significance of pressing others into the service of protecting her body. What emerged (through dreams and associations) was a powerful identification with an aspect of her family life in which her mother manipulated the children and her husband to rescue her from suicide. As a child, she was frightened of her mother's suicidal threats, but as an adult she was contemptuous: her mother was never serious. Prudence knew that she was far more destructive than her mother. Thus, she came to see that her thrill-seeking behaviour, her overt destructiveness, and her manipulation of others served to reinforce a sense of omnipotence, vengeance, and triumph over the mother she had actually been terrified of losing.

We continued to explore the tentative development of self-concern, and its opposite—the excitement of self-destructive fantasies. As she began reworking these fantasies, she repeated the drama by, on a few occasions, again purchasing a scalpel, and making veiled threats at her most vulnerable moments: for example, on Friday afternoons when facing a long weekend without me. These threats—designed to keep me with her or, failing that, to punish me for leaving her—slowly evolved into the wish for a fulfilling relationship with a long-time friend of the family who was recently widowed.

The termination phase of this intense treatment was the litmus test for her capacity to tolerate vulnerability, which she seemed able to do because she now had the capacity to anticipate painful loss. Throughout this process, she continued to explore and develop a sense of internal motivation for caring for her body, her emotional life, and her mind. She developed a healthy anxiety about her stunning capacity for omnipotence and the grandiose belief that she was indestructible. When in distress, she easily resorted to this kind of fantasy, but was consistently aware that she did this out of a need to obliterate her vulnerability. She successfully navigated the termination of our work and the intense feelings about our separation without cutting, weight loss, or other destructive activities. She put her feelings into words and confronted her conflicts in a more direct manner.

During our final session, she cried openly, expressed gratitude, and reminded us both of the time she imagined I was her father in a wheelchair. As I stood to shake her hand, a sudden inspiration took hold. With the kind of warmth and respect that comes from fighting alongside a comrade in a war, I let the fullness of my Southern accent come through when I said, "Farewell and good luck!"

Françoise Davoine, who writes about trauma and psychosis associated with war, reports that one of her patients, after she had recovered, said to her, "What saved me was your ferocity" (personal communication). Prudence was ferocious to herself and implicitly to those who hoped to help her. In the deep play of the transference (a dangerous drama in which the patient *creates* the scene she needs to reach), the therapist must let himself *be created* as the heretofore unknown partner to this crucial scene. My experience of paralysis in the critical moment of her cutting emotionally re-created and co-created the ailing father whose loss this little girl was both trying to defend herself against and trying to contact. Allowing this crucial experience—one that gave her access to the father she adored before this loss—requires an equivalent ferocity in the therapist, a capacity to hold the intensity of the emotional moment while insisting that it not become catastrophe.

This process of deep play leading to genuine emotional discovery—in this case, to the story of a family's tragic collapse following an accident—can indeed feel as if it takes place in a war zone. If it turns out well, swords may become ploughshares. Prudence's father's "Farewell and good luck" to her mother was vicious sarcasm—the root meaning of which is to tear the flesh, precisely the symptom of his daughter. My "Farewell and good luck" held a different paternal experience—that a loved daughter must grow up and that both parties must let themselves feel the bittersweetness of that fact.

References

Bateman, A., & Fonagy, P. (2004). *Psychotherapy for Borderline Personality Disorder: Mentalization-Based Treatment.* Oxford: Oxford University Press.

Blos, P. (1979). *The Adolescent Passage: Developmental Issues.* New York: International Universities Press.

Davoine, F., & Gaudillière, J. (2004). *History Beyond Trauma.* New York: Other Press.

Fenichel, O. (1945). *The Psychoanalytic Theory of Neurosis.* New York: W. W. Norton.

Jacobs, T. J. (1986). On countertransference enactments. *Journal of the American Psychoanalytic Association, 34*: 289–307.

Kernberg, O. F. (1975). *Borderline Conditions and Pathological Narcissism.* New York: Jason Aronson.

Klein, M. (1946). Notes on some schizoid mechanisms. *International Journal of Psychoanalysis, 27*: 99–110.

Loewald, H. (1960). On the therapeutic action of psychoanalysis. *Journal of the Psychoanalytic Association, 41*: 16–33.

Los Angeles Times (1994). Interview: meet our newest interviewer: how do you interview a guy who's made a career of talking about himself? Easy—let Spalding Gray interview Spalding Gray, 17 April.

Sandler, J. (1976). Countertransference and role-responsiveness. *International Journal of Psychoanalysis, 3*(1): 43–47.

Volkan, V. D. (1976). *Primitive Internalized Object Relations: A Clinical Study of Schizophrenic, Borderline and Narcissistic Patients.* New York: International Universities Press.

Volkan, V. D. (1979). *Cyprus—War and Adaptation: A Psychoanalytic History of Two Ethnic Groups in Conflict.* Charlottesville, VA: University of Virginia Press.

Volkan, V. D. (2004). Actualized unconscious fantasies and "therapeutic play" in adults' analyses: further study of these concepts. In: A. Laine (Ed.), *Power of Understanding: Essays in Honour of Veikko Tähkä* (pp. 119–141). London: Karnac.

Volkan, V. D. (2010). *Psychoanalytic Technique Expanded: A Textbook on Psychoanalytic Treatment.* Istanbul, Turkey: OA Publishing.

Volkan, V. D., & Ast, G. (2001). Curing Gitta's "leaking body": actualized unconscious fantasies and therapeutic play. *Journal of Clinical Psychoanalysis, 10*: 567–606.

Volkan, V. D., & Fowler, J. C. (2009). *Searching for the Perfect Woman: The Story of a Complete Psychoanalysis.* New York: Jason Aronson.

Volkan, V. D., Ast, G., & Greer, W. F. (2002). *The Third Reich in the Unconscious: Transgenerational Transmission and its Consequences.* New York: Brunner-Routledge.

Williams, A. (2004). Vanishing act. New York *Magazine*, 2 February.

Winnicott, D. W. (1971). *Playing and Reality.* New York: Routledge.

Creativity at the extremes: the 2007 Creativity Seminar

"The Berkshires are going Dutch", announced a local newspaper (*Berkshire Eagle*, November 15, 2006), which went on to describe how local cultural organisations were working together to feature Dutch art in the summer of 2007. The Dutch focus brought me back to memories of working in two Group Relations Conferences in the Netherlands in recent years. In 2004, although the languages of the conference were officially Dutch and English, Dutch was never spoken; the Dutch members seemed sensitive to their guests feeling excluded, and so used the more universal language. But in 2006, Dutch was spoken with a vengeance. Indeed, a resurgent nationalism seemed to find powerful expression in the choice of language in the conference. I found myself wondering what had happened in the societal dynamic of this lovely, cultivated country.

The brochure for the 2007 Creativity Seminar opened with the words of Anne Frank. "I'm so longing for everything . . . I feel as if I'm going to burst . . ." (quoted in Gilligan, 2002, p. 92). Carol Gilligan, in her book *The Birth of* Pleasure, notes the four exclamation points after Anne's first self-description—"Gorgeous!!!!" (p. 79)—and sees in the gradual attenuation of Anne's voice not only her extreme circumstances, but also the unfortunate fate of too many adolescent girls. That Anne's wish to "burst" had to be tempered by her reading of others' needs might indeed have reflected a gender-related dilemma, but one that must have been escalated immeasurably by the brutal danger outside.

Anne's diary is an example of creativity in extreme circumstances, and though they were unique to the tragic time in which she lived, one can also imagine those circumstances as an acute variant of a particularly Dutch conflict: both a stimulus to, and a constraint upon, creativity. Anne Frank's home country was created from the sea. The history of Dutch society reveals a collective commitment either to "pump together" or risk a catastrophic bursting. It even includes using the sea as a weapon; at points in its history, the Dutch met a flood of invaders with a counter-flood created by the strategic bursting of its dykes. For the Dutch, the sea was simultaneously a constant threat and the source of its wealth and power, both of which provided enormous impetus for societal co-operation, innovation, and a practical ethic of tolerance for differences.

Today, Dutch tolerance, the product of extreme circumstances, is, as Russell Shorto argues in *The Island at the Center of the World*, embedded in the diverse and creative culture of its most famous settlement, Manhattan. At home, however, its relationship to Muslim immigrants has strained Dutch society to the point of intolerance. A little more than a century ago, Vincent Van Gogh inflamed his landscapes with the extremes of his emotional life; many years later, his great-grandnephew, Theo, used his extreme art to inflame a suppressed and uncharacteristic nationalism in his society—and paid for it with his life. Indeed, "what happened" between the two Group Relations Conferences was Theo Van Gogh's murder by an Islamic extremist on 2 November 2004, in response to what was considered his provocative and blasphemous film, *Submission*.

In the chapter that follows, Marilyn Charles and Karen Telis consider a number of questions about the creative process as it unfolded in the work of the first Van Gogh. How do especially difficult outer conditions generate, shape, constrain or destroy creativity? How are the extremes of inner emotional life channelled into the creative act? How does Van Gogh's creative genius evolve in the course of a passionate and increasingly complex life?

References

Gilligan, C. (2002). *The Birth of Pleasure.* New York: Alfred A. Knopf.

Shorto, R. (2004). *The Island at the Center of the World.* New York: Vintage Books, Random House.

Pattern as inspiration and mode of communication in the works of Van Gogh

Marilyn Charles and Karen Telis

"There are two ways of thinking about painting, how not to do it and how to do it; *how to do it*—with much drawing and little color; *how not to do it*—with much color and little drawing" (

(Van Gogh, 1958, Letter 184, The Hague, April 1882)

The authors, two sisters, a psychoanalyst and a writer, meet at the writer's home in Provence, what Frenchmen call the midi. It is a place of natural intensity, with blinding sunlight, howling mistral, and an arid climate that cracks the earth. Even so, the earth gives forth its own distinct bounty, begrudgingly, to labouring farmers as relentless as the nature they combat. The sisters ride bikes along paths through meticulously planted fields and observe waves of lavender blowing in the breeze, golden blocks of sunflowers reaching skywards, purple and yellow squares of iris bounded by grids of fences laden with craggy vines. Viewed from a distance, the landscape becomes patchwork, in vast seas of colour.

The sisters drive into St Rémy through an alley of gnarled plane trees whose canopy protects the travellers from the sun's intensity. They remark to each other on their impression that Vincent Van Gogh is everywhere. Their vision of Provence is his, one assimilated from countless museum visits, study of reproductions in books, long acquaintance through biographies and letters. His experience in Provence informs their own. They seek him.

An exhibit in Arles—black and white drawings accompanied by quotations from his letters to his brother, Theo—is a revelation: Vincent in black and white, sweeping lines that convey a kinetic energy that the women believed as only extant in his oil paintings. The absence of colour—that quality most associated with Van Gogh—bares for the eye, as if through an X-ray, the skeleton of his work, the power of line.

Line communicates far more than neutral reproductions of the land and its people; there is heavy emotional content, not easily verbalised. The text on the walls—the artist's own attempts to translate the intent underlying his creations into words—raises questions about the creative process of visual art. The black and white drawings disclose what colour in the oil paintings had obscured; the shape, direction, and repetition of line are sufficient to convey meaning and excite emotional response. Dialogue ensues.

Provence is a feast for the eyes. From any hillside, we, the sisters, look out on a vast sea of colours. Lavender fields complement the brilliant gold of the sunflowers, broken by the craggy arched limbs of grapevines criss-crossing the landscape. The intensity and brilliance of the colour in the sun-drenched air bring to mind the paintings of Van Gogh that speak so eloquently to the magic of this place. Van Gogh's work is evoked once again as we drive under canopies of plane trees, majestically arching over our heads. We marvel at how vividly he has captured the feel of this vital elegance that holds us in its thrall.

In looking at the black and white renderings of the exhibit in Arles, we are caught by the kinetic energy of the patterning in the drawings (see Van Gogh, 2003). The movement and intensity make us almost giddy as we study the intricacy and melody of the lines sweeping and swirling across the page. We wonder what it had been like for Van Gogh to be so assailed by the sensory opulence of this landscape—this man from the cool, grey north—and what it had been like for him to encounter these chaotic patternings with such complexities of rhythm, and to then begin to weave in the added intricacies of colour. We also wondered what we might find in his writings that would help us better understand the rhythms and patterns that had inspired him to produce works of such rich and compelling complexity. We were guided in our efforts by two factors: first, our appreciation of the importance of historical and other contextual factors that helped to position Van Gogh and his art. Second, our appreciation of the vast and profound realm of non-verbal communications through which art achieves its power.

This was a domain that would become more important with the advent of "modern" painting, in which the artist comes to the fore in a new way (Maritain, 1953). Van Gogh came upon the art scene before the modern era, at a pivotal point when there were new possibilities that had been unimaginable. Technology was creating new issues and new questions regarding the place of the common man in the world, and photography had put the artist up against a new dilemma: if reality could be captured in a photograph, what was to be the artist's place in this new world?

The impressionists confronted this challenge, exploring new ways of seeing and explicitly attending to perception itself in their investigations. Later artists, such as Van Gogh, moved beyond the issue of what is seen, seeking out a deeper reality beyond the image itself. We can only imagine this search, its elements, and its urgency, if we look first at his origins. We need to have some way of locating Van Gogh as he arrived in Provence, not to the vivid sunny beauty that we encountered, but, rather, to a grey and snowy winter's landscape that must have been highly evocative of the flat monochromatic plains of his youth. In his letters to his brother, Theo, he described the landscapes he encountered there, noting the relationships between the elements in the visual field. His responsiveness to, and appreciation of, the power of the juxtaposition of formal elements show his awareness of the form underlying the structure of the whole. His ability to use these tensions between elements accounts for some of the power of his work.

Adding to these tensions were the continual paradoxes that marked Van Gogh's development. He was passionately interested in ideas, but was unable to follow a conventional path of learning. Similarly, although he identified strongly with his pastor father, he was unable to follow his footsteps directly. Rather, Van Gogh became a lay preacher, in this way, focusing his care and concern on the poor peasant, with whom he identified strongly. Eventually, he began to focus on drawing, thinking that through this medium he could show his concern for the human condition. He then encountered some of these same difficulties in his art, finding it very difficult to survive within the conventional schools of the time, but instead using what he could and then moving off on his own.

First and foremost a man from the north, Van Gogh travelled far to finally find his way to Arles. At the age of twenty-eight, he went to The Hague to study drawing. His subjects there were poor city life, soup kitchens, coal yards, poor fisherwomen, and bleak landscapes of Holland. This was the period of the drawings at Scheveningen. Then, in 1885–1886, he was in Antwerp, where he studied classical drawing at the academy and the works of Hals, Rembrandt, and Rubens awakened him to the power of colour. From there he went to Paris, where he began to come to grips with Impressionism. Wherever he went, Van Gogh had trouble finding a home. We can see in his self-portraits from Paris his social and psychological discomfitures. Then, in May 1886, Van Gogh was studying Seurat and Signac's pointillism, a technique based on a very elaborate colour theory. According to Gardner, Seurat had

> developed a theory of expressive composition in which emotions were conveyed by the deliberate orchestration of the action of color and the emotional use of lines in a composition. For example, 'gaiety of tone' would be created by using warm, luminous colors and placing the most active lines and shapes in the composition above the perspective of the horizon line. (Gardner, 1948, pp. 996–997)

Van Gogh took great interest in these theories, reading intensively and coming back to them repeatedly in his letters to his brother, Theo. He charted out the relationships between the elements of his compositions in the rough sketches with which his letters to Theo are speckled, detailing his ideas more explicitly in the text. Van Gogh's evolving technique in Paris overlaps with his memories of the countryside of his youth and the presence of labourers. His renditions of the countryside are very different from the French painters' more polished depictions. This issue of the relative refinement of the portrayal is an interesting one with Van Gogh. In his attempts to remain true to his vision of the peasant who is grounded in the earth, he is often misperceived as rough and unrefined; however, Van Gogh was actually very well read and was capable of drawing with a very refined hand.

Indeed, his rendering capacities have been compared to those of Rembrandt (Heinich, 1996).

In line with this misperception, we also might imagine that Van Gogh worked quite frenetically, yet infrared examination of some of his works from this period shows a pencilled grid underlying, which shows us how carefully and deliberately he sketched out his compositions (see Art Innovation, November 2002). We see Van Gogh learning, always learning, training both eye and hand, and then translating this learning more and more into his own unique idiom. This is the type of process that psychoanalyst Marion Milner (1957) describes in terms of "becoming one with the medium".

In his still-lifes of this period, one can see how Van Gogh's brush stroke evolved, after working with the impressionists and divisionists, into the use of rectangular bars of paint to sculpt his subjects. We can also watch the evolution of his art as he copied and recopied particular subjects over time, and they became progressively more idiosyncratic.

For example, Mirbeau (1891) suggests that Van Gogh's rendering of Millet's sower is such that " the movement is accentuated, the vision enlarges, the line simplifies until it has the signification of a symbol" (our translation). This alignment with the symbolic, spiritual realm of existence is configured in line with Van Gogh's origins.

In contrast to the more classical depictions of religion that Van Gogh encountered in Antwerp, the Dutch Protestants of his homeland did not relate biblical themes explicitly, but, rather, insinuated them into their art through the simple things of life through which God was made known. In Dutch landscapes, for example, there is frequently a dead twig, beautifully rendered, to remind us that we all will die. Knowing this tradition helps us to appreciate Van Gogh's devotion to rendering everyday life so that the meaning of life might be found. Looking at a work such as *The Potato Eaters*, for example, we can see how their hands seem to merge into the potatoes that have been taken from the earth. Noting the configural elements, we can see the refinement of Van Gogh's sensibilities in terms of the evocative nature of the placement, form, and prosody of a line. The placement of the figures is evocative of two pietàs placed side by side.

Van Gogh's work captivates us, in part, because it is so personal. His portrayals of the peasant are quite different from the more idealised views of Millet or Pissarro. Tracing his work over time, we can see how his style evolved, in line with his own view that a reverence for life demanded a more realistic depiction. He writes, on 30 April 1885,

> It would be wrong, I think, to give a peasant picture a certain conventional smoothness. If a peasant picture smells of bacon, smoke, potato steam . . . if the field has the odor of ripe corn or potatoes or of guano or manure—that's healthy, especially for city people . . . such pictures may teach them something. (Van Gogh, 1958, p. 370, Letter 404)

In reading Van Gogh's letters, we find him attempting to commune with nature so that he might speak to its true magnificence, poised between immersion in the experience and the need to distance sufficiently that he might capture it and also, ultimately, survive. We see a man caught between his need to have value and his very real difficulties in finding a place for himself in this life. We also see the young boy who so desperately sought his father's affection and approval. In his themes of poor peasant life, and also in his attempts to become part of the various communities in which he was living, we see Van Gogh seeking out the misfit—those who had been similarly discarded by society. Perhaps, in this way, he also hoped to redeem himself, a pattern he plays out repeatedly.

Unable to accommodate to the strictures of training or social custom, he veers off, at times quite explosively, on to his own path. This idiosyncratic way of being and perceiving marks both the greatness and the tragedy of Van Gogh's art. He seems to have been inevitably constrained by the limitations that prescribed particular ways of perceiving and expressing himself, but he was not able to obtain sufficient validation to make peace with his path.

Van Gogh's art captures some essence of this dilemma. Grounded in his own heritage of Dutch aestheticism, Van Gogh's work takes us back to the primacy of our own earliest experiences that are fundamentally sensory. We see in his art the types of primary patterns and rhythms that speak to us at a very immediate, sensory level. In the earlier works from the north, we are struck by the sombre tones and the intensity of the shading, with death always in attendance. In his work from Arles, in contrast, we find a profound lyricism. Death comes to be symbolised in various ways: for example, through the iterations of Millet's *Reaper* and through many drawings of cypress trees, which we will discuss later. One might see this lyricism as a function of Van Gogh's way of working, described cogently by Heinich (1996): "He absorbed nature into himself; he forced it to bend, to mold itself into the contours of his thought, to follow him in his flights, even to suffer his characteristic deformations" (p. 18).

Van Gogh's work is highly evocative, bringing us to the level at which we understand basic meanings, such as affect, which is recognised by its pattern, and communicated through its prosody. Shame, for example, is experienced in reference to an unmet anticipation. A child comes home from school, excited about the day, wanting to share it with her mother. But her mother is busy and pushes her aside. We see the trajectory of excitement meeting opposition, and then the fall. The eyes are shielded and the head goes down. Many people, if asked to draw the experience recounted, would draw it with an arc, and then a slash. Our minds translate an experience into lines that have meaning for us. So, then, it is the dashing of our interest or excitement that we experience as shame. We know it internally through its prosody and we recognise it when we see its various manifestations, such as the lowering of the head or the shielding of the eyes (which we see in the hooding of the eyes in some of Van Gogh's self-portraits). We also recognise it, at a very primary and largely unconscious level, through the rhythm of a line.

As we grow, the primary rhythms of human being and interchange are attached to experiences in ways that are both communal and idiosyncratic. We are aided in finding our way through these experiences by the amodal nature of non-verbal communication, in which

> the dimensions of experience such as shape, texture, and location in space, all come to carry meanings beyond any specific representation. We learn to "read" nuances of line in works of art as in faces. The slope, the turn, the sweep, the rhythm: each in some important way seems to mirror the type of affective prosody described by such disparate theorists as Stern (1985) and Tomkins (1962, 1987). Although we may not be able to decode them in verbal terms, these types of meanings become reference points [used in] . . . creative endeavors. (Charles, 2002, p. 111)

We then use symbols and categories as ways of naming and organising these experiences, and then communicating our understandings to others. For some people, who are visual and kinaesthetic in orientation, and are working at the level underneath the words, we find that the pattern becomes the primary means of communication. For example, Van Gogh describes in his letters his desire to communicate some essence of the quality of peasant life through his art:

> I have wanted to give the impression of a way of life quite different from us civilized people. All winter long I have had the threads of this tissue in my hands, and have searched for the ultimate pattern; and though it has become a tissue of rough, coarse aspect, nevertheless the threads have been chosen carefully and according to certain rules . . .
> (Van Gogh, 1958, p. 370, Letter 404, April 30, 1885)

Van Gogh was living at a time when the communicative functions of art were coming to a crucial turning point. Although his work cannot be properly characterised as "modern", in many ways he seems to have ushered in the modern era. One might conjecture that his inability or unwillingness to conform to the constraints he encountered made him perfect vehicle for this changing of the guard. One of the prevalent characteristics of modern art is the search for new forms through which to more overtly explore and express primary experience. As Rhode (1998) puts it, "Feelings require forms to articulate themselves" (p. 257). In Van Gogh's diaries, he expresses the desire to give form to his private experience so that he might communicate it directly an forcibly to others. He writes,

> In either figure or landscape I should wish to express, not sentimental melancholy, but serious sorrow. In short, I want to progress so far that people will say of my work, He feels deeply, he feels tenderly — notwithstanding my so-called roughness, perhaps even because of it.
> (Van Gogh, 1958, p. 416, Letter 218)

This desire to capture the essence of the inspiration requires the type of mastery of a medium that Van Gogh sought diligently. Drawing relentlessly, he trained his hand and his eye so that he might more accurately articulate his vision. We see him playing with new forms, such as the flattened field of Japanese art, becoming more explicitly concerned with pattern itself, and the organisation of the elements in relation to one another. We perhaps see this most pointedly in the drawings in his diary, where he focuses on the patterns of relationships between elements in the visual field, making extensive notes regarding the placements and juxtapositions of fields of colour as he plans out his paintings.

Contrary to the view of Van Gogh as impulsively creative, we can see in his diaries how very diligent he was and also how mindful he was of his own place in the world of art. As an artist puts more of himself into the work, there is always a tension between the desire to be valued and the fear of deprecation. This was a tension we can see in Van Gogh's life at every turn. Art historians have compared the quality of his drawings to those of Rembrandt, and yet Van Gogh felt continually frustrated by the technical limitations he encountered in himself. As he describes these tensions in his letters to his brother, we can see Van Gogh discovering himself within the medium he is exploring. "What a queer thing the *touch* is", he writes, "the stroke of the brush" (Van Gogh, 1958, p. 210, Letter 605, Arles, September 10, 1888). He seems to have been intuitively aware of the need to find himself within the medium, if he was to create something simple and profoundly true. This is the real power of art, when the artist finds himself within the medium so that the translation process is minimised and the vision comes through. In this way, the artist's being inscribes its own unique style or pattern upon the work, and we "read" his way of being through the finished product. Milner (1957) describes it thus:

> A work of art, whatever its content, or subject, whether a recognizable scene or object or abstract pattern, must be an externalization, through its shapes and lines and colours, of the unique psycho-physical rhythm of the person making it. Otherwise it will have no life in it whatever, for there is no other source for its life. (p. 230)

Trevarthen (1995), a developmental theorist, suggests that "art communicates powerfully because it makes systematic expression of deep and spontaneous 'images' or 'impulses,' that are subjective, emotional, and therefore immediately transferable" (p. 160). Van Gogh's work communicates at this very primary emotional level. Because the power of colour in his paintings tends to become foregrounded, one might not be as aware of the power of the formal elements of the work. And yet, in the black and white renderings, without the colour to distract us, we are struck by the affective intensity and prosody of the pattern itself. As we look more carefully at his paintings, then we can perhaps see more vividly the flow of the patterned strokes of his brush, which are themselves highly evocative.

Just as affect is a patterned phenomenon, "read" by the flow and prosody of the sensation, so, too, Van Gogh's highly patterned brush style seems to be read by us intuitively at a deep and primary level. His paintings communicate a highly pressured energy that can seem almost frenetic, yet he describes painting each stroke quite deliberately, with great care and precision. The emotion is carried in the stroke of the brush, so that we take in the tone and contour of the emotion without necessarily being conscious of the mode of transmission. As we look at his earlier works *vs.* his later ones, we can see and feel the gathering tension through the rhythm of the stroke.

As a psychoanalyst and scholar of art, respectively, we came upon these works from very different perspectives. For the psychoanalyst, seeing the formal, patterned aspects of Van Gogh's drawings—and thinking about the implications of integrating colour into this constellation—brought to mind the elements of perceptual organisation described by Rorschach (1942). Thinking about how differently colour *vs.* form are experienced (as noted by Rorschach and by Schachtel, 1966), we wondered about the more formal elements of Van Gogh's art that might be pushed into the background of our consciousness by virtue of the impact of the colour that becomes highlighted.

The writer trained in art history agreed that the drawings contained much pattern. Black slashes, two upside-down v's connected, repeated in clusters of different sizes, placed above the horizon line. She read these lines as crows, understood them to be a simplification, an artistic shorthand, a referent to an object exterior to the painting, a symbol. Twisting lines were easily decoded as "tree", "wheat field", and "crow", and parallel hatchings were decoded as hairs in a man's beard, the twill of a jacket. They discussed the kinetic response that the artist's placement of these lines on the paper excited in them; the v's of the crows appeared in clusters, the number in each cluster varied, creating a vibrant pattern that commanded their eyes to move back and forth, up and down, so that looking at the drawing became a rhythmic exercise.

For the psychoanalyst, these black and white renderings provided a new entry into Van Gogh's world. Might a focus on "pattern" provide a way to decode the artist's lines and to reveal a new element in the experience of Van Gogh's work? From this vantage point, the lines were charged with multiple meanings, symbolic and rhythmic. The lines thus provided kinaesthetic energy, but were charged with affect as well, an interesting juxtaposition to views of form *vs.* colour, in which it is colour that is viewed as the carrier of the affect, and form is viewed as the vehicle for its containment (see, e.g., Schachtel, 1966). Van Gogh's black and white renderings, in contrast, highlight the ways in which it is the pattern of the elements that carry the affective charge.

Given our different orientations, our quest sent us in three quite different directions: to Schachtel's (1966) discussions of differences between the experience of colour *vs.* form, and to Vincent's letters to his brother, Theo, in which he describes quite vividly his thoughts, feelings, and impressions, and, finally, to the drawings themselves. We used the dimensions described by Rorschach to help us think about the elements of perceptual style to which we respond in Van Gogh's art. Schachtel (1943, 1966), for example, highlights the experiential aspects of perceptual style, distinguishing between the more passive experience of colour that seems to impinge on us quite directly *vs.* the more active processes by which we construct forms from the visual field. Distinguishing between these two elements helps us understand tensions a person might experience between the ability to register emotion (colour) and to maintain sufficient equilibrium to construct meaningful forms. This task also reminds us to attend to the types of forms an individual constructs. So, then, we can think about the affective tone of the work; the quality of the portrayal, in terms of brush stroke, and so on; and also the content itself.

The determinants highlighted by Rorschach, such as " form, color, movement, [and] shading . . . represent different perceptual and experiential attitudes" (Schachtel, 1966, p. 4). Imagination, Schachtel notes, is an

> important part of perception, especially of that attitude of perceptual openness toward the world that enables man to perceive the new in the familiar and to break through the confines of a familiar perspective. Imagination does not form new images out of nothing; it transforms, recombines, varies known images. (1966, p. 65)

Responsiveness to expressive aspects of the environment often goes along with a tendency to humanise experience (Schachtel, 1966).

We see this type of perception in the human qualities with which Van Gogh's landscapes are invested, particularly in his later work. Van Gogh's absorption in the visual field, and in his painting, help to give his work this type of fresh perspective and also contribute to its kinaesthetic power, another dimension of perception highlighted by the Rorschach. We see the kinaesthetic experience of movement, for example, in a work such as *Starry Night*. Kris (1952) suggests that it is through these types of kinaesthetic reactions that art communicates a direct and experiential sense of participation, or co-creation. Kinaesthetic responsiveness is linked with empathic understanding, as we project something of self into our experience. Consider, for example, the quiet solemnity of Van Gogh's early drawings *vs.* the more jarring effects of his later work, such as *The Rock of Montmajour with Trees*, or the *Washerwoman at the Canal*, drawn in Arles in July 1888. We respond to the power of these works through our own sensitivity to the kinaesthetic realm.

Another element taken into account by interpreters of the Rorschach is shading. Looking once again at these two drawings, we can see how the earlier work shows a greater attention to subtleties of shading than in the later, more explicitly patterned, drawing. It is difficult to know to what extent this had to do with the greater darkness of the northern regions *vs.* Van Gogh's expressed intention to simplify his work in later years.

Rorschach (1942) links a focus on shading to a tendency towards depression and also to a desire for emotional control, factors Van Gogh struggled with increasingly over his all too brief existence.

As we followed our other path of enquiry and dived more deeply into Van Gogh's writings, we found a determined effort to simplify his art down to its basic essentials. We can wonder in what ways this effort was aligned with a more elusive effort to find an internal equilibrium: to make peace with himself and the social world. In September 1888, for example, he writes from Arles about his struggles to capture the real and the "essential" of what he discerns in nature (Van Gogh, 1958, p. 210, Letter 605, Arles, September 10, 1888). We can see Van Gogh's ambivalence, as he speaks of adding and retouching in order to add some "serenity" or "cheerfulness", but also speaks of the importance of allowing the stroke of the brush to stand, to speak for itself. "Ah", he writes from Neunen in 1883, a picture must be painted, and then why not simply? Now when I look into real life . . . I find a power and vitality which, if one wants to express them in their particular character, ought to be painted with a *firm* brush stroke, with a simple technique. (Van Gogh, 1958, pp. 457–458, Letter 439, Neunen, December, 1883)

Van Gogh was working at a time when art was evolving in profound ways. Acutely aware of the technical and philosophical debates being argued, his letters show him trying to come to grips with these issues that pull at once towards safety and towards an uncertain future. In spring 1983, he writes, "Sometimes I think I will make an experiment, and try to work in quite a different way, that is, to dare more and risk more" (Van Gogh, 1958, p. 537, Letter 265, The Hague, February 8, 1883). More and more, he seems to find himself up against his own internal need to follow his own vision, his own path. We can wonder to what extent following his own path was a conscious decision and to what extent Van Gogh was not able to stay within the strictures that had been laid out for him. We see this dilemma in all domains of his life. Perhaps he *had* to break the bounds, and yet, as he moved beyond the known, he had no external validation. In some sense, he was hounded into being. Although his work is in some ways very intentional, Van Gogh also seems to have become inundated with affect and driven by his vision. In his struggles to take his vision in hand and more explicitly "use" it, we see an interplay between his idiosyncratic processing of his experience and the final creation.

In a letter to a fellow artist, dated 1884, we find Van Gogh quite fervently following his own path. He is aware that his affective intensity puts him at risk of reactivity from critics and realises that the more he develops his own expressive style, "people will . . . say . . . *even more* frequently, that I have *no* technique" (Van Gogh, 1958, p. 397, Letter R43, Neunen, April 1884). In line with his heritage, his is an idealistic vision in which art is elevated beyond mere technical skill or knowledge so that it is not merely a product of human hands, but rather something that "wells up from a deeper source in our souls" (pp. 399–400).

We see Van Gogh poised at the brink of an era that was to signal striking changes in views of art, highlighting our tendency to organise primary experience into patterns (Langer, 1951). This is the realm of the non-verbal, termed by Ehrenzweig (1967) the "hidden order" of art, in which information is "known" at a primary and intuitive level, inviting a very different reading of the perceptual world than that determined by the conscious mind. In his later drawings, in particular, we see how intently Van Gogh was playing with form, pattern, and rhythm. Rose (1996) describes this internal order:

> Art invites an intuitive perception of an internal organization between parts and whole by way of such principles as symmetry, contrast, repetition, and rhythm . . . The dichotomy of form and content dissolves: content is embodied in form. (p. 64).

Looking, then, at a work such as *Washerwoman at the Canal*, in which the lines are so pressured that they deliver a message affectively and intuitively to the viewer, we can wonder, what is content? What is form? There is an interplay between the elements here through which form becomes content and these elements come to merge, mirror, and illuminate one another.

Philosopher Suzanne Langer (1953) notes that art "must be true in design to the structure of experience. That is why art seems essentially organic; for all vital tension patterns are organic patterns" (p. 373). These tension patterns recreate the basic rhythms of life (Rose, 1996), helping to sublimate loss "by perpetuating a *continuity of form* in the internal or external world" (p. 120). The forms created through this pattern of tension and release are evocative for us all, as we struggle to integrate our own losses. Rose (1996) contends that

> affective memories and symbolisations are the raw material for the creation of aesthetic forms. With the help of abstraction, they become objectified, elaborated, and sharpened until sublimation succeeds in transcending the personal and concentrating the dynamic of tension/ release with economic clarity. Thus, the jazz improviser Miles Davis [says]: "I listen for what I can leave out". (p. 122)

These words echo those written by Van Gogh in his later years as he worked toward a greater austerity in his art. Langer (1953) suggests that what distinguishes the artist is his intuitive recognition of forms symbolic of feeling, and his tendency to project emotive knowledge into such objective forms. In handling his own creation, composing a symbol of human emotion, he learns from the perceptible reality before him possibilities of subjective experience that he has not known in his personal life. His own mental scope and the growth and expansion of his personality are, therefore, deeply involved with his art (p. 390).

Van Gogh surely found in his art the possibilities he could not establish in his social world, focusing more and more on his art and its progress. While still in Neunen, his emphasis is on form. "What matters to me most at the point I'm at now is the question of form", he writes. "I think the best way to express form is with an almost monochrome coloring, the tones of which differ principally in intensity and in value" (Van Gogh, 1958, p. 349, Letter 394, April 1885). Van Gogh had a profound appreciation for tone. We may be most aware of the deftness of his ability to express emotion by what he called "symphonies of the colors" (Van Gogh, 1958, p. 472, Letter 444, Antwerp, January 1886), but he also had a quite extraordinary capacity to use the monochromatic elements to express emotion as well. His drawings show extraordinary nuance of tone, shading, and texture, pulling evocative threads in the viewer. As Zuckerkandl (1956) puts it, "Tones hold up for our perception, as real, a dimension of the world that transcends all individual distinctions of things and therefore all verbal language" (p. 372). We are thrust into the realm of primary experience—primary process—in which it is through the similarities and discontinuities of form and prosody that meanings are measured.

Van Gogh's appreciation for the complexities of tone and value was accompanied by an exquisite sensitivity to the kinaesthetic and physiognomic aspects of perception. In Arles, he speaks of the landscape in human terms, depicting oleanders as "raving mad" against a "funereal cypress" (Van Gogh, 1958, p. 47, Letter 541, Arles, September 1888). He works obsessively, trying to articulate in visual form the "character, the fundamental truth" of the scene. This "truth" is affectively intuited so that he experiences it as alternatively "a lover's insight" or as "a lover's blindness" for his work (p. 48).

Part of Van Gogh's extraordinary productivity (he produced more than 2,000 drawings and paintings over the span of barely ten years) seems to have come from his urgency to be more sufficient to the task of creation. "What I lack is practice," he writes in 1886 from Antwerp:

> I put the colors on somewhat too *painstakingly*, because I haven't had enough practice; I must hesitate too long, and so I work the life out of it. But that is a question of time, of exercise, till the touch becomes more immediately correct, the better one has it fixed in one's mind. (Van Gogh, 1958, p. 478, Letter 447, Antwerp, January 1886)

This is the realm of implicit understandings, where meanings are carried at very primary levels. Much as Milner (1957) describes, Van Gogh moves toward becoming one with his medium: "my brush goes between my fingers as a bow would on the violin, and absolutely for my own pleasure", he writes from St Rémy (Van Gogh, 1958, p. 216, Letter 607, St Rémy, September 1889). Even as he gains facility, however, Van Gogh is always pushing the limits of his capacity. "It gets more interesting", he writes, "if one is not satisfied with the skill gradually acquired, but aims seriously and thoroughly at originality and broadness of conception—the drawing of the mass instead of the outlines, the solid modeling" (Van Gogh, 1958, p. 487, Letter 449, Antwerp, February 1886). We see him grappling with form, trying to articulate the whole, so that in each brush stroke we find complexities of modelling, shading, and texture, captured in the lines themselves.

In line with the impressionist determination to explore the complexities of the visual image, Van Gogh played with the flat surface of Oriental art, but also tried to move beyond the surface appearance in order to capture something of the essence. Pulling in, once again, our lessons from the Rorschach and from psychoanalysis, we are reminded that it is not only the essence of the object that may be captured, but also aspects of the artist himself. We see that we cannot fully extricate ourselves from our work; we cannot remain entirely separate and also produce something of value.

Van Gogh copied prodigiously, amassing a great collection of illustrations. While at St Rémy, he copies the works of others with some misgivings, yet this task clearly has value for him. He had difficulty finding live models and so used black and white reproductions of the works of artists, such as Delacroix or Millet, to "pose" for him. He then improvised with colour, "searching for memories of *their* pictures—but the memory, 'the vague consonance of colors which are at least right in feeling'—that is my own interpretation" (Van Gogh, 1958, p. 216, Letter 607, St Rémy, September 1889). He likens his task to the composer of music, noting how musicians add their own personal touches. In similar fashion, he notes that in the domain of music, it is not only the composer who plays his or her work, but, rather, each interpretation can be a valuable product in and of itself. There is an aesthetic to the interpretation that, for Van Gogh, must stand on its own merits and, ultimately, can enlarge our appreciation of a theme as we see or hear it "played" from several angles. Ultimately, Van Gogh likens his copying to *"translating them into another tongue"* (Van Gogh, 1958, p. 227, Letter 613, St Rémy, September 1889), a view affirmed in the statement by Mirbeau, quoted earlier.

Van Gogh had an extraordinary appreciation of nuance and subtlety. One colleague wrote that Van Gogh often compared painting with music, even going so far as to take piano lessons to enhance his appreciation of the subtleties of tone and of value. Van Gogh made analogies about the relationships among colours from his under-standing of these relationships in the realm of music, likening the notes of the piano to particular shades. This attunement to lyricism and to relations between parts and whole are primary elements of Van Gogh's work.

In the subjects of Van Gogh's drawings, we find a juxtaposition of elements, as well. In spite of the prominence of the landscape in Van Gogh's paintings, he was utterly absorbed by the human figure, which seemed to stand always at its centre for him. He seems to have been struggling with man's place in the universe and with his own place in the world. *"People* are more important than anything else", he asserts, "I feel a certain power within me, because wherever I may be, I shall always have an aim—painting people as I see and know them" (Van Gogh, 1958, p. 473, Letter 444, Antwerp, January 1886). In grappling with the figure within the architecture of the whole, he says, "surely *that is* real painting, and the result is more beautiful than the exact imitation of the things themselves. Thinking of one thing and letting the surroundings belong to it and result from it" (Van Gogh, 1958, p. 428 Letter 429, Neunen, October 1885). Van Gogh's veneration of people and the simple basic processes of life go along with his desire to have children and become part of the human landscape and divine creation in that way.

He was a study in contrasts in many ways, not the least of which were his utter simplicity and humility contrasted with his fierce desire to create something of value.

As early as 1875, he writes to Theo, "Father wrote to me once, 'Do not forget the story of Icarus, who wanted to fly to the sun, and having arrived at a certain height, lost his wings and dropped into the sea'" (Van Gogh, 1958, p. 42, Letter 43, Paris, November 9, 1875). What poignancy, then, we find in Van Gogh's passion for yellow, for the corn-fields and flowers in the colour of the sun.

His torment at his inability to make his own way in the world is a recurrent theme haunting his letters to his brother. Caught between the need to create and the price his art exacted from him, Van Gogh anchored his comfort, spiritual wellbeing, and his very link to humanity in his ability to paint. The articulation of emotional realities seems to become his primary medium of exchange with the world around him, a world in which his work is not sufficiently valued even to pay for his supplies. Frustrated in his attempts to create a "real life" (Van Gogh, 1958, p. 544, Letter 476, Arles, March 1886), he saw his painting as a surrogate, but is reduced to begging from his brother, hoping that somehow, some day, his brother's investment will pay off.

In his writings to Theo, we see Vincent trying to make his peace with the possibility of constructing something of enduring value while not being recognised in his lifetime. At times, this peace seems inevitably out of reach. His lack of success at finding love or recognition seems to have increased his drive to forge a positive sense of self through his art (Graetz, 1963), and also fuelled his desire to create a "studio of the South", where he might find the human contact he so longed for with other "outsiders". He captured this dream of a containing artists' community in the works he created to adorn the walls of the yellow house.

Milner (1952) suggests that the drive to create meaning wells from an "internal necessity for inner organization, pattern, coherence, the basic need to discover identity in difference without which experience becomes chaos" (p. 84). Paradoxically, this also requires an ability to tolerate the chaos, the very type of disequilibrium that Van Gogh struggled with more and more as time went by. The emotional strain was complicated by the exigencies of daily living and also by the difficulties of the tasks he set himself. In his letters, we are constantly reminded of the many challenges he endured in trying to make a living at his art. We see him trying to manage and justify the financial difficulties, moving always towards the allure and enjoyment of his art and the hope of making some discovery through which to achieve the recognition he craved.

The urge to create can be mobilised by the very types of loss we find in Van Gogh's history. His search for an elusive sense of community spurred his creative endeavours in many ways. After his father died in 1885, Van Gogh seemed to turn to Millet as his spiritual father, using Millet as a model through which to transform himself by depicting the nobility and spirituality of the peasant, and then moving beyond copying, translating the image of the sower more and more into his own idiom. In his successive iterations of Millet's sower, for example, we see how Van Gogh increasingly develops his own unique idiom, the strokes of his pen lending power to the rendering. Over time, brush strokes, colour, and symbolism all come together, linking themes of youth with the fear and immanence of death that lurks more and more compellingly as time goes by.

Increasingly, these themes of life, death, awe, and redemption are catalysed by the expressiveness of his emerging style and by Van Gogh's increasing belief in his work. In September 1888, he writes quite emphatically about his belief that art should speak not from the perspective of the "delusive realist", but, rather, as "suggested by some emotion of an ardent temperament" (Van Gogh, 1958, p. 29, Letter 533, Arles, September 1888). He notes that this effect can be evoked in drawing, through the lines, though it is not clear whether he was aware of the enormity of the impact of line in his own work. The lack of external validation undermines his ability to believe in himself, at times distorting his views of self and world, so that in some moments his work pleases him whereas at other times he is repulsed.

In Arles, Van Gogh has more tolerance for his own idiosyncrasy than we find in the writings from St Rémy, where, his equilibrium shaken, he struggles quite pointedly between the extreme poles of absorption and repulsion. He describes to Theo being haunted by the idea of the sower. Although these "exaggerated studies" such as *The Sower* and *The Night Café* at times seem repugnant to him, they also seem to have the deepest meaning (Van Gogh, 1958, p. 33, Letter 535, Arles, September 1888). Van Gogh points to tensions between reason and feeling, noting that "true painters are guided by that conscience which is called sentiment, their soul; their brains aren't subject to the pencil, but the pencil to their brains" (Van Gogh, 1958, p. 417, Letter 426, Neunen, October 1885). He seems to be intuitively aware of the power and importance of absorption to the creative endeavour, recognising that the key to painting nature is to become absorbed by its beauty. In those moments, he finds that he can move beyond his concerns regarding the limits of his talents and "let myself go, never thinking of a single rule" (Van Gogh, 1958, p. 42, Letter 539, Arles, September 1888).

One way of trying to understand the tensions that Van Gogh experienced between immersing himself in the visual field as a way of trying to make sense of and do justice to it, *vs.* becoming overwhelmed by this immersion, is to look at the distinctions between an autocentric and an allocentric mode of perception, as described by Schachtel (1959). In the autocentric mode there is little or no objectification; the emphasis is on how and what the person feels; there is a close relation, amounting to a fusion, between sensory quality and pleasure or unpleasure feelings, and the perceiver reacts primarily to something impinging on him (p. 83). In the allocentric mode, there is objectification; the emphasis is on what the object is like; there is either no relation or a less pronounced or direct relation between perceived sensory qualities and pleasure–unpleasure feelings. The perceiver usually approaches or turns to the object actively and, in doing so, either opens himself toward it receptively or takes hold of it, tries to "grasp" it (p. 83).

Van Gogh seems to be intuitively aware of the emotional power and subtleties of meaning that can be communicated through colour and through the juxtapositions of fields of colour, and becomes more and more absorbed by the task of translating the beauty he sees into his own expressive language. Some paintings, he notes, speak "a symbolic language through color alone" (Van Gogh, 1958, p. 597, Letter 503, Arles, July 1888).

Although his intense absorption feeds his work, imparting to it some of its vital power, Van Gogh finds himself caught between inspiration and that edge too far. He finds nature almost too beautiful, leading to a "terrible lucidity" in which he loses his self-consciousness as well as his self-reference, so that he does not impose order on the scene but, rather, "the picture comes to me as in a dream" (Van Gogh, 1958, p. 58, Letter 543, Arles, September 1888).

Although this inspired lucidity enlivens him, it is also disturbing, as he fears the depression that will enter in its wake. When he is able to let himself go, his absorption in the beauty of the world and in the act of capturing this beauty seems to sustain him. But, he also becomes caught by the darker side of this beauty, as we see in his writings about *The Night Café*, in which he talks once again of his desire to communicate something of the affective experience, but this time to suggest "the powers of darkness in a low public house" in an atmosphere not of transcendent beauty, but, rather, "like a devil's furnace, of pale sulphur" (Van Gogh, 1958, p. 31, Letter 534, Arles, September 1988).

While in St Rémy, Van Gogh seems to become so absorbed that he loses himself and breaks down in the wake of bouts of painting. He becomes particularly intent on capturing the essence of the cypress, but is increasingly plagued by his emotions. His absorption is such that he finds himself unable to paint in the grip of such strong feelings and yet longs to paint the cypresses as he feels them. The feelings become so strong that he loses consciousness and, in the wake of these attacks, often is unable to work for weeks at a time.

In his diaries, he describes these desperate attempts to grapple with the emotional truth of the landscape before him, trying to represent inner realities by the contrasts, the "derivations, and harmonies and not by forms and lines in themselves" (Van Gogh, 1958, p. 547, Letter 477a, Arles, March 1888). Line and colour are not easily distinguished in Van Gogh's painting. He was continually confronted by the intensity, not only of the colour, but also of the formal elements of the landscapes surrounding him.

In his diaries, he despaired over the impossibility of attending to both colour and value at the same time. We see how he gets caught within his own processing limitations, and also how compelled he feels to push past those limits. "I must draw a great deal", he writes. "Things here have so much line. And I want to get my drawing more spontaneous, more exaggerated" (Van Gogh, 1958, p. 580, Letter 495, Arles, June 1888).

In spite of his great talent, Van Gogh describes being frustrated by the paucity of his talents in the face of nature's glory. Although he keeps to his own course, he continually undervalues his own work in comparison to that of others. Finding himself caught between his reverence for the simple things of life and his inability to do them justice, he writes to Gauguin about his frustration when he attempts to vivify the beauty of the natural world in his paintings. He derides himself for his failure to reproduce in his paintings the lustre through which the "ordinary" world seems illuminated, finding that "in my pictures I render it as something ugly and coarse, whereas nature seems perfect to me" (Van Gogh, 1958, p. 64, Letter 544a, Arles, October 1888). Yet, he can also appreciate his ability to capture the emotional realities he is encountering, which is perhaps his greatest genius. In that same month, he writes:

the élan of my boney carcass is such that it goes straight for its goal. The result of this is a sincerity, perhaps original at times, in what I feel, if only the subject can lend something to my rash and clumsy execution. (Van Gogh, 1958, p. 64, Letter 544a, Arles, October 1888)

It is in St Rémy that Van Gogh begins to write most explicitly about form and its importance. He criticises his earlier work for a lack of "individual intention and feeling in the lines. Where these lines are close and deliberate, it begins to feel like a picture, even if it is exaggerated" (Van Gogh, 1958, p. 217, Letter 607, St Rémy, September 1889). It is also in St Rémy, however, that he fights most intensely with the emotions that threaten to overtake him, as he struggles to do justice to the landscape. Van Gogh hopes that his appreciation of the olives and cypresses of Provence might be the avenue through which he can make a unique contribution to art. Although he fears his limits, he also seems to appreciate intuitively the importance of finding and engaging his own personal perspective, his own unique style. In these efforts, we see him caught between what Ehrenzweig (1967) describes as "art's conscious superstructure [that] may be largely composed by intellectual effort . . . [and] its vast substructure . . . shaped by (unconscious) spontaneity" (p. 266).

Van Gogh writes of this tension as early as the autumn of 1882 in The Hague, as he struggles with the hazard of "learning to paint" in such a way that one imposes painting on a scene rather than allowing the scene to speak for itself. He describes being dissatisfied with his accomplishments as they fall short of the grandeur of nature before him, and yet he can also find in his work an "echo" of what had captured him in the scene before him. Then, as he gazes at the picture and begins to look beyond its ultimate insufficiency:

I see that nature has told me something, has spoken to me, and that I have put it down in shorthand . . . There may be words that cannot be deciphered, there may be mistakes or gaps; but there is something of what wood or beach or figure has told me in it, and it is not the tame or conventional language derived from a studied manner or a system rather than from nature itself. (Van Gogh, 1958, p. 448, Letter 228, The Hague, August 1882)

Six years later, in Arles, Van Gogh comes into a greater mastery of his work, but struggles hard against the forces that threaten to unbalance him. He attempts to ground himself in the work ethic of his early upbringing, affirming the importance of doing difficult things, but also yearning for some comfort, as might be found through religion. At these times, he says, he often goes out during the night to paint the stars, or dreams of creating paintings depicting the phantom of community that so eludes him in his life. Much like his uneasy relationship with humanity, he describes his work as becoming more harmonious, but stumbles against elements of experience that impede his attempts to get his "brushwork firm and interwoven with feeling, like a piece of music played with emotion" (Van Gogh, 1958, p. 57, Letter 543, Arles, September 1888).

It is when he is on the brink of finally realising his dream of a "Studio of the South" with Gauguin that he seems to find himself stretched beyond his limits. He idealises Gauguin to an impossible extent. Ultimately, neither can tolerate this tension and the relationship ruptures, ending in Van Gogh's characteristically volatile fashion with a terrible outburst in which he cuts off his ear. Gauguin then makes his escape. One of the most difficult things for Van Gogh, in the wake of Gauguin's departure, was the loss of his dream of an artists' studio. He experiences Gauguin's departure as disastrous, the death of his dream of a refuge for fellow artists. He struggles to come to grips with his situation but still encounters moments of terrible disequilibrium and finds himself "twisted by enthusiasm or madness or prophecy, like a Greek oracle on the tripod" (Van Gogh, 1958, p. 134, Letter 576, Arles, February 3, 1889).

In the midst of all of this chaos, Van Gogh desperately holds on to his work, yet is struck increasingly by the strangeness of his experience. In March 1889, he attempts to describe his current state, which is quite variable, ranging from "indescribable mental anguish" to "moments when the veil of time and the fatality of circumstances seemed to be torn apart for an instant" (Van Gogh, 1958, p. 146, Letter 582, Arles, March 29, 1889). We see him becoming more and more preoccupied with the funereal cypresses and other symbols of death (Graetz, 1963). This is a time of tremendous turmoil, in which his landscapes vary from relative equilibrium to frenzy.

Near the end of his life, he struggles with the canvas that is to become *The Reaper*, describing himself as possessed by this endeavour, in part hoping this work might cure him. The reaper seems to become for Van Gogh a valiant and solitary symbol of his own defeat and of, perhaps, ultimate redemption. He envisions the reaper as both a "vague figure fighting like the devil in the midst of the heat to get to the end of his task" and also as an "image of death, in the sense that humanity might be the wheat he is reaping" (Van Gogh, 1958, p. 202, Letter 604, St Rémy, September 1889). For Van Gogh, this reaper is an important image, in some ways the polar opposite of the image of the sower that had preoccupied him earlier. Once again, we see the theme of redemption as he goes on to describe his vision: "there's nothing sad in this death, it goes its way in broad daylight with a sun flooding everything with a light of pure gold" (p. 202). As Van Gogh contemplates the completed work, there is an increasing sense of resignation in his description of the painting as

> an image of death as the great book of nature speaks of it—but what I have sought is "almost smiling." It is all yellow, except a line of violet hills, a pale fair yellow. I find it queer that I saw it like this from between the iron bars of a cell. (Van Gogh, 1958, p. 205, Letter 604, St Rémy, September 1889)

In retrospect, we can imagine that at this moment, Van Gogh might have accomplished his final task and come to a resting point. He then addresses his brother directly, telling him of his hope against a vaster sea of hopelessness. It is with great poignancy, then, that he writes to his brother of the common bonds that unite them in love across such a vast distance. We can see how compellingly Vincent is aware of having used painting as a means for comfort and restoration as he tells his brother of his hope that Theo will find in his family something of the solace Vincent could only achieve through the elements of nature and the common moments of daily peasant life he has rendered so lovingly.

Near the end of his stay at St Rémy, Van Gogh throws himself feverishly into his work, not knowing when his illness will preclude the work and hoping that the work will forestall the illness. Most chillingly, he fears his own cowardice in the face of what seems to be a developing process through which the increasing violence of the attacks might destroy his ability to paint. He finds himself caught between his urgency to paint, which at times seems suicidal, and a desperate need to find some respite on solid ground. He reminds his brother, somewhat wistfully, of the hope that had been invested in this journey to the South, "wishing to see a different light . . . because one feels that the colors of the prism are veiled in the mist of the North" (Van Gogh, 1958, pp. 207–208, Letter 605, St Rémy, September 10, 1889).

There is the sense that he has gone too far into alien territory and must turn back towards home in the hope that he might rescue himself from this terrible madness of the South. His father's admonition regarding the fate of Icarus lingers like a terrible refrain. Van Gogh tries to reposition himself, longing to look back on his time in the South as something remote and in the past. He imagines a future in which he will have had some success and so will be able to look back upon this difficult time with some distant regret at the terrible isolation and "wretchedness" he had experienced during this time when he had seen "the reaper in the field below between the iron bars of the cell" (Van Gogh, 1958, p. 210, Letter 605, St Remy, September 10, 1889). He has no way of contextualising his depression in the wake of his accomplishments, yet this may be an inevitable ebb in the wake of such tremendous creative passion. As Ehrenzweig (1967) puts it,

> The final result of creative work can never achieve the full integration that is possible in the . . . oceanic-manic phase of creativity. Depressive anxiety is the inevitable consequence. The creative mind must be capable of tolerating imperfection. Creative man awakens from his oceanic experience to find that the results of his work do not match his initial inspiration. (pp. 192–193)

Ultimately, Van Gogh seems to have given up the battle. He left the South, desperately seeking greater peace in the North. This peace was to elude him. In some of his late paintings, we get a sense of how trapped he seems to have felt, as he depicts images of slight figures caught between the bars of endless trees. On 27 July 1890, he finally took his own life. Although the wound he inflicted on himself was not immediately fatal, Van Gogh seemed determined to have an end to it. When his doctor told Vincent that he hoped to save his life, he replied, "Then it has to be done all over again" (Hulsker, 1990, p. 446). Reportedly, one of his last statements to his brother was "Misery will never end" (Goldscheider & Uhde, 1947, p. 14).

We can surmise that the misery did end and with it the life of an extraordinary artist. The legacy that Van Gogh leaves behind in his drawings, writings, and paintings, however, continues to enliven and enrich the lives of the generations that have followed. Because of the extensiveness of his writings, we are invited into the world of Van Gogh, to consider his life and art more pointedly from his perspective and to reflect on the experiences that he describes that culminated in such an impressive body of work. Most particularly, Van Gogh vivifies for us the primary, emotional, and formal patterned aspects of art, through which the artist speaks to us of both universal and particular truths, quite directly, through the power of the non-verbal realm.

References

Art Innovation (November 2002). www.art-innnovation.nl.

Charles, M. (2002). *Patterns: Building Blocks of Experience*. Hillsdale, NJ: Analytic Press.

Ehrenzweig, A. (1967). *The Hidden Order of Art: A Study in the Psychology of Artistic Imagination*. London: Weidenfeld and Nicolson.

Gardner, H. (1948). *Art Through the Ages*. New York: Harcourt Brace.

Goldscheider, L., & Uhde, W. (1947). *Vincent Van Gogh*. Oxford: Phaidon Press.

Graetz, H. R. (1963). *The Symbolic Language of Vincent Van Gogh*. New York: McGraw-Hill.

Heinich, N. (1996). *The Glory of Van Gogh: An Anthropology of Admiration*, P. L. Browne (Trans.). Princeton, NJ: Princeton University Press.

Hulsker, J. (1990). *Vincent and Theo Van Gogh: A Dual Biography*, J. M. Miller (Ed.). Ann Arbor, MI: Fuller.

Kris, E. (1952). *Psychoanalytic Explorations in Art*. New York: International Universities Press.

Langer, S. (1951). *Philosophy in a New Key: A Study in the Symbolism of Reason, Rite and Art*. Cambridge, MA: Harvard University Press.

Langer, S. (1953). *Feeling and Form: A Theory of Art*. New York: Charles Scribner's Sons.

Maritain, J. (1953). *Creative Intuition in Art and Poetry*. New York: McClelland.

Milner, M. (1952). The role of illusion in symbol formation. In: *The Suppressed Madness of Sane Men: Fifty-four Years of Exploring Psychoanalysis* (pp. 83–113). London: Tavistock, 1987.

Milner, M. (1957). The ordering of chaos. In: *The Suppressed Madness of Sane Men: Fifty-four Years of Exploring Psychoanalysis* (pp. 216–233). London: Tavistock, 1987.

Mirbeau, O. (1891). Combats esthétiques: Vincent Van Gogh. L' Écho de Paris, 31 March.

Rhode, E. (1998). The enigmatic object: the relation of understanding to being and becoming. Journal of Melanie Klein and Object Relations, 16: 257–272.

Rorschach, H. (1942). Psychodiagnostics. Berne: Hans Huber.

Rose, G. J. (1996). Necessary Illusion: Art as Witness. Madison, WI: International Universities Press.

Schachtel, E. G. (1943). On color and affect. Psychiatry, 6: 393–409.

Schachtel, E. G. (1959). Metamorphosis New York: Basic Books.

Schachtel, E. G. (1966). Experiential Foundations of Rorschach's Test. Hillsdale, NJ: Analytic Press, 2001.

Stern, D. N. (1985). The Interpersonal World of the Infant: A View from Psychoanalysis and Developmental Psychology. New York: Basic Books.

Tomkins, S. S. (1962). Affect, Imagery, Consciousness: The Positive Affects (Vol. 2) New York: Springer.

Tomkins, S. S. (1987). Script theory. In: J. Aronoff, A. I. Rabin, & R. A. Zucker (Eds.), The Emergence of Personality (pp. 147–216). New York: Springer.

Trevarthen, C. (1995). Mother and baby: seeing artfully eye to eye. In: R. Gregory, J. Harris, P. Heard, & D. Rose (Eds.), The Artful Eye (pp. 157–200). Oxford: Oxford University Press.

Van Gogh, V. (1958). The Complete Letters of Vincent Van Gogh with Reproductions of all the Drawings in the Correspondence (3 volumes). Boston: Little, Brown, 2000.

Van Gogh, V. (2003). Van Gogh à Arles: Dessins 1888–1889: Documents originaux—Photographies. Actes Sud: Fondation Vincent van Gogh-Arles.

Zuckerkandl, V. (1956). Sound and Symbol. Princeton, NJ: Princeton University Press.

Chaos is come again — creativity, chaos and change: the 2008 Creativity Seminar

A black man and a white woman, the potential for creative pairing and the forces that are threatened by it: Shakespeare's *Othello* and the political drama of the 2008 election.

Othello is not only a play about race; it is a play about apparent difference, real difference, and underlying commonality, about imagining "outside the box" and anxiously staying within it, about perception and apperception, about a dangerous interweaving and a tangled web.

Perhaps it is also about a tragic aspect of creativity, the inclination to psychologically create others, often without our noticing it, into the darker images of ourselves and then to violently separate from them. As someone once said about the dynamic of projection, "We don't see things as they are; we see things as we are." Often, we cannot stand it—at the cost of losing the more complex aspects of ourselves and of others.

At a time in the country's history when some felt that "chaos is come again", when a black man and a white woman invited us to imagine creative societal change, what happens to the creative process as it is felt and lived out by individuals? How does change, personal or societal, and its accompanying chaos affect creativity, and vice versa? Are projection and the encounter with difference actually a part of the creative process? How is creativity related to the security of what is and the promise and risk of what could be?

The following chapter steps down from the political stage to examine personal chaos and one troubled person's effort to staunch it, before any positive change could be undertaken. This young man's story takes us back to Winnicott's notion of transitional activity (1971), which he sees as the foundation for a person's creative relation to the world. But when the world intrudes with unbearable experience, when it becomes too different from what is needed for the ego to survive, when the movement of time takes one away relentlessly from the primary other, the first thing to be done is to stop time: this story illustrates how a person took up that crucial task through the medium and the activity of photography. What might this story tell us about creativity in times of chaos, both personal and social?

Reference

Winnicott, D. W. (1971). Transitional objects and transitional phenomena: clinical material. In: *Playing and Reality* (pp. 1–25). New York: Basic Books.

CHAPTER SEVEN

Photography as transitional functioning

M. Gerard Fromm

I n a paper titled "Silence as communication", Masud Khan (1963) describes an adolescent's breakdown into serious depression, the effort at psychotherapeutic contact, and, briefly, the phase of working back toward health. In a passing observation, he notes "the strange way this youth found his way back to mobility and aliveness through skating" (p. 179). Khan's use of the word *strange* is ambiguous. He is perhaps referring to a most commonplace phenomenon, observable during the course of many a therapy and in ordinary life as well: that people become invested in particular activities which carry deep unconscious meaning and which serve as vehicles for the resolution of unconscious conflict or for a restructuring of self- and object-images in the service of developmental advance. If there is a strange quality to any of this, it would have to do with how very personal and preoccupying this is to the person so involved, as viewed from the outside. Something extremely important seems to have been found upon which a surprising degree of concentration can be brought to bear naturally and with ease. We see it all the time in a child's play. Not infrequently, psychotherapy will catalyse these processes and offer the opportunity for their observation in more salient form because to the patient's natural developmental momentum is added the weight of a longing for recovery.

To state the issue this way, that is, in terms of recovery or integration, or a concern for the wholeness and vitality of personality, is perhaps to slant the argument of this chapter prematurely. First, it would be important to name the process—ordinary but none the less remarkable—that Khan observes: the investment of energy in an activity corollary to a process of finding and working one's way back toward health. One possibility here would have to do with compromise formation; an activity is found which allows the expression of problematic libidinal or aggressive feeling in a fashion concealed enough, from oneself especially, and, perhaps, modulated enough to diminish anxiety. Should such a transposition be mobilised in a therapy, this new compromise formation would, in effect, be a symptom substitution. Should the balances within this process move more towards secondary process and accommodation to aims more acceptable to oneself and others, such activity would exemplify a process of sublimation. The range between symptom and sublimation defines ego functioning, in so far as it is occupied with the insistence of a gratification in an unyielding environment, including, of course, the internal environment of values, attachments, prohibitions, and so on.

A second possibility here, related to, though significantly different from, the first, would broaden the description of ego functioning in its application to the kind of activity under discussion. Put simply, and in a way frequently true to the experience of people, such activity is invested with a drive toward mastery. It entails the need for some vehicle through which to restructure self- and object-representations formed originally in relation to intrapsychic conflict, trauma, or developmental arrest.

To give a simple example, an unplanned child was born to older parents, both fully involved in their work lives and whose other children were already in their teens. In early childhood, this youngest fell from a dock into the water and was rescued by a sibling. He also suffered from asthma attacks within which intense feelings of dependency and conflicts around separation were expressed and enacted. Although he lived very near the sea and the beach was a favourite local playground, he remained frightened of the water to the extent that he mastered swimming at a considerably later time than his friends. Once he did, however, swimming assumed a central place in the restructuring of a weakened sense of self. It became a vehicle for the integration of competence, self-sufficiency, maleness, the ability to separate and return, and, very importantly, the ability to face the feared constriction of breath and to accomplish a regularity of breathing. In his later years, following a marital crisis that he felt to be life threatening, so anxiety arousing that he felt he could not breathe, he managed the aftermath by spontaneously returning to swimming. Again, this activity stabilised him and renewed him as a strong person, capable of thought and self-sufficiency. During his therapy, swimming took on an additional function; it became a primary occasion for reverie, as though through involving his body in rhythmic mastering and calming activity he had created a physical setting in which to be in touch with himself.

Is there more to be said about the meaning of such activity beyond the functions of compromise and of mastery? This question will be posed here in terms of a transitional function; that is, the function or set of functions described by Winnicott (1951) as being served by a transitional object. Would it be fair to hypothesise a transitional function within some instances of this activity, and, if so, does the introduction of this concept add anything to our understanding? This chapter answers that question with a "Yes", and illustrates this thesis through one activity, photography, which is examined in a clinical case and an autobiographical account from the general field of the humanities.

Photography in relation to drive, ego, and the imaginary

The psychoanalytic literature having to do with photography is remarkably meagre. Colson (1979), in an excellent article entitled "Photography as an extension of the ego", was able to find only two previous articles on the subject (Fox, 1957; Sulzberger, 1955), which discussed the unconscious motivations of the photographer, from psychoanalytic case data, primarily in drive-defence terms. In these examples, photography is shown to have been used as the vehicle of unconscious voyeuristic and exhibitionistic wishes and of aggressive feeling, while providing simultaneously a safe psychic distance and a regulation of highly charged visual intake. Fox (1957) quotes Otto Fenichel: "Man's mechanical ingenuity has actually created a 'devouring eye' (the camera) which looks at and incorporates the external world and later projects it outward again" (pp. 101–102).

All of this makes straightforward sense. We are bombarded with images daily; we lean towards easy reliance on them and sometimes ravenously seek them out. We have all known, or perhaps at times been, the person who must have images of a place in order to have been there: photography as a kind of consumption and a certifier of our presence. We have all enjoyed a phase of infancy in which great pleasure was experienced in the satisfaction of a purely visual hunger. And photography is equally obviously a vehicle of the erotic. By its very nature, it penetrates and exposes. It looks into what is always to some degree private, and invites, through the simple existence of a photograph, the look of a public. As for the aggressive component, Sontag (1978), in an exceptional set of essays on photography, comments:

> However hazy our awareness of this fantasy, it is named without subtlety whenever we talk about 'loading' and 'aiming' a camera, about 'shooting' a film . . . [T]here is something predatory in the act of taking a picture. (p. 14)

Colson's (1979) contribution takes the question of the psychological use of photography beyond the terms of instinctual conflict. In his analysis, he outlines three broad areas in which ego functioning may be enhanced and supported by the use of photography. The first of these has to do with the individual's fundamental relationship to time and to change. Noting that photography tends to blossom as a personal interest during adolescence or in early parenthood, the latter in order to record the explosive growth of infancy and childhood, Colson concludes that "People take up photography at times of rapid change in their lives when the photograph is most clearly expressive of the wish to hold time still, to have greater opportunity to consolidate the ordinarily fleeting experience of the moment" (p. 274). Colson thus relates photography to the ongoing mourning processes of life; photographs themselves transmute this pain into the pleasure of nostalgia and anchor in an external prop one's internal relationships to a person or a time felt to be lost.

Colson next takes up the particular way in which vision, as structured through photography, enhances both the definition and the

discovery or rediscovery of reality. He argues that both object constancy and protection against either overwhelming or simply numb-
ing amounts of visual stimuli are served by the fixing of the visual
image. One step further, he notes the rediscovery and the re-enrich-
ment of reality achieved by a creative focus on the object: the narrow-
ing of cues, the stripping away of over-learnt familiar contexts, the
capturing of fleeting tones, and so on. This latter mode links up with
the child's spontaneous exploration of the world and offers, if it can
be achieved, the ego's replenishment or refreshment of interest in all
that goes on around one.

Finally, noting Freud's occasional analogy between photography
and the topography of the mind, Colson enlarges upon the drive-
defence theme and suggests that photograph records the peripheral
preconscious perception, selected for its link with the unconscious, yet
available now enduringly for conscious study. Hence, the photograph
includes the forbidden wish, the inhibition against awareness of the
wish, and the ego's effort to overcome that inhibition.

Rapaport (1959) has succinctly pointed out the great contributions
made by ego psychologists, particularly Erikson, toward a truly psychoanalytic theory of reality. Colson's observations regarding photography astutely extend this enterprise as it pertains to this sometimes
deeply meaningful image-making activity. Photographs are the prod-
ucts of a visual scanning of the world, ending in a visual fix between
subject and object. Implicit in this is the role of vision as integrator of
experience. Indeed, Spitz's work (1965) would probably locate the
template of the photographic impulse in the joining of the visual with
the tactile in the infant's development. He writes, "the nursing situation is not merely an experience of gratification. It initiates the transition from exclusive contact perception [the feel of the nipple and the
holding] to distance perception [the seeing of the mother's face]"
(p. 75). Spitz is addressing here the way in which the image of mother,
and especially of her face, becomes embedded in a rhythm of gratification, frustration, stimulation, and soothing. This cycle is the ground
of object constancy, of the shaping of amorphous tensions into recog-
nisable needs, and of an awareness of time via sequences of events
and experiences of delay, anticipation, and satisfaction.

Within this cycle, vision becomes a fundamental integrative
modality. Very early on, everything is actively looked at and increasing pleasure taken in that looking. The child's smile soon anchors that

pleasure in the rudimentary affectionate dialogue of human images. Erikson (1977) puts it simply: "Seeing is hoping" (p. 41), and hopes more often than not fulfilled promote the equation between seeing and having. Hence, photography draws powerfully on those precursors within ego development having to do with the role of the visual in the integration of sensory experience and the mastery of frustration and of separation.

There is also, however, a darker interpretation of the ego's reliance on the visual. The paradigm for the *imaginary* (Lacan, 1977) is the child's mirror image, and the leap away from the inner experience of fragmentation and personal insufficiency to a fixing on, and an embracing of, the external image for an essentially false definition of self. For Lacan, the inevitable developmental rupture between subject and object, the gap that constitutes separateness, is managed either by fascination in the imaginary or by delivery into the *symbolic*. The imaginary, as Eigen (1981) writes, "marks the self's attempt to master trauma in a false way, usually through the subtle assertion of some mirage of self-sufficiency" (p. 421). In the imaginary, the subject finds to his delight a one-to-one, point-to-point correspondence between subject and object. The gap is closed. There is a surface-to-surface truth, which may be embraced as the whole truth, as long as depth and alternative angles are denied. For Lacan, this is the ego, and mastery is the effort to shape oneself towards an image with consequent splitting and alienation of self. Eigen (1981) describes this process as the subject's becoming "an imitation of himself (and others) by molding his reactiveness in terms of image forms that aid his quasi-spurious sense of self-sufficiency" (p. 419).

For Lacan, the imaginary represents a limiting or nullifying illusion, a closing of the self from the transformative possibilities of genuine self-responsiveness and of genuine otherness. Winnicott gives a different valence to illusion, having to do with its creative or wholeness-supporting possibilities. For now, it will be enough to underline, as Eigen puts it, "Lacan's basic distrust of the visual that, in part, leads to his situating the symbolic primarily in language. For Lacan, vision is the site of seduction par excellence" (p. 421).

Lacan lends a balancing interpretation of photography as an extension of the ego. To the tone of industry and triumph within the concept of mastery (take, for example, Paul Rosenfeld's comment that

Life appears always fully present along the epidermis of [the] body: vitality ready to be squeezed forth entire in fixing the instant . . . and not a tool, save the camera, is capable of registering such complex ephemeral responses, and expressing the full majesty of the moment. (Quoted in Sontag, 1978, pp. 206–207))

we must contrast something more deflated and perhaps cynical. We must consider the possibility that reliance on the imaginary depletes and impoverishes not only the self, but the other as well, the out-there-ness that constitutes external reality. We must question the seductive possibilities in the camera's apparently sincere mediation between subject and reality.

Sontag (1978) writes, "A way of certifying experience, taking photographs is also a way of refusing it" (p. 9). Photographs put a machine between subject and object. One may not so much live in the reality as acquire it or fend it off, in either case asserting a spurious control, as though relief from the vastness, the surroundingness of the world might be gained through the photographic conquest of it. Taking a picture becomes an act of self-abstraction and leaves an orderly world, the comforting duality of the one who sees and the thing seen. No matter how intimate the scene photographed, photography substantiates the irreducible fact of distance. No matter how sensual a photographic content, the charge eventually lets go its hold.

The making of a photographic image offers the illusion that something of reality has been captured. There are at least two parts to this: first, that what is seen is actually real, and second, that reality can be captured. Sontag (1978) writes that

photographic images do not seem to be statements about the world so much as pieces of it, miniatures of reality that anyone can make or acquire . . . A photograph passes for incontrovertible proof that a given thing happened. (pp. 4–5)

And yet, of course, photographs prove nothing. By themselves they have something of a catatonic quality—mute, still, apparently disengaged from the ongoing processes of life, posed or arranged to suit the wish of the viewer. Their allure lies in the conjoint offering of a something, an image, and a nothing, a silence. Photographs will not speak to us; thus, they offer the imaginary possibility that nothing need be said.

Taking photographs is, from this angle, an act of framing the world. The apparent reality of the photograph is a reality of discrete segments, a particularising and an atomising of life, a stripping away of context and continuity (Sontag, 1978). And, in that other sense of the word *framed*, photographs trap reality in a potential falsehood of appearances. The essential seduction of photography, its place in the imaginary, has to do with the embracing of image as though it were experience and as though it were knowledge, the equation of seeing with living and with knowing. Sontag (1978) writes,

> Photography implies that we know about the world if we accept it as the camera records it but this is the opposite of understanding, which starts from *not* accepting the world as it looks. . . . In contrast to the amorous relation, which is based on how something looks, understanding is based on how it functions. And functioning takes place in time, and must be explained in time. Only that which narrates can make us understand" (p. 23)

She notes Franz Kafka's similar comments about the distractions of surfaces and the obscuring of inner essences. The latter, Kafka adds, cannot be captured visually; they must be "grope[d] for . . . by feeling" (quoted in Sontag, 1978, p. 206).

Kafka here returns us to the groping and the feeling of pre-visual, non-visual experience, and to the bodily, cognitive, affective unintegration before recourse to an imaginary structuring. There is a paradox here: vision assumes its initial meaning and power as the integrator of image, feeling, touch, time, expectation, and so on, but the hyper-cathecting of the visual disintegrates; it splits. It poorly substitutes for, and actually alienates further, a fully sensual and a fully thoughtful groping with inner and outer reality. Put a different way, the same reality confirmed by and enhanced by photography can also be reduced by it. In the latter case, the ongoing developmental task of integration between inner and outer degenerates into a relationship of simple interest, or, perhaps, subjugation, an impoverishment of relatedness between person and world, a non-participation, a kind of anaemia resulting from the chronic hunger for reality contact actualised futilely via more and more images of decreasingly nourishing emotional value.

What kind of experience within psychological development does nourish the integrated relatedness of self and other? Winnicott's answer to this brings us to the set of objects, phenomena, and functions that he calls "transitional".

A young man

"The first thing about John," said his sister, "was that he was a mistake." He was an unplanned child, seven years younger than his sister and eleven years younger than his brother. For a sustained period during his early childhood he suffered digestive difficulties. Essentially, he could not take in without pain; he ate fussily, vomited often, and required special strained foods. He could be quite charming and elicited considerable spoiling from his sister and mother. He also developed a will "like iron" and a "ferocious temper", exercised especially with his disturbed, aggressive older brother. His father was a strong-willed, impulsive man, ambivalent about his marriage and away from home for long periods of international employment. The description of his mother anticipates a discussion of photography: evocative, but hard to bring into focus. She was described as bright, observant, vague, preoccupied, impractical, bizarre, anxious, sensitive, shadowy, loving, "a dreamer". At a local clinic, she arrived "dressed in a long flowing black formless gown with a black riding hat and black earlaps". When her younger son was four, she was hospitalised with a circulatory problem, which was to grow in severity until her death from a heart attack when John was fifteen.

About his mother, John later said, "I remember my mother taking care of me. I was very close to her. I'd get upset if she were going out. I'd beg her not to." His sister commented, "John was so insecure that he would kiss our mother all the time." Reportedly fearing a heart attack, John's mother was unable to effectively limit the misbehaviour of either of her sons, and when the father eventually returned home, he met his children's aggression with aggression of his own. John said, "My brother and my father had some bad fights. It really scared me. They'd punch each other. My mother couldn't stand the violence. She'd scream and go crazy. I thought they were going to kill each other."

When John was six, a case of mumps left him completely deaf in one ear. His early school years, in some ways unremarkable, included expressions of affection towards girls or women that were perceived as "bugging" them. Noteworthy is his recollection that "Once I heard my teacher's name announced [on the radio] and I thought she had been killed. In school the next day I went to hug her and she pushed me away." He began to daydream in school and to argue about rules.

When John was ten, he was hospitalised for an appendectomy, and soon thereafter his mother was hospitalised for further surgery on her circulatory disorder. John, because of his age, was prohibited by the rules of the hospital from visiting her; a few days later he sprained an ankle, was X-rayed at the hospital, and managed to find his way to his mother. John's peer relations continued to deteriorate, and any attachments that held some potential came to naught with each succeeding move of the family. As John approached thirteen, his mother suffered two heart attacks. John's reaction was violent. "I remember arguing with my mother while she rested in bed. The maids told me to stop because she needed the rest. My father got angry with me and told me I was killing my mother by arguing so much . . . I was going through a lot of bad stuff in my head. I was uncomfortable with my mother and fought like hell with her. I screamed at her over silly things. It was a sexual thing. I was repulsed by it, and that's why I fought against her. I used to get images of her fooling around with other men. Also I could feel myself changing physically and was afraid she might see that I was developing."

John was taken for an interview at a local mental health clinic. During the interview, he felt that the interviewer was "doing something sexual" to him. The subsequent clinic report noted that John "had night fears, slept in his mother's room, played with dolls, was fearful of heights and elevators, had been enuretic until the age of eight, was very compulsive about germs, and hated girls". John had also developed somatic concerns, particularly regarding his chest and heart. The clinic's recommendation for psychotherapy was not followed up by the family, preoccupied as it was with John's mother's illness. John's father also was making a sustained effort at family involvement at this time, and this seemed to settle John and to offer him something on which to build. He did well at his Bar Mitzvah and got a job as a newspaper delivery boy.

Just after his fourteenth birthday, John was sent to a private boarding school. His behaviour there seemed foolish and scattered; he felt homesick and increasingly depressed. While John was at home on a spring vacation, his mother had to have her leg amputated because of gangrene. Several weeks later, she suffered a near-fatal heart attack. Within days, John provoked a fight at school, was pushed into a glass door, and received a serious gash on his wrist. One week later, his mother died. That summer, John took up photography.

This new and solitary interest found fertile ground in a natural proficiency, such that John was asked by one of his teachers to give lessons on processing and printing photographs to younger students. Much of his life at this point John spent behind a camera or in the darkroom; he also slept a great deal. Following a bad experience with marijuana, he became anxious in a sustained and progressive way: "I felt I was in a dream. I began to feel lonely and depressed and thought I was falling apart. It got worse as if something snapped. My head was in a whirlpool. . . . I began to feel peculiar. . . . I felt disconnected from my body as if I were another person looking at myself." He also felt that his food might be poisoned. Following a series of abortive efforts at school, at therapies, and at relationships, which included his first sexual experience, John was hospitalised at age nineteen in a state of acute anxiety, paranoia, and suicidal preoccupation.

There are three features of his behaviour in this new treatment setting that quickly became salient. First, he was preoccupied with making and retaining connections to people but avoided any deepening involvement. Soon after arrival, he worked hard to orientate himself to places outside the hospital. He made many contacts with people associated with the private school he had attended, which was near the hospital. He made innumerable phone calls and attached a brittle importance to the unrestricted and efficient flow of messages to him and from him. He left the hospital grounds frequently (the hospital being an open, voluntary, and longer-term treatment setting), and reacted with great upset if the staff had not saved dinner for him, as though they had severed their connection to him in his absence. He would bring back to the hospital "friends" he had made, each in need of help. Practically everything sent or given to him, including food from the hospital dining room, was kept in his room, and it soon became a mounting shambles of debris and smells.

The second and third features of his hospital behaviour seemed closely related psychologically, but evoked strongly divergent affects in others. John seemed to enact at every turn an omnipotence, focused towards others and towards himself. With regard to others, the degree of wilfulness, stubbornness, and rebelliousness in his behaviour was extreme. He fought constantly about each and every rule of the hospital. He demanded to be made an "exception". He pushed and bickered his way towards a relationship of nearly unrelieved antagonism with staff and patients alike. The interpersonal evolution of mutually hostile, distant, and paranoid relationships was clearly in process.

John also, however, enacted most strikingly and most poignantly an omnipotent relation to himself. This seemed to be the centre of distress for him and the primary opening he offered for others' empathy, rather than simply their antagonism. He wilfully embarked on an effort to reverse the progressive direction of time, to go back rather than forward, and, failing that, at the very least, to stop permanently in a present. To his therapist he said, "I'm forgetting how upset I was six months ago. I've got to get back there, but it's all slowly fading from my memory . . . The obscurity in my head is increasing." Any forward movement, anything "constructive", "even putting one foot in front of the other" aroused anxiety. Through argument, mannerism, confusion, and pseudo-deafness, he fought any comment from his therapist that he experienced as advancing him or displacing him from the single thought he was trying to hold.

John seemed to strive for a state of suspended animation. He enacted this literally by, on several occasions, freezing in one physical position for long periods of time. He described this experience to the staff as having to do with extreme anxiety; "for him to be distracted during such moments means that he must begin retracing his thoughts from the beginning no matter how long this takes". A neurologist wrote, "John calls his mannerisms 'contortions.' They consist of facial and head movements, anchoring of a foot, periods of immobility, and speaking words backwards. John explains these as means of controlling and rejecting certain thoughts and actions, and keeping himself from seeing, feeling, or smelling anything". To his therapist he said, "I have stopped noticing the change of seasons . . . Soon it will be summer. Then a whole year will have passed, and I will not have been conscious of it at all. Suddenly I will wake up and I will have been asleep for a whole year." Following his therapist's short vacation, John said, "I haven't been here in a long time. I haven't seen you for a week. I've been standing still since you left." The one thing he seemed to want from his therapist was a "trick", something "to spark his memory and help him recover the past". Understandably, then, the most calm phase of his therapy was the lengthy and detailed history-taking process.

In the early part of his hospitalisation, a member of the house-keeping staff took it upon herself to clean his room of its accumulated stale food, papers, and assorted junk. Inadvertently and without his knowing it, she threw away what she took to be a rag; it was actually what remained of his baby blanket. During one of the moves his family had made early in his life, his first baby blanket had been lost. This second one had assumed meaning in his life much later, at age twelve, which was also the time of his mother's first heart attack and of John's mounting antagonism toward her. Of this latest incident, the staff remarked that John "suffered criticism for retaining the blanket, but it meant enough to him to endure the criticism. He spent hours digging for the blanket in the town dump and would get stuck and not be able to get out at closing time. . . . He seemed to feel that he had lost a part of his body, and that, since the garbage at the dump is not burned, it would forever remain buried, and this was quite unendurable".

The transitional function of photography

About his short opera *Oedipus*, the composer Igor Stravinsky (Stravinsky & Craft, 1963) remarked that "[c]rossroads are not personal but geometrical, and the geometry of tragedy, the inevitable intersecting of lines, is what concerned me" (p. 7). Not necessarily tragic, but of enormous psychological consequence, is a point very early on in life when two lines begin to diverge, or better, when something that is one begins to become two. Stravinsky accents the icily dramatic inevitability in the tragic geometry, its being situated in an irreversible time dimension unsparingly visible to the audience, if not to the protagonists. This early psychological development—from one to two—also occurs in and over time, but human beings are not necessarily fated towards psychic depletion in a purely linear relation to time and to the other. Instead, there is the transitional process.

Classical psychoanalysis has always had a place for timelessness, as well as for omnipotence and for the equation of distinct things. The mathematics of the unconscious can be seen as a preoccupation with this particular point in psychological development, that is, how one becomes two and *vice versa*. Indeed, displacement and condensation seem, at their root, related to these operations: displacement as one becoming two, here enlarging into a here-but-especially-there, and condensation as two becoming one, there merging into here. But it was Winnicott's observations and, to be sure, his sensibility that led him to give these primary processes a particular developmental significance and a quite different valence. Winnicott's (1951) point of departure was an ordinary, rather overlooked, yet intriguing detail: that young children develop an attachment to a special object, such as a blanket, which becomes particularly important at times of separation or deprivation, for example, at bedtime. Winnicott noted the rights assumed by the child over this special object, its being cuddled, loved, hated, held without change, and animated into a warmth-giving or otherwise vital and real thing. He recognised this object as the focal point of a precious and totally unselfconscious experience, an experience, as he saw it, intermediate between inner and outer reality.

Winnicott thought of this experience as a resting place; it has been called a place of solace (Horton, 1981). But also central to Winnicott's conception is the idea of primary creativity. Winnicott intuited that each successful feeding, each environmental provision that was well adapted to the baby's needs, fitted in with, in an inherently matched way, the infant's need and desire. It answered that desire and shaped it, and, in doing so, it offered the infant the illusion of magical control, or better, of a primary capacity to create what was needed. Winnicott would view this as eventuating in basic trust, but from the inside: the infant's trust in his capacity to make or find what he needed in and from a tentatively sensed out-there-ness. The transitional object is the tangible shape into which this area of illusion evolves. It is neither fully self nor fully other; Eigen (1981) describes it as "without any sharp sense of exteriority" and as "an incipient other, otherness in the process of being born" (p. 414).

In other words, the earliest experiences of the bifurcation between self and other, the dividing lines, are mitigated and recycled by transitional functioning. Successive experiences of merger, emergence, re-merger, and re-emergence lead the infant toward a bit-by-bit toleration of separation anxiety, confidence in his creative power, and comfort that what is needed can be created out of or found in the tangible stuff of the incipiently not-me.

Winnicott saw the need for an area of transitional functioning or, as he later called it, a potential space as existing throughout life. He included the arts and religion as areas of this sort for many people, areas of deep and intense experiencing and of personal imaginative involvement. Rose (1980) in *The Power of Form* elaborates the place of the transitional process in ordinary living, particularly in the ego's constructions of transient forms to give meaning and expression to the current state of dynamic equilibrium between the fluidities of self and reality.

> As in its early form as the transitional object, in its developed form as the creative imagination, the transitional process remains an essential instrument of adaptation. It samples the pluralism of reality, withdraws and re-advances, attempting to extract coherent configurations composed of both self and non-self elements. . . . In contrast to repression and denial, these abstractions offer new perspectives from which to explore and enhance, rather than circumscribe, the appreciation of reality. (p. 117)

Rose calls this aspect of ego functioning "the creativity of everyday life" (p. 115). The transitional process forms islands of stability out of the flux of reality, which both rescue and form a secure base for reimmersing oneself in that flux. Offering an apt metaphor for the current presentation, Rose notes Bergson's comment that "the Forms which the mind isolates and stores up in concepts, are then only snapshots of the changing reality" (p. 25).

The clinical material presented earlier suggests several interpretations of the place of photography in this young person's life, among them an interpretation of its transitional function. Before commenting on that, some of its other likely functions might be noted. For example, photography seemed to provide John with the contact-from-a-distance necessary for him to feel safe from his own and from others' aggression, while still feeling a minimal human relatedness. It might have expressed, in sublimated form, that aggression, connected perhaps to his earlier demand for a constant and a silencing contact with others. Photography might also have represented for John an excited effort to find and intrude on the betraying other, the inner mother of adolescence who was to be caught in the act of deserting him for someone else.

Finally, photography might have served as a vehicle of externalisation through which something corresponding to his inner affectivity could be found, held, and focused outside himself. In contrast, inner states felt as such had, from early life, been sources of distress (his digestive problems), of agitating vagueness in relation to his mother, of obscurity and disorientating momentum (his own psychotic decompensation), and especially of unseeable deterioration (his mother's progressive illness). Better to anchor one's experience in what can be externally perceived and held.

Photography provided him with multiple external images, more tangible and less threatening than the internal images that had plagued him for much of his life: images of other men with his mother, of his pubertal self in his mother's eyes, and of the shadowy, cherished, and departing mother herself. Furthermore, this management and projection of internal stimulation had as its complement the management of external stimulation via the compartmentalising of reality into so many discrete pictures and their laboured development in the darkroom. All of this one might conceptualise as John's use of photography to defend against painful and dangerous inner states while also maintaining a tenuous and precious contact with reality.

Purely on the circumstantial evidence of John's story, it also seems likely that photography, for John, was intimately connected with his history of traumatic separations from his mother, and that its discovery at the time of her death represented his best effort at dealing with her loss. From this angle, one can see a continuity of transitional objects. His second baby blanket became vitally important to him at age twelve, the time of his mother's first serious heart attack and of his frantic hostility toward her; photography became important immediately following her death. Clearly enough, photography can represent an effort at undoing separation. Time seems halted and distance overcome; both of these were conscious desires for this young man. A photograph seems to offer a poignant experience of being with, a union sheltered from interruption and unconcerned with aging. This aspect of photography, its apparent defeating of time and motion, its basic stillness, cannot be overestimated in terms of its lending itself to transitional functioning. John's life seemed always in relentless, progressive, and sometimes invisible movement toward loss; photography grasps at a quiet and visible permanence.

A photograph is also a capturing of the light that really touched somebody (or some thing). Hence, it is a potential relic (Sontag, 1978). There is a trace of the other in it. But it is also, of course, a creation of the subject. The photographer selects, according to intuitive affective criteria, the angle, composition, and lighting that will hold an experience at its most personally and most tolerably expressive. This sense of creative power is heightened further by the feeling that the world itself is one's medium, its ordinary changes, from afternoon to evening, for example, offering an explosion of new light for new images. The creative power of the photographer thus exploits change, transforming it into a resource and subduing it as a threat. The medium of photography seems inexhaustible, and everything feels photographable. Any picture can be invented and brought within range.

Perhaps more than any other art form, a photograph is at once me, the photographer-creator, and not-me, the photographed other. Winnicott might say that the question posed (rhetorically) many years ago by John Szarkowski of the Museum of Modern Art ("Are photographs mirrors on the inner world or windows on the outer world?") is not to be formulated. Photographs intermix elements of both, and, in that way, they can assume an extra chilling power, like Francis Bacon's glass-covered portraits or the shiny black Vietnam War Memorial, at which one looks to find and know the other, but also inescapably sees on it and in it oneself. Photography is intermediate experience, simultaneously an inventing and an accepting of reality. In this sense, photographs are analogous to the cave paintings discussed by Modell (1968, 1970); they are the creative self's natural accidents. They transform that which already exists, and, hence, they implicitly reflect an acceptance and an opening on to what is outside the self.

Photographs as images obviously include the fact of distance; they relate more to experience that includes distance perception rather than primarily a tactile mode. They substantiate a gap between subject and object that, in part, longs to be overcome. As the story of John suggests, transitional phenomena can occur as part of a consuming wish to return: in John's case, to return to that precious area of experience before the question, is this my mother or is this me, is formed, before it was possible to conceive of living or dying without her. Photographs as images offer a special vehicle for that return, in so far as our earliest form of thinking is primarily visual and imagistic. Lewin (1968) calls this period "our pictorial past" (p. 10), a crucial vestige of which is the dream. Photographs offer an object, a person, a setting, or simply an affective note from which, one may hope, something important will materialise, as if the real scene photographed will capture a ghost upon development. Photographs seem to offer what John hoped

for from his therapist, a spark that may catch on to, light up, and ener-
gise to movement an experience. In a sense, though photographs
refuse to speak, they silently beg to, and to be spoken with. Sontag
(1978) states, "The very muteness of what is, hypothetically, compre-
hensible in photographs is what constitutes their attraction and
provocativeness" (p. 24). She calls this the "talismanic" use of photographs, an attempt "both sentimental and implicitly magical . . . to
contact or lay claim to another reality" (p. 16).

There is a distinction between contacting and laying claim to. It
parallels the distinction Modell (1970) makes regarding the transitional object as a "great psychological divide" (p. 244), with a progressive side that implicitly acknowledges that which is outside the self
and a regressive side which omnipotently denies separation. John's
hospital behaviour seemed fraught with omnipotent strivings in the
service of undoing separation, and his desperation and decompensation testify perhaps to the failure of transitional processes to sustain
him. He recurrently pushed the illusion of his power to the point of
delusion, the point where others were either forced to validate externally an impossible demand or to invalidate it, directly or accidentally,
and deplete his sense of relatedness to the world.

Even in, or perhaps especially in, such personal chaos, we find
clinically the patient's effort to represent the trouble and to do something about it: to represent, to make present again in a form, so as to
have it live for starting over. This is the necessary illusion of transitional space, that one has the power to call something back or call
something to life again because it is desperately needed. This is also,
at times, the aim of the photographer. Clarence John Laughlin writes,
"I attempt, through much of my work, to animate all things", to "free
the human contents of objects" (quoted in Sontag, 1978, pp. 186–187).
Sontag (1978) calls photographs "incitements to reverie" (p. 16); "The
ultimate wisdom of the photographic image is to say: 'There is the
surface. Now think—or rather feel, intuit—what is beyond it, what the
reality must be like if it looks this way'" (p. 23).

I am suggesting here that the spontaneously discovered activity of
photography served a transitional function for John. Born of affects
associated with separation, photography mitigated his potential
for catastrophic anxiety and a turning away from reality. It eventuated
in tangible objects, each of which contained intermixed elements
of self and other, and each of which carried in bounded form deep

experiential potential. Photography, to some degree, relieved John of the ongoing and, for him, unbearable strain of reality acceptance by allowing him the sense of his creative capacities to invest the world anew and to make and hold aspects of it, without concern for it or for himself.

Activities serving transitional functions occur regularly in life and in therapy. Their handling within a psychotherapy requires sensitivity on the therapist's part, analogous perhaps to the sensitivity involved in a mother's handling of the child's security blanket. By describing the environmental provision in terms of sensitivity, however, I do not mean a preciousness or an exaggerated delicacy on the therapist's part. In fact, the therapist's preciousness would be a mishandling, an under-mining of the fact that transitional experience includes an important separateness and what one can feel and make out of that for oneself. There is an essential privacy to it. I mean, instead, the therapist's private recognition of the transitional processes served by a particular activity of the patient and the working with their functions and course, in some distinction to their meaning. One of Winnicott's (1951) most intriguing and challenging notions has to do with questions not to be asked regarding the transitional object. He first put the issue in the following way, italicising this entire statement himself:

Of the transitional object it can be said that it is a matter of agreement between us and the baby that we will never ask the question: 'Did you conceive of this or was it presented to you from without?' The important point is that no decision on this point is expected. The question is not to be formulated. (p. 14)

Questions not to be formulated seem incompatible with both the values of psychoanalysis—the ideal that the examined life is the good life—and its need for a method as unsparing as is resistance itself. However, in this statement, Winnicott was getting at the fundamental and necessary place of magic in a child's life (Modell, 1968), the way in which Freud's (1920g) grandson, in playing out and being in charge of a drama of separation and return using that spool, was *really*, from an internal point of view, making his mother go and return. The symbol was identical with the person and its handling affected her. Most importantly, it worked; again from the child's point of view, he *experienced* his power to live without mother and to bring her back, and nothing about this experience compromised developing reality-testing functions. There was no autistic turning away from the actual mother upon her return or any movement toward a quasi-delusional insistence on idiosyncratic definitions of reality. The activity and the experience were *transitional*, phases on the way to other levels of development.

A therapist recognising the transitional function of his patient's activity is recognising a private, unselfconscious experience actualised through a vehicle. It is a spontaneously lived activity, an engagement that is, to some degree, disrupted by the self-splitting processes implicit in an analytic focus, the way a person will fall from a bicycle if he focuses on how he is riding it. The transitional object is also irreducible. The whole point of it, at that basic level of symbolic identity, is that there is no thing behind this thing. It does not reduce to self or to other, and, as representative of an integration between these dualities, it constitutes a third, an alternative to the exclusivities of self and other, fashioned from absence and from the remnants of dyadic living. Transitional experiences need not give way to a therapy; they are not symptoms or transference displacements. And the whole issue of their meaning, in that narrow sense of the thing behind the thing, risks analytic intrusiveness and engulfment.

As therapists, just as the good enough mother does, we must permit our patients their experiences of separateness and their valuing of something other than us. Our usefulness lies more appropriately in noting the course of transitional experiences and activities: their beginnings, their settings, their accoutrements, their sensations, their interruptions, their natural endings, their newly evolving forms, and so on. Finally, we can note the circumstances precipitating a turning toward transitional experience. Transitional process always serves important functions in a person's ongoing struggle to relate inner and outer reality. The articulation of these realities, or of the current intrapsychic and interpersonal developmental conditions holding sway, is a more useful therapeutic focus than is the transitional phenomenon itself.

Transitional phenomena, of course, come *into* a therapy as well (see, for example, Greenson (1974) on transference and transitional phenomena). This topic will not be developed here, except to say that it was Freud's genius to invent a clinical situation in which reality might be left behind temporarily and one's dream life (and, therefore, a life confidently known as inner) contacted. One aspect of this situation is its diminished reliance on the visual: the analyst sits behind the couch. It was the genius of those after Freud, who worked analytically with more severely disturbed, more reality-disorientated patients, to invent a clinical situation in which an actual outer image is offered, the image of the therapist, to which one can begin to relate from an optimal distance. Inner and outer are kept physically distinct because, for such patients, they are not psychologically distinct. Approximating the photograph, the therapist's image is relatively silent, relatively still, relatively constant. It exists within a frame, which marks off, spatially and temporally, a setting of some potential. It also registers the affective relationship of a given moment between subject and object.

Gradually, through transference experience, which might be seen as the superimposition of self- and object-images and image fragments upon this new image, the therapist becomes part of the transitional process. What is at first clearly not-me is used as though it belonged to me and takes on aspects of me. What is also clearly not-mother comes to stand in her place up to a point. The therapist's image is given a complicated life. The action of a psychoanalytic therapy moves from the distinctness of the therapist's image to its ambiguity as it is intermixed with elements from the patient to again its relative distinctness as a new other. The image as image is destroyed in the process because the person of the therapist repeatedly comes to life. He speaks, moves in time, breathes, feels. The therapist's image may come to be held as a positively toned inner experience, but the experiential place of his images is also returned to the patient in words. Words, like pictures, make presence out of absence; they also offer, in Khan's (1960) photographically resonant phrase, the relief and clarity of "narrative focus" (p. 140). Words carry the possibility of resolution via understanding; in a sense, they extend and complete the process of personal experiencing that static images can most powerfully but can ultimately only incite. In his poem "Turning", Rilke (1914) writes, "Work of sight is achieved / now for some heart-work / on all those images, prisoned within you; / for you overcame them, but do not know / them as yet".

The indispensable and the irreplaceable

I will close with a brief discussion of another person's discovery of photography upon the death of his mother. In 1981, Roland Barthes'

Camera Lucida was published (the author having been killed shortly before when he was struck by a car while crossing a street). This last short volume is charming, amusing, elegant, wonderfully French, and finally very moving. Barthes purports to offer a study of photography, of its essence, by approaching it from the point of view of an uninstructed man of letters: a thoughtful, circumspect, proudly naïve point of view carried off through a supreme confidence in his intelligence, sophistication, and remarkable access to his feelings.

Barthes observes that a photograph that matters to him as a spectator involves the intermingling of two elements. The first he calls the "studium", which has to do with a general field of interest. One's interests always have reasons behind them more or less consciously available as one scans one's tastes and values. The "studium" is the product of education and of culture; it is also an action of the subject. In this chapter, the "studium", the study, the general field of interest is photography and also transitional phenomena and also psychopathology. John, himself, has to do with a different second element.

Barthes goes on:

> [B]ut at the moment of reaching the essence of Photography in general, I branched off; instead of following the path of a formal ontology (of a Logic), I stopped, keeping with me, like a treasure, my desire or my grief; the anticipated essence of the Photograph could not, in my mind, be separated from the "pathos" of which, from the first glance, it consists. . . . As *Spectator* I was interested in Photography only for "sentimental" reasons; I wanted to explore it not as a question (a theme) but as a world: I see, I feel, hence I notice, I observe, and I think. (p. 21)

> The second element will break (or punctuate) the *studium*. This time it is not I who seeks it out (as I invest the field of the *studium* with my sovereign consciousness), it is this element which will disturb the *studium* I shall therefore call *punctum*; for *punctum* is also: sting, speck, cut, little hole—and also a cast of the dice. A photograph's *punctum* is that accident which pricks me (but also bruises me, is poignant to me). (pp. 26–27)

These observations, and others, of Barthes serve as a kind of simultaneously earnest and playful academic scaffolding for a very personal experience. After his mother's death, he is sorting through photographs of her with little expectation of finding anything meaningful. Doing this represents a "painful labor . . . To say, confronted with a certain photograph, 'That's *almost* the way she was!' was more distressing than to say, confronted with another, 'That's not the way she was at all'" (p. 66). Barthes experienced this painful out-of-reach quality in his dreams as well: "I dream about her, I do not dream *her*" (p. 66). But amid many photographs about his mother, he comes across one that, to him, is her. This photograph is an old, faded one showing his mother as a girl of five standing with her brother, two years older, next to a small wooden bridge in a glassed-in conservatory called a Winter Garden. Barthes finds in this child, photographed seventeen years before his own birth, the mother he knew:

> The distinctness of her face, the naive attitude of her hands, the place she had docilely taken without either showing or hiding herself . . . a sovereign *innocence* (if you will take this word according to its etymology, which is: "I do no harm"). . . . In this little girl's image I saw the kindness, which had formed her being immediately and forever . . . (p. 69)

Barthes remembers her illness and thinks of her death:

> During her illness, I nursed her, held the bowl of tea she liked because it was easier to drink from than from a cup; she had become my little girl, uniting for me with that essential child she was in her first photograph. . . . Ultimately I experienced her, strong as she had been, my inner law, as my feminine child. Which was my way of resolving Death. If, as so many philosophers have said, death is the harsh victory of the race, if the particular dies for the satisfaction of the universal, if after having been reproduced as other than himself, the individual dies, having thereby denied and transcended himself, I who had not procreated, I had, in her very illness, engendered my mother. Once she was dead I no longer had any reason to attune myself to the progress of the superior Life Force (the race, the species). My particularity could never again universalize itself (unless, utopically, by writing, whose project henceforth would become the unique goal of my life). From now on I could do no more than await my total, undialectical death. (p. 72)

Barthes then reflects upon his loss:

> It is always maintained that I should suffer more because I have spent my whole life with her; but my suffering proceeds from *who she was*;

and it is because she was who she was that I lived with her. . . . I might say, like the Proustian Narrator at his grandmother's death: "I did not insist only upon suffering, but upon respecting the originality of my suffering"; for this originality was the reflection of what was absolutely irreducible in her, and thereby lost forever. It is said that mourning, by its gradual labor, slowly erases pain; I could not, I cannot believe this; because for me, Time eliminates the emotion of loss (I do not weep), that is all. For the rest, everything has remained motionless. For what I have lost is not a Figure (the Mother), but a being; and not a being, but a *quality* (a soul): not the indispensable, but the irreplaceable. (p. 75)

Barthes' thoughts and feelings here are so deeply personal that any comment about them feels presumptuous. Neither is there any utility in probing these statements. Instead, they are offered as an example of a man facing life's most momentous transition: his foreseeing of his own not-so-distantly future death as he has just seen the death of the person who gave him life. In the midst of this particular transition, the psychological contours of which are uncharted territories for our science, he finds a photograph which revives him, revives her, offers a presence through which to comprehend an absence, and mingles perspectives of past and future and of adult and child in powerful ways. On viewing a photograph of a young man condemned to death for the attempted assassination of Secretary of State Seward in 1865, Barthes (1981) is caught short:

> The photograph is handsome, as is the boy: that is the *studium*. But the *punctum* is: *he is going to die*. I read at the same time: *This will be* and *this has been*. . . . What *pricks* me is the discovery of this equivalence. In front of the photograph of my mother as a child, I tell myself: she is going to die: I shudder, like Winnicott's psychotic patient, *over a cata-strophe that has already occurred*. Whether or not the subject is already dead, every photograph is this catastrophe. (p. 96)

For Barthes, each photograph brings together a particular life, a moment of aliveness, and a particular death, a moment that is over. He persuades us to accept that our lives, like photographs, are pure contingency and that a state of peace or rest is, perhaps more deeply than Freud (1923b) suggested, the precipitate of a particular and an embraced loss. This transitional object, for a mature man at the end of a life, works very differently than does the transitional object of early life. It does not, for example, generalise the warmth of mother and open out onto the softness of objects in the world. Rather, it particularises and condenses a variable, lived experience into a perceived set of details. Neither does it offer the illusion of the power to create what is needed; instead, it offers a dispensing with illusions and a willingness to settle things because one has already had what was needed. There is, however, within Barthes' response to the photograph, the core transitional experience of a joining within a parting. Barthes sees in the child-mother's image the "anterior future" (p. 96) of a unique person, and upon the completion of her life he feels an accepted depletion and the eventual completion of his own life. A sense of wholeness and strength comes in feeling the circularity of life's cycle, in the opportunity to remember and to return her kindness.

Barthes' distinction between the indispensable and the irreplaceable reaches towards a statement of the transitional function. Winnicott (1960) repeatedly illuminated the indispensability of good-enough mothering at the beginning of an infant's life and the consequences of its failure. One such consequence is the compulsive, sometimes saving, frequently catastrophic effort to relive the failure situation, to replace the indispensable. This is the irony of severe psychopathology. Good enough mothering, conversely, is dispensed with. It becomes gradually less necessary because the child has taken in the mothering functions and has access to transitional processes. The other's presence and sustaining activity can be done without; the capacity to be alone (Winnicott, 1958) has been achieved. But because good enough care leads to a *personal* relationship, that relationship is toned, shaped, and framed by the particularities of both parties. The dispensable mother is, thus, personally irreplaceable. Life's first transitional object, if things go well, could be said to be found somewhere along the way between the indispensable mother and the irreplaceable one. Barthes shares with us a last transitional object; as it happens, it is also a photograph.

Notes

1. Excerpts from *On Photography* by Susan Sontag. Copyright © 1973, 1974, 1977 by Susan Sontag. Reprinted by permission of Farrar, Straus and Giroux.

2. Excerpts from *Camera Lucida* by Roland Barthes, translated by Richard Howard. Translation copyright © 1981 by Farrar, Straus and Giroux. Reprinted by permission of Hill and Wang, a division of Farrar, Straus and Giroux.

References

Barthes, R. (1981). *Camera Lucida*. New York: Hill & Wang.

Colson, D. (1979). Photography as an extension of the ego. *International Review of Psycho-Analysis, 6*: 273–282.

Eigen, M. (1981). The area of faith in Winnicott, Lacan and Bion. *International Journal of Psychoanalysis, 62*: 413–433.

Erikson, E. H. (1977). *Toys and Reasons: Stages in the Ritualization of Experience*. New York: W. W. Norton.

Fox, H. (1957). Body image of a photographer. *Journal of the American Psychoanalytic Assocciation, 5*: 93–107.

Freud, S. (1920g). *Beyond the Pleasure Principle. S.E., 18*: 1–64. London: Hogarth.

Freud, S. (1923b). *The Ego and the Id. S.E., 19*: 1–66. London: Hogarth.

Greenson, R. (1974). On transitional objects and transference. In: *Explorations in Psychoanalysis* (pp. 491–496). New York: International Universities Press, 1978.

Horton, P. (1981). *Solace: The Missing Dimension in Psychiatry*. Chicago, IL: University of Chicago Press.

Khan, M. M. R. (1960). Regression and integration in the analytic setting. In: *The Privacy of the Self* (pp. 136–167). New York: International Universities Press, 1974.

Khan, M. M. R. (1963). Silence as communication. In: *The Privacy of the Self* (pp. 168–180). New York: International Universities Press, 1974.

Lacan, J. (1977). *Ecrits: Selected Writings of Jacques Lacan*. New York: W. W. Norton.

Lewin, B. (1968). *The Image and the Past*. New York: International Universities Press.

Modell, A. (1968). *Object Love and Reality*. New York: International Universities Press.

Modell, A. (1970). The transitional object and the creative act. *Psychoanalytic Quarterly, 39*: 240–250.

Rapaport, D. (1959). A historical survey of psychoanalytic ego psychology. In: *Identity and the Life Cycle* (pp. 5–17). *Psychological Issues*, Monograph 1. New York: International Universities Press.

Rilke, R. N. (1914). Turning. In: *Poems 1906 to 1926*. London: Hogarth Press, 1957.

Rose, G. (1980). *The Power of Form: A Psychoanalytic Approach to Aesthetic Form. Psychological Issues*, Monograph 49. New York: International Universities Press.

Sontag, S. (1978). *On Photography*. New York: Farrar, Straus, & Giroux.

Spitz, R. (1965). *The First Year of Life*. New York: International Universities Press.

Stravinsky, I., & Craft, R. (1963). *Dialogues and a Diary*. Garden City, NY: Doubleday.

Sulzberger, C. (1955). Unconscious motivations of the amateur photographer. *Psychoanalysis, 3*: 18–24.

Winnicott, D. W. (1951). Transitional objects and transitional phenomena. In: *Collected Papers: Through Pediatrics to Psychoanalysis* (pp. 229–242). New York: Basic Books, 1958.

Winnicott, D. W. (1958). The capacity to be alone. In: *The Maturational Processes and the Facilitating Environment* (pp. 29–36). New York: International Universities Press, 1965.

Winnicott, D. W. (1960). The theory of the parent–infant relationship. In: *The Maturational Processes and the Facilitating Environment* (pp. 37–55). New York: International Universities Press, 1965.

Miracle workers — transformation through creativity: the 2009 Creativity Seminar

F ifty years ago, William Gibson's *The Miracle Worker* opened on Broadway. It ran for 719 performances and received six Tony awards. It is the story of a young teacher, Annie Sullivan, who through devotion, ingenuity, and a kind of matching ferocity (see Chapter Five), leads her blind, deaf student, Helen Keller, into language. The breakthrough moment pairs two sensations on Ms Keller's hand: water and Ms Sullivan's finger tracing the word for water. Ms Keller's dramatic Wah-Wah indicates the birth of a sign, and, thus, the first step toward a life in the symbolic world.

While Bill Gibson was working on *The Miracle Worker*, he was also founding the theatre programme at the Austen Riggs Center, a programme that continues to the present. Bill joined Joan Erikson in her mission of bringing people in turmoil into artistic activity. (And he joined his wife, Margaret Brenman-Gibson, the first fully trained non-medical psychoanalyst in the United States, in the collective mission of establishing Riggs as a fully open setting for treatment.) With her own mixture of devotion, ingenuity, and ferocity, Joan created a department in which raw materials were available for interaction with sensations, memories, and feelings toward a creative moment and a new horizon.

What do we know about these moments, and about the people who facilitate them? How do we think about these transformative interactions? The 2009 Creativity Seminar—dedicated to the memory of William Gibson, who passed away that year—took up these questions, as do the two papers that follow: first, Ellen Handler Spitz's meditation on the teaching and treatment implications in *The Miracle Worker*, and then my own description of these two processes in the work with a student–patient at the Center.

CHAPTER EIGHT

To teach and to treat: meditations on *The Miracle Worker*

Ellen Handler Spitz

"I t's less trouble to feel sorry for her than it is to teach her anything better." This powerful sentiment from William Gibson's *The Miracle Worker* immediately links educational and therapeutic tasks; it also captures the fierce valuing of learning over sympathy that Gibson lived out in his work as theatre director at the Austen Riggs Center in Stockbridge, Massachusetts many years ago. When Dr Gerard Fromm asked me to speak on *The Miracle Worker* at the Austen Riggs annual Creativity Conference in honour of playwright William Gibson, who passed away in November, 2008, at the age of ninety-four, and who was a great friend to psychoanalysis, I demurred at first because I am not an expert on the life of Helen Keller, or, indeed, on blindness, or on disability; yet, I have thought deeply about the film, and I hope that what follows may prove meaningful. It is, of course, a brilliant work, and all I can do is to offer a few of my own perceptions; I must emphasise at the outset that, in what follows, I shall be speaking about the 1962 film with William Gibson's script, just as it is, and not its relation to historical fact. We shall be treating it *sui generis*, as a work of art, *tout compris*.

Last term, my colleague Professor Jay Freyman, a classicist, and I taught a seminar on "The nature of learning and the art of teaching" at our campus of the University of Maryland. In it, we screened this film, as it seemed to us that *The Miracle Worker* had to be an indispensable part of our enquiry. But why? What makes it such an important and timeless classic on the nature of learning and the art of teaching?

Ninety minutes long, black and white, deceptively simple, the film held our students rapt (the class, twenty humanities scholars, watched it together, as a group). Although they had been captivated by a plethora of engaging material, including films such as *Goodbye, Mr. Chips, To Sir with Love, Farewell, My Concubine, Stand and Deliver, Dead Poets Society, The Paper Chase*, and many readings ranging from Aristophanes, Plato, and Montaigne to Jacques Barzun, Gilbert Highet, and Muriel Spark (*The Prime of Miss Jean Brodie*), I doubt that, for most of them, anything trumped *The Miracle Worker*.

Our special focus was as stated, and, along with this particular film, we asked our students to read Montaigne's classic, justly famous essay of 1575 "Of the education of children", a supremely relevant text. Now, at Austen Riggs, the manifest focus is not on teaching and learning *per se*, but, rather, on therapy and treatment, which are different. Or are they? If they are different, how are they different and in what ways different? Bennett Simon (1978), for example, has noted in *Mind and Madness in Ancient Greece* that Plato treats madness and ignorance as maladies of the same kind. Simon writes, "Plato's unique contribution is the ideal that man can achieve control over the irrational by a special kind of training and education" and that "analogously, Freud's unique contribution was the development of [a method] leading to permanent, internal reorganization . . . a method of understanding, leading to self understanding" (p. 207). This juxtaposition frames my essay.

In pondering the film and what it portrays and in considering how different and similar these realms of endeavour are and in what ways they overlap (education and treatment, the teacher and the therapist), we might note that the Greek stem *therap-* carries the basic meaning "to serve"; hence, its English derivative, "therapist", likewise carries the connotation of service that is, the therapist renders service to the body or mind of the patient. Indeed, the ancient Greeks so used the stem to mean, "render medical service" (Professor Jay Freyman, personal communication, 30 July 2009).

Annie Sullivan, young and inexperienced (Helen Keller was her first pupil), is brought to Tuscumbia, Alabama, by a set of desperate parents because their little girl, Helen, blind and deaf, needs to learn. The stakes are high. If she cannot learn, the alternative under consideration by her family is to send her to an institution that might destroy her spirit and possibly spell her demise altogether.

Creating mayhem in her parents' gracious southern mansion, Helen appears to us on screen as a feral child—dirty, unkempt, uttering unintelligible shrieks—and she wantonly transgresses the most fundamental bounds of civility. There seems no way to get through to her. We witness her as she drives her family to the brink of distraction (her father tries to write at his desk but she sweeps everything he has opened on to the floor in a heap and then treads on it; she perambulates the family's formal dining room table at meal times, scooping up food from other people's plates with her unwashed hands and stuffs it greedily into her mouth.) Far more horrifyingly, just before Annie Sullivan arrives, Helen has been stopped in the nick of time after being found on the lawn attacking another child—a black child of one of the family's servants—with a knife. Thus, she is seen as succumbing daily to rampant bouts of frustration and aggressiveness. She seems progressively uncontrollable. Her mother, moreover, senses her state of mind acutely and even articulates it by lamenting that Helen is "slipping away", as she puts it, and that she, as her mother, knows no way to bring her back. The new teacher, therefore, enters a scene that daunts beyond measure.

Helen's mother, however, understands her daughter to some degree, and I think this makes a difference that we cannot ignore. Kate Adams Keller, southern gentlewoman that she is, responds intuitively with unfailing warmth to Helen, believes in her intellect, and, of course, loves her deeply. She, like the successful teacher, who, very soon, will take this awareness much further, has gradually developed certain insights about Helen and has grasped, I believe, a crucial element in her present situation, which, however, I doubt she herself would have been able to articulate in the terms I am about to use. What Kate Keller realises is that what once may have sufficed as palliative, soothing, and even as minimally communicative for Helen (in other words, all the motherly cuddling, holding, and touching that she has supplied since the child's infancy) no longer suffices. As Helen grows progressively older, a hug, an embrace, while it feels good, simply cannot and does not perform the healing functions it did when she was younger.

As we mature, Helen's mother intuitively realises, we evolve mentally and experience ever more urgent needs for meaning, for sense making, for connections on multiple psychic registers, cognitive and symbolic, as well as physical. This sensitive mother, therefore, loving her daughter and in despair, sees Helen as a beloved child who is vanishing day by day into an impenetrable world of darkness and silence and wishes passionately to redeem her and to recall her to life. She knows at the same time, with a profound sense of helplessness, that what *she* herself has to offer no longer works. Helen needs a teacher.

Just before Annie's arrival, there is a telling scene with the entire family in the living room. This occurs just after Helen has behaved aggressively towards the other child outdoors. Holding a doll seems to calm her momentarily but, while her parents, her grandmother, and her stepbrother argue about her fate and dispute with one another about what to do with her, and as the new baby wails in its cradle, Helen grows increasingly agitated. Upset with the doll now, she begins banging it against things and people. There is much we could make of this behaviour, but what actually happens is that her mother, watching her carefully, notices that she has touched the doll's face and then her own face, especially her eyes. Taking Helen's hand, Kate holds her fingers up to her own face and touches them to *her* eyes. Helen, she grasps, is identifying with the doll and the doll with herself and also with her mother (which is, of course, a very prevalent use of the doll as has been well described in the clinical literature of play and psychoanalysis), and Kate Keller realises that Helen wants her doll to possess eyes of its own, just as they both do.

Filled then with hope and with that ever-present maternal desire to set things right, Kate reaches for her sewing basket and immediately attaches two buttons to the doll's face. With that, she hands it back to Helen, and, as soon as the child touches these raised forms in their proper places on the surface of her doll's head, her unhappy face brightens with a momentary smile of bliss. Such a gift! Watching, we feel a corresponding sense of joy, as well as awe, amazement, relief, and, at least for me, a renewed appreciation of that splendid phrase of Donald Winnicott's: "meeting and matching the moment of hope".

Even before this, during the opening credits of the film, we find a purely visual sequence that also conveys Kate Keller's extraordinary attunement to Helen. It is a windy day, and freshly laundered sheets are billowing on the line. Helen runs in and out among them, and we can almost join her sensuous pleasure as the soft cottony textures caress her skin, emitting their sweet scent, and the breeze, wafting its loveliness, blows the fabric all about her young body. As she sashays in and out among the hanging sheets, some of the clothespins fail to hold, and one of the sheets comes tumbling down, enveloping the little girl, who rolls delightedly on the ground enwrapped by its folds. Her mother rushes out to her. We think, Oh, no! Will she be worried that the child is being smothered and stop her? Or, will she be angry that the clean sheets are on the ground and therefore being soiled and stop her? But, not at all: intuiting the child's pleasure, Kate Keller takes her blind, deaf child into her arms, embraces her, and rolls together with her in the grass.

I think we absolutely need to make significant connections between these two scenes and the climactic and apparently miraculous one in the end when Helen relates the water that spills over her hand from a pump to the fingered sign for water and to the repeated syllable that signifies water. The child's earlier moments with her mother with the sheets and with the doll's eyes, even before her teacher arrives on the scene, form significant precursors to that later dramatic event. Learning builds on prior experience, and, as the greatest educators (think of John Dewey (1934)) have shown, an awareness of, and a sensitivity to, this step-by-step aspect of the learning process should be a part of every teacher's thinking and methodology, consciously utilised, not left entirely to chance. I wonder how a notion like this might work in relation to clinical practice, and whether certain insights might optimally precede other insights and, if so, whether and how a clinician might arrange such a progression. Would such a thing be desirable even if it were possible? Or, rather, in the realm of treatment and therapy, could it be that the order of insights which evolves in any given treatment situation just *is, ipso facto*, the right and best one for that particular patient? (Unlike, say, learning to write in the Roman alphabet, where one must first learn to form letters before one can go on to words and then sentences.) In other words, how much leading and planning is there in clinical work as opposed to other forms of teaching, and might that be seen as a significant realm of difference?

Annie Sullivan builds on Kate Keller's previously established rapport with Helen. Yet, Annie does not understand this for a long time. At first, she sees the girl's parents as an unmitigated obstruction and nothing more. Of course, in advance, we all see with clouded vision, whereas, in retrospect, we trace our progress rationally, or so we think, from an arbitrary point in the past to a subsequent triumph. When we do so (as I am doing a bit right now), do we mitigate, I wonder, our sense of awe and our ascription of success to the miraculous? Do we take away from Annie's aura as a "miracle worker"? I think, in fact, we do not. No matter how much we understand and explain, there is always that which evades our reason. A thoughtful teacher, therefore, tries to be aware of precedents but always tries leave the door ajar mentally so as to welcome the unexpected and to embrace that which cannot be imagined beforehand. Just so, Annie, later on in the film when she is in the cabin with Helen and cannot get the disorientated girl to respond, uses a little servant boy as an auxiliary to coax her into learning. What a brilliant spontaneous ploy of creative improvisational teaching this is, utterly unanticipated and unpredictable!

We also need to remember that Helen is born a normal infant and, as we witness at the start of the film, she loses her sight and hearing to a near-fatal illness before the age of two. Kate Keller reminds herself how bright little Helen was as an infant and even insists that she could articulate syllables and imbue them with meaning. The attending doctor, moreover, assents to these impressions. He, too, remembers Helen as lively, alert, and full of promise. Even if such descriptions are retrospectively exaggerated, they give us a sense that, when Annie Sullivan arrives in the picture, she has before her not merely the manifestly wild, wilful, and unkempt creature who frantically—using the senses left to her—probes her face and clothing, smells her hands, and pummels her suitcase to catch its vibrations, but a complex, gifted human being, whose hidden history can be tapped for positive future growth. Annie knows, furthermore, that what this child is doing at that first meeting is expressing her curiosity and giving vent to her frustrated desire to figure things out.

So, this is another valuable lesson and one all too often forgotten: that *whatever* has happened in the past, *whatever* has been there—as psychoanalysis famously reveals—is never wholly lost. Aspects of it can be brought forth, worked with, and transformed. Yet, we often fail to consider this in teaching. It is, of course, a very ancient idea, expounded by Plato and instantiated perhaps most cogently in his dialogue, "Meno" (1937a), in which Socrates patiently demonstrates to a slave boy that he possesses the wherewithal to discover, despite his initial logical mistake, the correct way to compute the side of a square having an area twice the size of another one with two-foot-long sides. So, the ideal teacher—we see here—regards her student as possessing rich treasures of past experience and untapped abilities that can be brought to bear on the task at hand, as well, of course, as past experiences that might hinder that task and which, therefore, must likewise be brought forward in order to dislodge and mitigate their obstructive force.

Annie Sullivan arrives by train. It is 1887. Just fifteen years after the railroad incident in Russia that sparked Tolstoy's imagination and eventually became *Anna Karenina*. Two years before the great World's Fair in Paris that featured the Eiffel Tower. Surprisingly young and inexperienced, a product of illness, poverty, and successive personal losses, this young person travels bravely away from what has been her familiar territory at the Perkins School for the Blind in Boston to take on her first pupil. Unlike the Kellers, she is a northerner, Yankee, Irish. And this is not without consequence, for, unlike many southern women of her era, to wit, Kate Keller, Annie has never been trained to be deferential, coy, pliable, and to obey orders without comment or protest. She represents, at least superficially, a huge contrast to her employers. Fighter, survivor, as fierce and stubborn in her own way as the barbaric little girl she has come to teach, Annie proves an exceedingly good match for her pupil. This, too, deserves comment. Matching counts. No teacher, however good, is right for every student, just as no therapist makes a suitable fit for every patient who presents for treatment. Moreover, as T. Berry Brazelton, the distinguished paediatrician, has observed (1994), mothers sometimes give birth to babies who are so temperamentally different from them that primary bonding comes at the cost of great discomfort both for baby and mother right at the start of life.

Unlike the genteel, well-heeled Kellers, Annie, hailing from the industrialised north, from the asylum, the orphanage, is used to no mollycoddling, no nonsense. After what she has witnessed and lost in her own life, as well as because of her cultural background, she is loath to tolerate the pampering of children. Unlike Helen's parents, she knows blindness at first hand. She arrives wearing dark glasses, after having suffered nine operations on her weak eyes. In sum, Annie

Sullivan comes to Helen not with love, not with affection (like the girl's mother), but armed with a history that braces her and, at the same time, affords her the wherewithal to be unusually open and available, to be patient, to withstand the storm. She points out that she does not love Helen. Helen is her pupil, not her child.

Which raises an interesting question, I think, for the teacher–student relationship, and possibly for the therapist–patient relationship as well. Does love have a place in it? Obviously, as in all dyads, feeling ebbs and flows. But what we sense in *The Miracle Worker* is something special. It is an alternation on this teacher's part between certain forms of emotional distance and closeness that foster alliance, permit it to form, and then to flourish. The distance, importantly, springs neither from anxiety nor from arrogance, neither from pity nor from guilt, but is the result of an adaptive maturity on Annie's part. Porous and firm, this hard-won maturity affords her a unique perspective on Helen. Annie peers through Helen's defences (her primitive behaviour, her tempestuousness). What she locates there and keeps fixedly in the forefront of all her teaching is curiosity, cleverness, verve, spunk, and independence, all of which remind the teacher of herself.

Stunningly, after the longest and most painful scene in the film—the first dining room scene—Annie recalls herself as a little girl pleading to have the chance to go to school. She never forgets this.

So, is this love? Does the ability to identify, and to wish to help, constitute a kind of love? Or would it be a mistake to call it that, as Annie herself clearly thinks? I want to leave this an open question to which we shall return later. But two relevant points first.

Related to the notion of "love" is, of course, the notion of "like", and I find it fascinating that, towards the end of the film, there is an interchange when Captain Keller (just, in fact, as he and his wife seem to be hell-bent on undoing, by their persistent over-indulgence, much of the progress Helen has made with Annie) asks sceptically and with pique, "Miss Sullivan, do you like the child?"

To which Annie replies, "I'm beginning to. Do *you*?"

But to this question, I am afraid, there is only a telling silence.

Second, I want to remind us momentarily of Freud's famous cases, many of which ended up as failed treatments. Think, paradigmatically, of "Dora" (1905e). Surely, as any careful and unbiased study of Freud's clinical practice reveals, the propensity to regard patients—

whether one is fond of them or not—principally as fascinating *in vivo* research experiments into the workings of the human psyche must result in less than optimal outcomes. One *must* care for the other person in the dyad. But how? How in teaching and how in therapy? These are questions *The Miracle Worker* invites us to ponder.

From the start we can tell—from Annie's warm send-off in Boston and her wearying days- and nights-long train ride south, filled with flashbacks, memories, and dreams—that her genius as a teacher is going to spring directly from her awareness of her own past and her unconscious use of it, particularly of her own childhood. How analogous is this, we might ask, to the use by a therapist of transference and countertransference in the clinical situation? Unlike Helen's mother, who draws almost exclusively on maternal love and intuition, Annie has been, to an extent, just where this child is now—in darkness, cut off. She knows what it means to want passionately to understand something that seems beyond reach. Thus, we see the vital importance to teachers of mining and making use of not only their students' past experiences, but their *own* lives in order to reach their students. Very early on, for example, shortly after they meet, Annie makes a facial expression signifying pleasure and places Helen's hand over her mouth and cheeks so that Helen can imitate the expression while Annie vigorously nods. She does this for both "good" and "bad", thus using herself as a way of connecting with the child.

No matter what Helen does, Annie is not afraid of her. I want to underscore this point. Annie is not only not afraid of Helen, she is not intimidated by the rage, helplessness, pity, disgust, and shame that, sometimes, Helen's behaviour evokes in others. From the first moment of their meeting, when Annie has just been brought from the railway station and Helen is waiting on the veranda, Annie willingly permits Helen's intrusiveness. She allows the child to grope hungrily at her body, her face, her wardrobe (Helen pulls off her gloves and later tries on Annie's hat and coat and even, momentarily, her underwear), and Annie tolerates it all. She stands by during the little girl's indiscriminate rifling through her neatly packed luggage, all because she recognises and values the curiosity that fuels it. Moreover, when Helen discovers the doll Annie has packed as a gift for her and Annie sees that it is accepted, she seizes the moment and without delay begins to teach her. Thus, immediately, within the first hour of her arrival, Annie is showing Helen how to sign with her fingers: D, O, L, L.

Perhaps another clinical analogy is apt. Might we think of an analyst peering through armamentaria of defences to understand what cannot be directly expressed? A child who breaks something, or who hits another child, is not only breaking and hitting but is also speaking, or, rather, *trying* to speak, though these actions, and Annie Sullivan, in her teaching, wants to understand this "speech" of the unhearing, unsighted child who uses only touch, smell, and taste and to help Helen both to understand the world around her and also to make her own wishes known. Like a therapist, she reacts, then, not only to manifest but to latent content. She seeks to address—if you will—not only the question the student is asking openly in class, but the one not being asked but that is troubling deep down.

Rather than fleeing emotionally from Helen's bizarre outbursts and ignoring or indulging her out of anxiety or panic, rather than fuming in impotent, guilty rage like Helen's militaristic father, Captain Keller, with his frequent rather callous self-serving references to southern bravery during the Civil War, or trying to pacify and reward her with tender embraces and sweets, like Helen's mother, Annie attends with specificity to the disturbing acts. *What*, precisely, is Helen *doing*? And *why*? What is she trying so desperately to communicate? We may be reminded, apropos, of certain brilliant early child analysts such as Hermine von Hug-Helmuth (1871–1924), and later, of the previously mentioned Donald Winnicott, who, in a classic paper, "The anti-social tendency" (1956), interprets childish transgression as inevitably encoding a plea, a message, a *cri de coeur*. Annie, as we see in this film, transforms each one of Helen's acts into an occasion for teaching and learning. Each trespass becomes a teaching moment.

After all, there is excellent cause for rejoicing in Helen's wildness. Just think of its alternative: imagine an unseeing, unhearing child who has lost hope, an apathetic child who has succumbed to withdrawal, depression, and to both physical and mental decline. As long as this little girl continues to fight back, to feel hungry, to grab her food, to touch and probe and explore the external world, as long as she asserts herself (however inappropriately), Annie knows she has a chance, that her pupil is still "alive". She can be worked with and helped to harness that flow of energy more positively.

Once again, we can find implications beyond the specific circumstances of the film. Ought ordinary teachers, perhaps, try to feel less threatened and react less punitively toward high jinks and the sowing of wild oats in their students? Ought we recognise the wondrous creative potential of all this energy? I wrote a piece some years ago on 1980s New York City subway car graffiti (spray painted by roving gangs of mainly adolescent boys) and tried to argue this point. Wouldn't you, after all, rather have a bellicose student in your class than an apathetic one? Uncannily, Annie Sullivan, having suffered near blindness, sees so clearly what no one else in Helen's milieu, with far better eyes, can see. Looking beyond each manifest trespass to the latent desire that motivates it, Annie responds to Helen's deepest wish—that is, *her wish to learn,* her wish to understand, to know, to communicate: as E. M. Forster famously put it, to connect.

"I want her to have eyes," Annie says. Nothing else will do.

Let us turn now to the famous dining room scene. There are two, but I mean the first one. We need to remind ourselves of how important the dining room is as a site and focus on its huge symbolic value. It is the place were the family, day-by-day, gathers to commune and to share nourishment. Food is smelled, touched, and tasted here, so that all three of Helen's intact senses are given priority in this space. It has, therefore, special meaning for her even beyond its centrality to the family at large. When pandemonium breaks loose in it, we sense a major structural upheaval, and this is proved by Annie's insistence, almost immediately afterwards, that Helen be removed from the family home and brought under her absolute control.

Horrified by Helen's crude behaviour and lack of table manners, Annie stops her from stealing food from her plate at dinner. She means to have this child sit down appropriately on her own chair, eat from her own plate exclusively, and do so with proper utensils. Eventually (off camera), she will teach Helen to fold her napkin. Helen, never having been exposed to such normal demands and standards, is understandably furious. We witness an almost unbearable sequence as the spirited girl defies her teacher. We cringe as Helen hits her, slaps her hard in the face repeatedly, pulls her teacher's hair, spits out food into her face, knocks off her glasses, kicks at the floor, hurls spoons, one after another, and creates devastation in this otherwise orderly space. The incorrigible girl pushes Annie to the point where the teacher is panting, her hair and clothing in disarray, and yet she refuses to submit. The patience of a saint would be sorely tried. Waiting outdoors with the rest of the family while this is going on, Helen's Aunt Ev remarks to the others as they listen to sounds of skirmish and dishes clattering to the floor, "This could go on all afternoon."

Annie never backs down. She knows she cannot. Having faced her own version of such feelings, she is prepared not only to identify with them unflinchingly but, beyond this, to *use* them and to capitalise on them. (Apropos, there is a wonderful moment earlier in the film when Annie, at a moment of ire, shakes her doll, the very doll she has brought along for Helen, instead of shaking the child herself. In that flash, we see the way *her* symbolic functioning matches that of Helen's and how the identifications go back and forth and are so rich and complex.) Refusing to be distracted, Annie focuses her attention on the issue of discipline and on the question of what good can come of all this turmoil; what, optimally, does she want Helen to *learn* from this experience?

One thing Helen learns right away is to hate and fear Annie, a reaction the teacher will have to overcome in order to form a working alliance with her. And we segue now into the topic of discipline, which was, for our students at the university, the film's central issue. They felt that *The Miracle Worker*, perhaps more than any other film or text they had encountered, conveys with clarity the value of discipline and its role in the learning process. Discipline, *The Miracle Worker* demonstrates, is a necessary step on the path to knowledge, but never an end in itself. Annie says this explicitly later on to Helen's parents when she states that obedience without understanding is worthless. Michel de Montaigne would have heartily concurred.

Because of Annie's refusal to back down in their fierce battle in the dining room, Helen now shrinks from her. And this gives us another valuable insight: the insight that it might well be necessary for both student and teacher to experience and weather negative feelings of great strength towards one another during the learning process. When growth is occurring, the earth must shake and even crack a little, voices cannot always remain calm, and turbulence might gain sway over tranquillity. In clinical practice, one speaks of the negative transference and of the value of a patient's being able to hate the analyst during certain phases of the treatment. The analyst must survive this so as to continue working.

A crucial element in the work is that it must occur apart from Helen's family. Annie, you remember, insists on this as a condition of her stay, but her dictum is strenuously opposed by both of Helen's parents. She prevails, of course, and Helen is brought to a cabin in the woods (on the family's estate) where Annie can work uninterruptedly with her. Again, we might make an analogy to clinical practice, for we know that both Anna Freud and Melanie Klein, early practitioners of child psychoanalysis, advocated for the removal of their child patients from the parental home during therapy sessions. At first, this was fiercely opposed; parents wanted their children treated at home. They wanted to maintain their customary control.

Interestingly, the idea of getting the child out and away from parental influence in order to facilitate learning has a long pre-psychoanalytic history. It is advocated, famously, not only by Plato in the "Republic" (1937b), but also in the essay by Montaigne (1575) on the education of children that I mentioned at the start of this chapter. Montaigne argues boldly that parental love for children entails a natural indulgence and display of tender feelings that cannot but be highly detrimental to their education, and that the good tutor, therefore, must remove his pupils from such influence, from what he deems the orbit of soft parental leniency. One might extend this notion to the parameters of doctor–patient relationships more generally and recall the warning that, for similar reasons, that is, the intrusion of tender and complex emotions, a doctor should not operate on his own children. Yet, Freud analysed his daughter Anna and, likewise, Melanie Klein her children, and many children today in the USA and in the UK are being home-schooled. We might think, moreover, of Suzuki training in violin and piano, where parental involvement is obligatory. If familial love is detrimental, what then should a teacher feel, optimally, for her pupil, and *vice versa*? And, as we asked earlier, what should an analyst feel for her patient?

At the end of the film, we begin to understand, perhaps. When Helen has had her moment of epiphany and, with Annie's patience, tolerance (and intolerance), fortitude, focus, and with her Socratic method of bringing out what is already there in the child, and with all the pain that has gone before, she makes her thrilling discovery at the water pump of the connections that will serve as foundation for her ongoing knowledge and for communication throughout her life (the real Helen Keller went on to attend Radcliffe College, 1894–1904), we, as audience, undergo a parallel experience of ecstasy and revelation. We comprehend that what has just happened, this culmination, and this new beginning, which Annie Sullivan has helped Helen Keller to achieve, is permanent and profound. Irreversible knowledge. Something has changed forever.

Going back to the quote I gave at the beginning of this essay, if it is true that "Freud's unique contribution was the development of [a way] to permanent, internal reorganization", then surely, I think, we have to say that this description sounds strikingly like what Annie Sullivan has just accomplished with her young pupil: permanent internal reorganisation.

And so, Annie Sullivan calls Helen Keller's parents over to partake in this triumphant scene, and with tears and with many embraces, the film draws to its radiantly hopeful close. In what can only be interpreted as an expression of gratitude, Helen signs the word for "teacher". Later that night, as Annie sits rocking in her chair on the balcony in the starlight, the little girl, in her nightdress, comes outside looking for her and, reaching for her teacher, she slowly and deliberately approaches her and plants a kiss on her cheek. Annie takes her pupil into her arms and rocks gently with her. A lullaby ends this movie. It is the same one we heard at the beginning, thus returning us to the maternal love with which we started and without which the miracle, the breakthrough, the wonder, might not have happened.

References

Brazelton, T. B. (1994). *Touchpoints: Your Child's Emotional and Behavioral Development, Birth to 3*. New York: DaCapo Lifelong Books.

Dewey, J. (1934). *Art as Experience*. New York: Paragon Books, 1979.

Freud, S. (1905e). *Fragment of an Analysis of a Case of Hysteria*. S.E., 7: 7–122. London: Hogarth.

Montaigne, M. de (1575). *Essais*. France: Simon Millanges, 1580.

Plato (1937a). Meno. In: *The Dialogues of Plato*, B. Howett (Trans.). New York: Random House.

Plato (1937b). Republic. In: *The Dialogues of Plato*, B. Jowett (Trans.). New York: Random House.

Simon, B. (1978). *Mind and Madness in Ancient Greece*. Ithaca, NY: Cornell University Press.

Winnicott, D. W. (1956). The anti-social tendency. In: *Through Pediatrics to Psycho-Analysis* (pp. 306–315). London: Hogarth Press, 1987.

CHAPTER NINE

Unconscious creative activity and the restoration of reverie

M. Gerard Fromm

Activity

"Concepts can never be presented to me merely; they must be knitted into the structure of my being, and this can only be done through my own activity" (Follett, 1930, quoted in Milner, 1957, p. xi). So begins, epigrammatically, Marion Milner's intensely personal study, *On Not Being Able to Paint* (1957). This moving articulate reverie lays out for us the human subject in the process of finding her subjectivity, a process of both excitement and peril. As a psychoanalytic text, it is without precedent and without duplication since. As Podro (1990) writes, "What has been largely absent (within psychoanalytic considerations of painting) is an insight into how the activity of painting itself was a matter of urgency and of satisfaction: how painting was itself valuable to us" (p. 17).

It is precisely this "urgency" that catches a dimension of creative activity akin to the clinical, and, indeed, so attuned that one easily finds clinical examples of activity, in some distinction to interpretation, as critically important vehicles for the mastery and integration of unconscious feeling and for, in Kohut's terms (1977), the restoration of self. This largely unconscious process might offer another angle on what it means to work through. But the emphasis in the Follett quote on "my own activity" could obscure the degree to which creative activity always takes place in some relational context, within which such activity might also be quite vulnerable. In this chapter, I hope to illustrate the creative use of activity to deal with developmental challenges, but also how dependent that creativity can be on a primary relationship in the person's life.

In Chapter Seven, I noted a passing observation made by Masud Khan (1963). Describing his adolescent patient's effort to recover from a serious breakdown, Khan commented on "the strange way this youth found his way back to mobility and aliveness through skating" (p. 179). I gave two further examples of this process of the investment of energy in a particular activity corollary to a person's working their way towards the restoration of psychic health. The first had to do with the range of psychological and developmental functions the activity of swimming served throughout a man's life. The second had to do with a young man's discovery of photography at the time of his mother's death. The latter story suggested the developmental connection between the activity of photography and a first transitional object, a blanket cathected powerfully in early childhood in a context of maternal illness.

These clinical examples persuaded me that what Erikson called "the silent doings of ego synthesis" (1956, p. 57) could be extended to include the silent work of transitional activity. This work, like the young man's photography, temporarily relieves the subject of the unbearable strain of reality acceptance by allowing him the sense of his creative capacity to invest the world anew and to make and hold aspects of it. For the young photographer, his creative ability to stop time mitigated his serious potential for catastrophic reaction to the loss of his mother and the dangerous possibility that he might turn permanently away from the reality of such a depleted world. For the swimmer, this activity, among other things, created a space for essential reverie in a time of crisis.

These examples and others invite our attention to organic activities of self-healing. I am quite sure that there are many important functions for an activities programme within a treatment centre, but perhaps this is one of them (J. Erikson, 1976)—not so much as an activities "therapy", which risks disruption through interpretation, but through the provision of space and support for personally found and personally meaningful activity. At stake here is the whole question of sublimation as an unconscious healing process. As a treatment value, the importance of which might be directly proportionate to the degree of disturbance of the patient, its jeopardy in this era of very short-term and rigidly structured treatment programmes is of great consequence.

On Not Being Able to Paint

Another way of speaking about this "gyroscopic function" (Sandler & Sandler, 1986) and as well about the "silent doings of ego synthesis" (Erikson, 1956, p. 57) would be in those terms relatively unique to Milner, Winnicott, and others in the "middle school" of British psychoanalysis. These terms accent the human subject's ongoing task of relating inner and outer experience. It was Winnicott's (1951) genius to bring together a paediatric and psychoanalytic attention on the unnoticed but obvious experience of early childhood around security objects. He quickly realised that these "objects", such as the teddy bear, occupied a psychic position for the child between inner experience and outer experience; they were, thus, "transitional", less important as objects in themselves than as the vehicles for necessary psychic and physical activity. This activity intermingled the benignly omnipotent early sense of self with the realities of separateness and differentiation. As such, it prefigured and precipitated the birth of fully symbolic activity.

Elsewhere (Fromm, 1989), I have noted some of the theoretical links between Winnicott's work and Erikson's, two brilliant paediatrically orientated psychoanalysts working simultaneously on different sides of the Atlantic. Echoing Erikson's more elaborated explication of the mutuality in the developing life cycle, Winnicott argues that the human individual is never free from the strain of relating inner and outer experience. It can be argued that it was Milner's genius to have illustrated what he meant before he said it, and to have shown us that such integration is not only the carrying out of an essential function, but, at least for some, the source of creativity.

In *On Not Being Able to Paint* (1957), one of several autobiographical books, Milner studies creativity from the vantage point of herself as a "Sunday painter" making her own efforts to learn to draw and paint. Milner discovers, in first-hand ways that come through with the authenticity and freshness of a person speaking to herself, some of the parallels between the painter and the analytic patient. As Anna Freud writes in the Introduction to Milner's book:

> Both ventures, the analytic as well as the creative one, seem to demand similar external and internal conditions. There is the same need for "circumstances in which it is safe to be absent-minded" . . . there is the same unwillingness to transgress beyond the reassuring limits of the secondary process and "to accept chaos as a temporary stage". There is the same fear of the "plunge into no-differentiation" and the disbelief in the "spontaneous ordering forces" which emerge, once the plunge is taken. There is, above all, the same terror of the unknown. (Milner, 1957, p. xiii)

Milner captures the oppressiveness and the reassurances of conscious logic and preconceived ideas when it comes to creativity. She describes the defensive interference with, and the reach to closure of, the creative process when the uncertainty could not be borne further. Note, again, that all of this describes what is at stake emotionally in the *activity* of painting, rather than, as is often the case in psychoanalytic discussions of this subject, in what a particular painting might mean, either as a set of images or as a psycho-historical event. There is a correspondence here with the work of Kris (1982) and Bollas (2002), who speak of the establishment of the process of free association not as a prerequisite for psychoanalytic therapy, but as its basic therapeutic action and outcome.

Milner's table of contents captures the simplicity and the truly personal nature of the encounter between the inner and outer worlds: "What the eye likes", "Being separate and being together", "The plunge into color", "The necessity of illusion" (p. vii). In one of her later chapters, she discusses personally invested activity as the "medium" for the relating of inner and outer life, and so introduces what, to my mind, is a psychoanalytic term of equal importance to that of the "frame". In the following lengthy extract, she outlines this concept, including its developmental and treatment significance, and, almost in passing, suggests a diagnostic schema of some interest to analysts working with pre-oedipal psychological conditions:

> The problem of the relation between the painter and his world . . . became basically a problem of one's own need and the needs of the

"other", a problem of reciprocity between "you" and "me"; with "you" and "me" meaning originally mother and child. But if this was the earth from which the foundations for true dialogue relations with the outside world should spring, did they always get established there? . . . It looked as if for many people they only became established partially, that there were always certain areas of psychic country in which they failed; and what was established instead, as always when dialogue relationship fails, was dictatorship, the dominance of one side or the other. It seemed that in those areas in which one had lost hope of making any real contact with the outside world one of three things could happen. First one could try to deny the external demand and become an active, dictatorial egoist, actively denying the need of the other, trying to make one's own wishes alone determine what happened. Secondly one could become a passive egoist, retreating from public reality altogether and taking refuge in a world of unexpressed dreams, becoming remote and inaccessible. Thirdly, one could allow the outside world to become dictator, one could fit in to external reality and its demands, but fit in all too well; the placating of external reality could become one's main preoccupation; doing what other people wanted could become the centre of life; one could become seduced by objectivity into complete betrayal of one's own side of the matter . . .

This idea of being seduced by objectivity raised again the whole question of the actual ways in which one's relation to the outside world develops, from the moment of birth onwards. It suggested that such a dictatorship of the external could be set up in infancy, even with the best of intentions on the part of the adults, simply by inability to give time for the wish to enter into relationship to come from the child's end; thus the establishing of reciprocity could fail simply because the child's time rhythms of need and wish are different from the adult's. Or not only could it fail from wrong timing, it could fail through inability to establish communication, since the child's small gestures of relationship are so easily overlooked or misunderstood. Of course this failure of relationship is inevitable at times, it is part of the agonizing side of being a child; but here came in the particular aspect of the free drawing method that apparently made it partly able to compensate for that failure, able to act as a bridge between the public and the private worlds. For by it one could find an "other", a public reality, that was very pliant and undemanding; pencil and chalk and paper provided a simplified situation in which the other gave of itself easily and immediately to take the form of the dream, it did not stridently insist on its own public nature. . . . So by means of this there could

perhaps come about the correcting of the bias of a too docilely accepted public vision and a denied private one. And apparently it could
come about just because there was this experience of togetherness
with one's medium lived through together. Because of this one could
reclaim some of the lost land of one's experience, find in the medium,
in its pliability yet irreducible otherness, the "other" that had
inevitably had to fail one at times in one's first efforts at realizing
togetherness. Granted that it was a very primitive togetherness, one
that allowed the other only a very small amount of identity of its own,
yet it did seem able to serve as the essential basis for a more mature
form in which both other and self have an equal claim to the recognition of needs and individuality; just as psycho-analysis does through
the analyst acting as a pliant medium, giving back the patient's own
thought to him, in a clarified form, rather than intruding his own
needs and ideas. (pp. 116–118)

Milner (1969) describes in detail the treatment of one of her more
seriously disturbed patients and the importance of this patient's painting in her recovery. The patient speaks of her illness as a "breakdown
into reality" (p. 10). Thus, she captures one side of the catastrophe
potentially suffered by the developing self too early disillusioned
about its capacity to relate to the outer world; this area of illusion is
either forced towards delusion, says Winnicott (1951), or towards a
collapse of the self into a depleted relation to reality. In contrast is
the essential, if silent, partnership between child and primary care-
taker, whose easy adaptation to the child's needs provides an ordinary experience of omnipotence, the experience of "I want, I have",
which becomes the grounding for a confident, creative relationship
to the world. It is this relational background to the breakdown
and restoration of creativity that I will now try to illustrate through
parallel reports of a patient's psychotherapy and her work with her art
teacher.

Breakdown and engagement

The patient is someone for whom this idea of a breakdown into reality made sense. Her breakdown in life, which occurred shortly after
she left home to attend college, felt to her like the final movement in
a gradual loss of the formerly sustaining illusion that she was

emotionally connected to others. In college, she fell into a deep alone-ness without the psychic ability to conjure up any feeling of inner life or relatedness. In this state, she could never allow herself to relax or even to sleep fully; instead, she felt compelled to frantically grasp for people.

Talking about the chaotic and clinging relationships in her life during her effort to live alone, the patient became reflective: "Even some of the bad experiences with people were still experiences, like paint thrown on the blank, empty canvas of my life before and since." She once thought of herself as a puppet who had a life as long as someone was pulling the strings. Early in her therapy, she saw herself as without a puppet master, collapsed on a dark stage, helpless, alone, but free and beginning to discover an inner life, at first only through the experience of self-inflicted pain.

One of the patient's first statements in therapy was, "I always felt that I have been totally uninteresting. I'd never be the topic at the dinner table or at school. I don't have anything of a self that interests people, that strongly grabs people. I have no energy to do that. I'm a dead and deadening person. I don't make waves." This statement fitted with an early impression I had of her: that, given her attributes and experiences so far in life, she could be seen as quite an interesting person, but that she had totally lost interest in herself. Her statement contrasts strongly, however, with the series of tidal-wave dreams that almost immediately followed, dreams that conveyed her inner convic-tion that she could not manage what was indeed intensely alive within her by herself.

The patient felt that her teachers had never listened to her and recalled how her peers had teased her as "spacey". I came to feel that part of her difficulty might be thought of as a disturbance in the capac-ity for reverie. Early on, the therapeutic action of the work seemed to have to do with moments of silence or lull in the hour, moments when her demand for me to fill that space betrayed her conviction of total lack within herself. It was a good sign when she eventually became surprised, even delighted, to find that "something comes next". The therapeutic task had to do with the transformation of the patient's "spaciness" into free association (Bollas, 2002), and the way that the therapeutic relationship legitimised this process as not only produc-tive (which was a highly charged value for her), but also a vital func-tion. She had been an amateur, though accomplished, singer, but had become terrified of forgetting her lines. Her conviction that her mind would not work automatically to remember her lines related to this disturbance of reverie, and reflected also what she took to be her family's belief that she would not work naturally to become an educated person. Within this way of seeing things, however, I felt it important to hold for myself the distinction between nurturing and relying on an organic integrative drive and the more problematic idea that the patient's growth could be taken for granted, that she and it would go on by itself.

This understanding of my patient brought me back to a passage in the Appendix of Milner's book *On Not Being Able to Paint* (1957):

> The expressive word "reverie" has been . . . largely dropped from the language of psycho-pathology, and the overworked word phantasy made to carry such a heavy burden of meaning. "Reverie" does emphasize the aspect of absent-mindedness, and therefore . . . the necessity for a certain quality of protectiveness in the environment. For there are obviously many circumstances in which it is not safe to be absent-minded; it needs a setting, both physical and mental . . . a physical setting in which we are free, for the time being, from the need for immediate practical expedient action and . . . a mental setting, an attitude, both in the people around and in oneself, a tolerance of something which may at moments look very like madness. . . .
>
> Just as sleep dreaming is necessary (said Freud) to preserve sleep, so both conscious and unconscious daydreaming is necessary to preserve creative being awake. Clinical psycho-analytic experience suggests that many of the impediments to going forward into living are the result of a failure of the child's environment to provide the necessary setting for such absent-mindedness. For it seems likely that, in this phase of not distinguishing the "me" and the "not-me" we are particularly vulnerable to the happenings in the inner life of those nearest to us emotionally. (pp. 163–164)

This patient "always knew" she could not take care of herself in college. She had felt sheltered, spoiled, nagged, and defined by her parents' idealised images of her as well as their demonized images of her sister. On the other hand, she felt that she had never been trusted, taught or, in a certain sense, left alone to find herself. She knew "for sure" that when the puppetry was over, she would collapse, as indeed she did. She did not know that this edge of her life, this flat-earth moment of leaving home for college, might well have been such an edge because it had been, in quite different ways, for both of her parents. She had come to a critical moment of identity formation, the late adolescent version of "distinguishing the 'me' and the 'not me'", and she was indeed "particularly vulnerable to the happenings in the inner life of those nearest to [her]" (Milner, 1957, p. 164).

The patient was certain that she could not meet this developmental challenge. She knew that she would be utterly alone and utterly resourceless, despite a fine intelligence, talents, a pleasant-enough personality, and her family's material resources. She also sensed that her family's difficulties with ordinary dependency and loss might lead them to attack, as she herself did, those feelings in her. Thus, she experienced this moment of separation not only as falling into space, but as leading to rage and narcissistic disappointment should she try to return. This absence of play in the intrapsychic and familial systems, this absence of in-between space and room for experiment and rapprochement, seemed to guarantee for this patient enormous anxiety and almost certain failure at the task of separation.

An interesting feature of both parents' earlier life development was the way in which their own areas of necessary illusion had suffered assault. In early adulthood, the patient's father felt terribly traumatised by seeing "too much too soon" as a young military recruit. On the other side, the patient's mother felt crushed by her own mother's cruel life lessons, one of which used her daughter's doll as vehicle for the instruction. This harsh and possibly envious action seemed to echo a generation later in the patient's nihilism and her experience of external life as crushing her internal life. As a kind of generational transmission (Fromm, 2012), her mother's longing to resuscitate the lost potential of the mother–daughter relationship might well have expressed itself in her description of the patient as a baby: "Like a doll; people were shocked that she moved."

On Not Being Able to Paint opens for us a window on to anxiety-driven resistances to engagement in a creative relation to the world. In this patient's treatment, this seemed to be the first and, in some ways, the most fundamental problem. It seemed to me that my task was to offer "a setting for absent-mindedness" (Milner, 1957, p. 164), an opportunity for a silence that might become generative. To do that, I would have to be fully present with her, and this turned out to be, at least at the beginning, the most difficult part of the work. The patient created in me the experience of her, in her own extreme terms, as "dead and deadening", as superficial and disconnected, and as trying to cover that inner sense of emptiness with half-hearted demands that I feed her. At one point, a friend had harshly accused her of "sucking my blood", needing too much, but my experience of her, in spite of her demands, was that she did not suck at all; as she said, "I don't grab." This way of being seemed like the current version within the analytic setting of an actual and sudden early childhood illness that the patient had suffered, in which listlessness and no appetite were serious symptoms.

This is almost certainly what led me to welcome those occasions when tension developed in the hours or when direct questions occurred. I found myself taking those rare opportunities to become declarative with her, to show her my own separate thinking and emotional life, with the hope that they might actually become resources to her. For example, after a desultory and sullenly dependent session, a session in which she complained that she felt "on a string" with other people and yet also complained that she did not feel as if she was on a string with me, she burst out with, "What are we doing? What's progress?" I said to her that the notion of progress might be complicated by her own and others' expectations of her, but that I would think of progress for her as bringing her head, heart, and gut together and letting herself be herself, apart from what others might have in mind for her. At moments like this, she seemed to call me into presence for her, after which she was slightly more able to relax into the session. Soon after this, she said, "I can't believe I've tried so hard to please people, to be the perfect child . . . I feel now that I'm hiding in the dark, not doing things for other people but not knowing yet what I want for myself."

Early painting

The treatment setting made available a number of programmes, including an activities programme to which, early on, her skills and interests brought her. It offered a wide array of creative possibilities and was staffed by artists and craftsmen who offered the patient the true experience of apprenticeship within the role of student or worker, rather than a role organised around treating an illness. The patient found her way to the art teacher, an older man, himself a successful artist, devoted to the process of painting as a daring breaking through to what is authentic in a person and, therefore, inevitably beautiful. The quotes below are from his notes (Garel, personal communication).

As it turned out, he, too, was encountering with this patient the problem of engagement, and, like me, experienced himself as held resolutely outside while being offered a small glimpse of a true inner life. She began with her teacher by talking of her past painting experience and asking him for acrylic paints. But in response to the teacher's question about what size canvas she wanted, she produced "a little, twisted piece of driftwood, about two inches long and a quarter inch in diameter. Still puzzled, I watched her take out a very fine brush with tiny bristles, her own that she had brought with her, and in a quite short time, working intently and steadily, she transformed the little wood into an exquisite object, improvising a complex, detailed design as she was painting." It was to become a piece of jewellery.

Realising that he was working with a talented person, the teacher asked the patient about her jewellery, but she shrugged off his question with a disinterested, "I don't know." When she returned to class, she painted two abstractions, which seemed to her teacher sensitive but also busy and decorative. He offered her his responses. "When I talked to her about the dynamics of space, I could feel my words bouncing off her as she looked at me stonily. It appears that this is a girl who does not like criticism or suggestions and so I decided to just let her go her own talented way."

Later, she painted a simple, silhouetted nude girl, a work that her teacher thought was exceptional, but "she seemed to ignore my praise, so I more firmly decided that it might be best, at the moment, to just let her express her own independence in any direction . . . I let her choose her own pattern of work. It seems that my relation to her is one of leaving all decisions up to her and just being around. Apparently she accepts me if I don't interfere with her very limited tolerance of outside direction." These comments precisely paralleled my experience and position in the early part of this patient's psychotherapy.

Over time, the patient actually asked her teacher for help. In attempting to draw a person, she could not understand how to give the figure a certain body posture. She sought his instruction, but, once she got it, she made no further attempt at working on the painting.

Instead, she took all of her art materials back to her room. She asked her teacher if this arrangement suited him, and he agreed on the condition that she show him everything she did there, including what she considered to be her failures, so that they could discuss them. This approach puzzled her, though she agreed to it. For a while, she brought him very little new work, instead showing him the painting assignments she had produced in art classes earlier in her life. Her teacher recognised their technical merit, but added, "I don't teach this way. I expected her to develop and change, but this would be an experiment and distillation from her own needs."

In the month prior to a break in her therapy because of my summer vacation, the patient did not experiment with, or go deeper into, her painting. Instead, she mobilised her taste and craftsmanship in the extensive production of tiny ceramic beads, which she would string together into necklaces, and then of many unusual and personally designed note cards. She painted both, the former with dabs of colour in abstract design and the latter with pastel hues of watercolour that faded into each other, forming a subdued and elegant background design.

Rupture and reciprocity

As one might expect, the summer break in therapy seriously disrupted this patient's tentative efforts to integrate her inner and outer life, and she fell back into sullen detachment and the driven, shallow craving for attention characteristic of earlier times. In parallel fashion, she did not paint at all during my several weeks' absence. When I returned, we began a critical phase of her treatment. This phase began with her wish to see a different therapist, but her then proceeding in her sessions as though she were working with me. After a while, she again brought up her wish to discontinue her work with me and to see someone else. We made little progress in understanding or even elaborating her reasons for this wish, and I found it important to make clear to her my position, which was that it did not make sense to me to work with her if she did not want to work with me. I added that I hoped she would learn what she could in the process of coming to a decision.

Throughout this, it seemed impossible to get to her feelings about my having been away or about our work together at all; we could only see clearly that she was frightened of her anger towards me. On the day that she had scheduled her meeting with a consulting therapist, she found herself recalling a dream from earlier in the summer. Interestingly, I, too, had found myself thinking about this dream. In the dream, the staff and patients of the treatment centre were welcoming a new medical director. Some of the staff were naked, and the patient was embarrassed to notice that neither I nor the medical director had penises. To distract everyone from this embarrassing exposure, she took off her shirt and displayed her large breasts.

In the sessions during this phase of consultation, I worked more steadily towards interpreting the transference. This greater focus on what might be happening in the room between us led to a more confrontational mood in the patient. Eventually, she asked me when we had begun therapy; I told her the date. She said that she did not want to think about how bad she felt then and how isolated she was. I recognised in this her acknowledgement that treatment had helped her feel a bit better, and I added that therapy is difficult because it involves thinking about painful feelings. She belligerently said that she got nothing from therapy. Although she had still not talked explicitly about the trouble she was having with me, she made it clear that she had decided to change therapists and that she was now just going through the motions and doing her duty with me. It was also clear that she felt that the consulting therapist was simply doing his duty with her and that we were all going to try to get her, in one way or another, to continue seeing me.

I confronted her about this. I told her that she did not believe me when I said that I did not want to work with her unless she wanted to work with me. I added that she was angry with *me* because *she* was just waiting, as though I could open up what her trouble was for her. She quickly switched the subject to a friend who "might be playing with my mind". I asked her if she saw the connection between that statement and her feelings with me now. She erupted. "Both have to do with men; I hate them and I hate you." She added, "I feel a love potential but that's risky." I said to her that it is hard for her to look at her decision about therapy and to open that up with me because she worries that I will play with her head. For the first time she consciously considered, with a mixture of enjoyment and anxiety, the possible relationship between her feelings towards me and toward other men in her life.

She then faced me and said, "Where do you think I am in treatment?" I said to her that I thought she had made a good start at scratching the surface, not realising that I was capturing in my language her habit of savagely picking at her skin, just as she picks at, in a more figurative sense, her shortcomings. She then asked me if I saw any progress at all, and I told her specifically the progress I thought I saw, both outside of her therapy by the reports of others as well as herself, but also inside her therapy. She then asked me what I saw as the important issues for her in her therapy. I told her that therapy was an unfolding and so I could not really predict what might become crucial for her, but that I could see clearly something about her relationships with men, particularly a feeling of so much anger that she was afraid it could not be dealt with. I added that I thought that had to be worked out directly with somebody.

Obviously, these exchanges are a bit unusual in psychoanalytic therapy. My responses were not primarily interpretative, because I did not feel authorised by the patient to do so. In particular, I did not interpret the impotence she was convinced of or intending to create in me. Instead, I felt that my patient had reclaimed her status as client and needed to be met at the frame of her treatment, at the place of a potential contract, where she could feel clearly the limits and the potential of our work together. It was important, I thought, to survive as her therapist (Winnicott, 1969) in the face of her massive passive aggression, and to register my presence as a person who could think about her across the gap of the summer break and through the waves of her pent-up anger. I felt that the possibility of a restored capacity for creative reverie in my patient depended on the security that might come from her feeling these boundaries as well as her true choice about joining or not.

After this, the patient said to me, "Why haven't we talked this way until now? We've piddled away this time." I acknowledged her complaint that I had let her be wasteful; I added that it simply might not have been safe to talk this way until now, having in the back of my mind that all of this had to await my leaving for vacation and my return. She left this session saying, "I've noticed that my feelings seem more real lately. When I cried with my friend yesterday, they were not my usual tears of self-pity, but tears of actual closeness with her."

In the next session, she reported feeling manipulated by me. Why was I telling her these things now? Was I trying to hold on to her? I said to her that I told her these things now because she asked, and this was the first time that she had done so. I added that until now she might have been taking care of me, protecting me from her need to get to this anger. I reminded her that the main thing she was doing in the dream was taking care of me in my inadequacy. She said that the preceding day she had felt "a wave of something". In saying this, she noted the word "wave", because waves were always in her dreams. There was a tone of pleasure and recognition at the metaphor we had created together. "A wave of fear and of being dependent on somebody I don't trust; I didn't like it at all and then I became afraid that under the surface there might be awful things." One particularly disturbing sexual thought from her past had come back to her instantly the day before when I had said to her that she had scratched the surface. It seemed clear that, although she did not feel at all sure about the meaning of this thought, she had been stuck with her own frightened and encapsulated interpretation of it for many years.

We then spoke about the dream that had occurred to both of us during the consultative process. Eventually, I told her what I thought the dream might mean in the context of our current work: that if I do not have a penis, I am no threat to her, but I also cannot help her because I have no potency. She found herself then considering again her idea that she had grown up with people whose self-esteem injuries had led them to insist that she reflect their goodness and their potency. She could not believe that I would not want that myself, and so this work must be manipulative. Neither could she yet formulate that she might want this kind of narcissistic gratification from me and that her collapse during my absence might relate to that unmet longing.

When she came back the next day, she said, "I *have* been protecting you. It's like in that dream." She took a further step in realising that in the dream she was covering me by exposing herself. She could see parallels in other relationships, particularly with men, and she could see her identification with her mother as a protector. She felt her father needed protection, needed to know that he was loved. She said, "I'd hate it too if someone didn't want me. Maybe I project that here." She was referring to making me feel unwanted, but she could also begin to consider that perhaps she had felt unwanted by me when I went away.

The patient appreciated her new tentative ability to be angry with me, but then worried that she could become "vicious". She hoped I could manage her anger, then added, "And don't let me babble." I said, "Fair enough, but now we know that your babbling has been your way of protecting me", a form of verbal self-exposure unconsciously covering her fantasy of my impotence. She said, "So therapy is about this relationship and what goes on here." I said that it was, and she said with sudden affection, "That's a new perspective; I'll have to think about that."

Later painting

During this extended, post-vacation phase of her psychotherapy, her art teacher also struggled with re-engagement. Again, the following quotes are from his notes. She showed him: "a drawing of hands, almost in prayer, actually more pleading than in prayer, with a chalice and lit candles. This took up most of the paper, but in the four corners were beautifully done small vignettes, some with couples and bare, spiky trees, all depressed scenes. I praised the drawing, but added that this showed a deep expression that her lovely decorative jewelry does not deal with. She wanted to know what I meant by that. I explained that jewelry design shows nothing of her problems, which must be a big part of her life now. She stated angrily, 'I have no problems!' . . . and then said quietly with a frown, 'Maybe I do.'"

With the approaching student exhibition and with her teacher's recognition of her feelings coming through in her painting, the patient got back to work, always in her room, but steadily and regularly showing her work to her teacher.

> She listens carefully to my criticisms and though she says very little, only asking me to repeat things that she doesn't understand, she will then act in her room in a way that is a direct result of our talks. My suggestions are never related to changes that should be made on the picture she shows me, but rather to general concepts of what I think art should be and demands that her talent can handle to give her work more depth.

> She then brought in a very pleasant abstraction, nice and tasteful. I praised her for it, but I also spoke about the need for conflict in a picture, conflict that was resolved rather than avoided. Though I only talked in abstract terms, her next picture had pictorial expression as

well as abstract conflict. Instead of just being shapes with opposing forces, there was a strong depiction of flames and smoke. The picture following that is even more specific . . . constantly more expressive involvement.

The patient was very interested in displaying her paintings in the student exhibition. To her teacher's surprise, she continued intense work after the show had begun.

Everything she has done since (the exhibition) is just in pencil and is not as elaborately finished in color: mainly expressive for herself and to show me, not concerned about impressing people. She has told me that she feels much better since she began to express her feelings in drawings and sometimes she writes on the back of these pictures: "depressed", "feeling lousy", a whole litany of such words. Though these pictures come out of depression, they are all very vigorous, definite and bold, drawn by applying great pressure, actually angry force in depicting complicated scenes . . .

Besides these, she also does some drawing in a journal . . . I was surprised that these drawings were quite mild, really casual doodles, just small drawings that were interspersed between voluminous writing, something she would do while thinking of what else to say. I presume that her emotion was put into the writing, the drawings being unimportant expressions . . .

One day at lunch the patient asked her teacher to look at a sculpture she had made.

Intrigued, I went to her room, and saw a huge three-dimensional spider. It had a diameter of about nine feet, made up of bits of junk and rags into a convincing form with an interesting fierce head. What then was most impressive was that she went to one corner and began manipulating long strings attached like reins to the hind legs and made the creature move ominously. It was humorous yet threatening. I enjoyed it and congratulated her.

A few days later I came into the art room and saw a beautiful acrylic abstraction with wild color and experimental textures, free painting that was unlike any student I was familiar with. I thought it might be hers though she hadn't done any painting here before. It showed the special talent and skill she had shown in other work. Sure enough it was hers, and when she came, she showed me how she got the unusual textures by using a steel comb we use to clean dry paint-brushes. It was the first time she had ever done an acrylic painting and she had immediately *played* with the new medium.

This blossoming capacity for play, as well as the energetic reveal-ing of herself in her painting (now done in the public space of the art room) and in her sculpture, followed immediately upon her decision to continue her psychotherapeutic work with me. We entered a phase of much deeper contact with her feelings and greater self-awareness. She had a long phone conversation with her father and found herself with many very positive childhood memories of their relationship. For the first time, she cried hard in her session as she felt her long-buried love for him and her feelings of loss in that relationship. These memories were powerful and specific. She got herself into something of a wild argument with two female friends over an apparent betrayal involving a young man, but she came out of this saying, "I was happy about it. For the first time, I made noise with my feelings. I never felt so involved with so many people, so cared about."

With the agreement of her psychopharmacologist, she decided to discontinue her antidepressant medication and declared to me, "This is the place where I'm going to work things out." She seemed pleased, relieved, and much stronger, as though her medication had repre-sented her own and perhaps her family's fear of depression and their need to force a functioning they were sure could not happen from inner resources or relational work. Now, the patient *wanted* to look inside, despite thoughts that had seriously scared her, all of which found their way into her paintings. With this new-found wish to dig, she largely dropped her habit of picking at her skin, and the nagging question "What's wrong with me?" became a more bold "What's happening with me?"

The restoration of reverie

What I hope to have illustrated in this lengthy clinical report is, to return to Milner's language, the establishment of reciprocity in a psychotherapeutic encounter. The pattern of simply "fitting in", of "placating . . . nexternal reality" (Milner, 1957, p. 116) seemed to be the patient's unconscious way of being with me, and also seemed to be what she expected me to do with her. All of this had parallels in her painting and in her relationship to her art teacher. The idea of drift-wood captured an important piece of her self-image. She had felt cut adrift by her parents (as she soon would by me during my vacation) and headed for the inevitable failure on her own that a programmed upbringing, at least as she felt it, implied. To claim her life and trans-form it, she needed to be let go of, to see where those dream waves might take her, and then to learn the inevitability and the value of fail-ure. Her art teacher insisted on her showing him *all* her work, includ-ing failed efforts, so that learning might occur. In her psychotherapy, the work with my potential failure, as a consequence of my really fail-ing her in my absence, was equally important. As Khan (1972) writes of a similar patient,

> I help her because I fail her and am not shamed by her accusations but accept her anger as right and just. And what is even more important for her is that I accept my failures and am not devalued in my eyes by them. Nothing could be more damaging to her growth and discovery of herself than an *ideal fit* in the clinical alliance. (p. 277)

This patient did indeed seem to have broken down into reality during my absence, unable to sustain what she was capable of creatively during that time, with telling exceptions: she kept stringing things together (her beads) and she created in her lovely note cards the idea of communication across a distance. On my return, she presented as lifeless, until I could find a way to integrate my own and her affect into the hours, to throw those paints on to a blank canvas. Contrary to her fantasy, this allowed her to feel that the treatment rela-tionship was durable enough to re-engage with. It was during this work that couples and conflict came into her painting, that she actu-ally listened to her teacher, that aggressive energy was put into the action of drawing, and that words became interspersed with her pictures. Her teacher wrote that she doodled in her journal "while thinking of what else to say". In other words, we see here a restored capacity for reverie, and drawing as transitional activity. Her spider sculpture reworks the puppet metaphor, now from a new position of affect, perspective, and agency, even as it also captures anxieties about devouring and being devoured in the transference. Along with her daring return to painting, it illustrates her rediscovered capacity for vigorous play, a capacity mirrored as well in the confrontational, deep-play exchanges between patient and therapist.

Not long after the events described above, the patient had a poignant dream in which she was holding in her hands two tiny, fragile, but beautifully speckled eggs. In the dream, she felt terribly frightened that any movement on her part might lead one egg to crush the other. Whether these eggs represented her parents or her embattled sibling relationship or her longing to be held by her mother or her fragile but precious connection to me, this dream captures an action of loving care-taking and consequent paralysis. This intrapsychic situation, in which the subject, to use Winnicott's phrase, is a "caretaker self" (1960, p. 142), forecloses the integration of a real affective life, especially the mobilisation of aggression in encountering the world. Thus, the patient's recovery from the psychic disaster of my leaving her seemed to require a phase of transgressing each other, and our mutual survival (Winnicott, 1969), toward an outcome of making sense of the transference relationship. This work re-established the treatment in a "third" position (Muller, 1996), in which the vicissitudes of early relationships, and their coming to life in the transference, could be held by the therapy rather than by the patient. To get there, the patient had to find and use the analytic relationship as a medium, to fully experience its pliancy, durability, and richness, and to discover the potential creativity in actions she assumed to be purely destructive.

In his paper on Milner's idea of "answering activity", Parsons (1990) reconsiders Ferenczi's (1928) concept of the elasticity of psychoanalytic technique. He describes it as

> the analyst's allowing himself to yield, to be moved by the patient: not so that the patient shall necessarily come to agree with him, but to allow some new position, unknown so far to either patient or analyst, to be discovered. (p. 420)

This seems an apt way to describe the work with this patient. Parsons finds in Milner's work a language for psychoanalytic creativity and a conviction about its centrality to genuine processes of growth and mutuality. He concludes by saying,

> Technique is about how to do something. If creativity is something that happens between analyst and patient, in which they both participate, its theoretical basis will be of a different sort. A theory of

psychoanalytic creativity will not be a theory about the best way of doing something, but about how to make something possible between people. (p. 423)

References

Bollas, C. (2002). *Free Association.* Cambridge: Icon Books.

Erikson, E. (1956). The problem of ego identity. *Journal of the American Psychoanalytic Association,* 4: 56–121.

Erikson, J. (1976). *Activity, Recovery, Growth: The Communal Role of Planned Activities.* New York: Norton.

Ferenczi, S. (1928). The elasticity of psycho-analytic technique. In: *Final Contributions to the Problems and Methods of Psycho-analysis* (pp. 87–101). London: Hogarth, 1955.

Fromm, M. G. (1989). Winnicott's work in relation to classical psychoanalysis and ego psychology. In: M. G. Fromm & B. L. Smith (Eds.), *The Facilitating Environment: Clinical Applications of Winnicott's Theory* (pp. 3–26). Madison, CT: International Universities Press.

Fromm, M. G. (2012). *Lost in Transmission: Studies of Trauma Across Generations.* London: Karnac.

Khan, M. (1963). Silence as communication. In: *The Privacy of the Self* (pp. 168–180). New York: International Universities Press, 1974.

Khan, M. (1972). Dread of surrender to resourceless dependence in the analytic situation. In: *The Privacy of the Self* (pp. 270–279). New York: International Universities Press, 1974.

Kohut, H. (1977). *The Restoration of the Self.* New York: International Universities Press.

Kris, A. (1982). *Free Association: Method and Process.* New Haven, CT: Yale University Press.

Milner, M. (1957). *On Not Being Able to Paint.* New York: International Universities Press.

Milner, M. (1969). *The Hands of the Living God.* New York: International Universities Press.

Muller, J. (1996). *Beyond the Psychoanalytic Dyad.* New York: Routledge.

Parsons, M. (1990). Marion Milner's 'answering activity' and the question of psychoanalytic creativity. *International Review of Psycho-Analysis,* 17: 413–424.

Podro, M. (1990). 'The landscape thinks itself in me'. The comments and procedures of Cezanne. *International Review of Psycho-Analysis,* 17: 401–408.

Sandler, J., & Sandler, A.-M. (1986). The gyroscopic function of unconscious fantasy. In: D. Feinsilver (Ed.), *Towards a Comprehensive Model for Schizophrenic Disorders* (pp. 109–123). Hillsdale, NJ: Analytic Press.

Winnicott, D. W. (1951). Transitional objects and transitional phenomena. In: *Through Paediatrics to Psycho-Analysis* (pp. 229–242). New York: Basic Books, 1958.

Winnicott, D. W. (1960). Ego distortion in terms of true and false self. In: *The Maturational Processes and the Facilitating Environment* (pp. 140–152). New York: International Universities Press, 1965.

Winnicott, D. W. (1969). The use of an object. *International Journal of Psychoanalysis, 50*: 711–716.

Creative collaborations: the 2010 Creativity Seminar

The 2010 Creativity Seminar was dedicated to the memory of Evelyn Stefansson Nef, who passed away at the age of ninety-six, several months before the seminar. Evvie's amazing life, as she tells us in her 2002 autobiography, was a series of creative collaborations, with tragedy as their springboard. Her furrier father had just discovered her sewing talent when, in the midst of her adolescent blossoming, he passed away suddenly from a heart attack. The unthinkable escalated as Evvie's mother reacted with deep depression and never spoke another word for the rest of her life. However, Evvie soon put her sewing skills to good use in the service of making clothes for Bill Baird's puppets, and both careers were launched.

Later, she fell in love with and married the Arctic explorer Vilhjál-mur Stefansson, with whom she collaborated on expeditions, teaching, and books. Still later, she became a psychotherapist, collaborating with her patients—and sometimes art was a major part of their work together—towards their growth and well-being. In late life, she brought her clinical interests and philanthropic generosity to Austen Riggs through her support for the Creativity Seminar and the Erikson Institute more broadly. She loved the arts; Marc Chagall painted a mural in her Georgetown home, and Yo-Yo Ma played at the most wonderful birthday parties the Berkshires has ever seen. She remains with us in spirit.

More than once, Erik Erikson acknowledged that his wife of sixty-six years, Joan, made important contributions to everything he did. Erik's ideas, shared daily with Joan, needed her facility with English for their best expression, not to mention their evolving formulation. And, from the other angle, Joan conceived the Center's Activities Department as a creative rather than clinical space, with Erik hearing the insight about identity in her intuition. They worked together so closely that sometimes neither could quite tell where one person's work ended and the other's began. Not unusual in creative collaborations, Joan was often Erik's hidden partner.

The 2010 Creativity Seminar began with another version of this synergistic partnership, one that had its start four decades ago when the young actress Margaret Ladd first saw a play in the Riggs theatre. Stunned by the emotional honesty with which the patient-actors inhabited their roles, and realising the potential of this work, she and her playwright husband, Lyle Kessler, conceived the Imagination Workshops, through which troubled people across the country have had transformative opportunities to engage with every aspect of drama ever since. At the beginning of the 2010 seminar, the eminent actor and Riggs Board member Sam Waterston joined Margaret in performing a scene written by an Imagination Workshop member.

The psychoanalyst Donald Winnicott famously commented that psychotherapy takes place in the "overlap" between "two people playing" (1971, p. 38), which locates psychotherapy itself as a creative collaboration. How is it that, in creative collaborations, one plus one is vastly more than two? What makes these relationships work? What allows people—talented or accomplished as they might be separate from each another—to positively explode creatively once they begin to collaborate? The chapter that follows examines these questions as they were lived out in one of the most famous creative collaborations of all time.

References

Nef, E. S. (2002). *Finding My Way: The Autobiography of an Optimist.* Washington, DC: Francis Press.

Winnicott, D. W. (1971). *Playing and Reality.* New York: Basic Books.

CHAPTER TEN

Two of us: inside the Lennon–McCartney connection

Joshua Wolf Shenk

" I thought, 'If I take him on, what will happen?'" John recalled as he remembered his first encounter with Paul (Davies, 1968a, p. 33). How did John Lennon and Paul McCartney make magic together? On the surface, it seems simple—they covered for each other's deficits and created outlets for each other's strengths. Paul's melodic sunshine smoothed out John's bluesy growls, while John's soulful depth gave ballast to Paul and kept him from floating away.

These points are true as far as they go. John and Paul did balance and complement each other magnificently, and we can pile example on example. When they were writing "I Saw Her Standing There", Paul offered this opening verse:

"She was just seventeen,
Never been a beauty queen."

"You're joking about that line," John shot back, "aren't you?" (Badman, 2000, p. 50). He offered this revision:

"She was just seventeen,
You know what I mean"

There it is: innocence meets sin—an inviting, simple image takes a lusty, poetic leap.

Lennon and McCartney did, to use the precious phrase, *complete* each other. "Paul's presence did serve to keep John from drifting too far into obscurity and self-indulgence," said Pete Shotton, a Liverpool boy who stayed in the Beatles' circle, "just as John's influence held in check the more facile and sentimental aspects of Paul's songwriting" (Hertsgaard, 1995, p. 112).

But images of completion and balance miss an essential energy between Lennon and McCartney: the potential energy of creative partnerships that they, as much as any pair in history, exemplify and illustrate. We tend to think of them in terms of arithmetic: two people added together yield magnificence. This is the idea of partnership as chocolate and peanut butter—tasty, obvious, easy.

However, Lennon and McCartney were more like an oyster and a grain of sand. Their power together did not derive simply from individual ingredients, but from a dynamic of constant mutual influence. Indeed, even "influence" understates the case, as it suggests two distinct actors operating on each other. Lennon and McCartney did affect each other, change each other, goad, inspire, madden, and wound each other, but they also each contributed to something that went beyond either individual, a charged, mutual space of creation—those pearls your ear probably recognises and leans toward as much as to your parents' voices.

On a warm, humid July day in 1957, fifteen-year-old Paul McCartney came around to see a local band called the Quarrymen play in the fields behind St Peter's Church in the suburbs of Liverpool. John Lennon, who was twenty months older, fronted the six-piece band. He had his glasses off as usual; he was vain like that, though his vision was lousy. His hair was piled up and greased back in the style of post-Elvis "Teddy Boys". He played banjo chords on his guitar, ignoring the two bottom strings. For much of the set—part rock and part "skiffle" (a flavour of 1950s folk)—he passed over chord changes he did not know and made up lyrics as he went along. When he did the Del-Vikings doo-wop "Come Go With Me", he threw in an image from the blues: "Come and go with me . . . down to the penitentiary". McCartney thought it was ingenious.

Afterwards, in the church hall, Paul picked up a guitar himself, flipped it over to play left-handed and showed off the songs he knew—Eddie Cochran, Carl Perkins, Little Richard. He had the lyrics down (including the complete lines to Cochran's "Twenty Flight Rock", a song others had a hard time even deciphering) and knocked off the chords perfectly (including a quick and delicate shift from a G to an F chord that made jaws drop). Then he went over to the piano and pounded out some Jerry Lee Lewis. The boy had polish *and* heat. He wore a white jacket with silver threads—he looked like Elvis, John thought. "Right off, I could see John checking this kid out," said Shotton (who played the washboards for the Quarrymen). Another friend said that John and Paul "circled each other like cats" (Spitz, 2005, p. 97).

Clearly, these two boys had chemistry—that ineffable quality of attraction that feels like a primal, physical force and that often descends like a lightning strike. As with the passion of love, or the nature of creativity itself, science has struggled to account for chemistry. Humans might, or might not, have pheromones that affect connection (though smell does demonstrably play a role in sexual attraction). Mirror neurons might, or might not, play a role in empathy and rapport. In their book, *Click*, Ori and Rom Brafman (2011) offer many powerful stories of what chemistry looks like, but when it comes to analysing it, their first adjective is "magical". Hardly the stuff of white coats and laboratories.

Of course, we celebrate, even venerate, these "chemical" connections, and for good reason. They give us a big kick. Magnetic resonance images (MRIs) show that the brain region responsible for dopamine absorption lights up in couples that say they are in love, comparable to the influence of narcotics. By contrast, social disconnection provokes activity in the region responsible for physical pain.

But intense connection also brings a peculiar discomfort. People "madly" in love show symptoms directly comparable to mania, depression, anorexia, and obsessive–compulsive disorder. Serotonin levels actually fall in passionate love (which, not incidentally, has a short lifespan, as opposed to the mellower, longer lasting "companionate love"). The behaviour in passion also carries profound psychological risk. Arthur and Elaine Aron's experiments on what they call self-expansion show that people literally lose a sense of distinction between themselves and a close other. As the psychologist Sandra Murray (1999) has shown, love would not work at all without "cognitive restructuring", or helpful illusions that dispel the inherent fear of rejection and pain.

John Lennon saw the two sides of his attraction to Paul McCartney quickly and clearly. "I dug him," he said, and he wanted him in the band. But he had his concerns. "I half thought to myself, 'He's as good as me,'" he told the journalist Hunter Davies in 1967. "I'd been king-pin up to then. Now, I thought, 'If I take him on, what will happen?'" (Davies, 1968a, p. 33. (In one sense, Lennon obviously meant: "If I invite him to join the group." But the double meaning of "take him on" is worth noticing.) In a 1970 interview with Jann Wenner, Lennon described his dilemma even more plainly:

> I had a group. I was the singer and the leader; then I met Paul, and I had to make a decision: Was it better to have a guy who was better than the guy I had in? To make the group stronger, or to let me be stronger? (Wenner, 2000, p. 133)

With hindsight, it is clear that it was not an either/or. Bringing Paul aboard made the group much stronger and it made John much stronger. It gave him part ownership of a priceless enterprise. That mathematics adds up to infinite value. But we are missing the point if we look at Lennon's thinking as a mistake. Actually, he put his finger right on the core emotional dynamic. What Paul represented to John — for good and for ill, for excitement and for fear — was a loss of control. All through his relationship with McCartney, the power between them would be fluid, a charged, creative exchange that fuelled them and frustrated them, leading to creative peaks and valleys of recrimination and estrangement.

And it can all be traced to their first encounter. "The decision was made to make the group stronger," Lennon told Wenner (Wenner, 2000, p. 133). Had he decided to keep the power all to himself, he probably would have forsaken his power entirely.

In a 1995 interview, Mick Jagger was asked how he and Keith Richards lasted so long as song-writing partners, when Lennon and McCartney split. His answer was simple: a team needs a leader. (He did not go so far as to explicitly identify himself as that leader, but he made it perfectly clear.) By contrast, John and Paul, Jagger said, "seemed to be very competitive over leadership of the band. . . . If there are 10 things, they both wanted to be in charge of nine of them.

You're not gonna make a relationship like that work, are you?" (Wenner, 1995, p. 723). His point sounds like an MBA case study— fitting, maybe, from a rock and roller who studied at the London School of Economics.

But successful creative pairs suggest that power roles are often murky. The domineering and dynamic Gertrude Stein seemed to run over her mousy, housekeeping partner, Alice B. Toklas. Stein literally appropriated her partner's identity—wrote in her name—to create a self-serving portrait of herself. But close observers often saw Toklas take Stein by the lapel, directing her as deftly and surely as an actor onstage. In many ways, Stein's creative life began when Toklas recognised her—when, in Stein's words, Toklas said "Yes" to her work.

Sometimes, apparently rigid power roles actually facilitate something more open. Quayle Hodek and Kris Lotlikar, co-founders of a leading renewable energy firm, decided at the start that one of them would be CEO and have the final say. This, Hodek told me, allows them to operate without fear of paralysing conflict. The irony, he says, is that his ostensible deputy calls many more shots day-to-day. Even Mick Jagger and Keith Richards at times operated more fluidly than Jagger claimed. *Exile on Main Street* was recorded in Richards' house in the south of France, and on the terms he preferred (a loose arrangement, edging into chaos, built on jams and endless takes). Many consider this album the team's masterpiece.

But no pair illustrates the fluidity of power—and the power of fluidity—better than John and Paul. At its worst, theirs was an alienating, enervating struggle; at its best, the dynamic was playful and organic. Jagger is probably right that it led to their split. But who said you measure the strength of a collaboration by its longevity?

The tension between Lennon and McCartney was rooted in their distinct styles and personalities. As a boy, the precocious and creative John Lennon always needed, he said, "a little gang of guys who would play various roles in my life, supportive and, you know, subservient. I wanted everybody to do what I told them to do," he said, "to laugh at my jokes and let me be the boss" (Davies, 1968a, p. 13). He needed both to connect and to dominate. "Though I have yet to encounter a personality as strong and individual as John's," said his friend Pete Shotton, "he always had to have a partner." (John so entwined himself with Pete that he called them "Shennon and Lotton" (Hertsgaard, 1995, p. 14).)

When John put a band together, he brought his mates in, often simply *because* they were his mates, but left no doubt about his status. Shotton, for example, did not have a particular talent for music and did not like it much. When he told Lennon he needed to be out of the band, John broke Pete's washboard over his head. It is not likely we could find a clearer display of power in primates on the savannah.

For some time after Paul joined, John stayed out front. Among the band's many early names were "Johnny and the Moondogs" and "Long John and the Silver Beetles". When "The Beatles" went to Hamburg, the contract named John as the payee. In the late 1950s, Paul pitched a journalist on the band; he began his description of the boys with John, "who leads the group . . ." (Davies, 1968b, p. 61). But the letter itself—a piece of Paul's relentless promotion—speaks to his own power style. He was more social, more affable, more outwardly and consistently energetic. Where John oscillated between intense shyness and raw aggression (he beat his girlfriend, for example), Paul had a knack for working people that was as savvy as it was sweet.

From the start, Paul looked up to John, "posing and strutting with his hair slicked back", remembered Cynthia Lennon, "to prove that he was cool" (Lennon, 2005, p. 61). But he also took the microphone and worked the crowd. In Hamburg, "most people among the fans looked upon [Paul] as the leader," said Astrid Kirchherr, a German student who befriended the band. "John of course was the leader," Astrid continued. "He was far and away the strongest" (Davies, 1968a, p. 85). What is interesting, though, is not the question of who ran the show, but the subtlety of strength itself, the many ways power can be exercised between partners.

Consider the moment Paul's brother, Michael, cited as an illustration of his "innate sense of diplomacy". It was in Paris in 1963. The Beatles' producer, George Martin, had arranged for them to record "She Loves You" in German. When the band missed their studio appointment, Martin came around to their suite at the George V hotel. They played slapstick and dived under the tables to avoid him. "Are you coming to do it or not?" Martin said. "No," Lennon said. George and Ringo echoed him. Paul said nothing, and they went back to eating. "Then a bit later," Michael said, "Paul suddenly turned to John and said, 'Heh, you know that so and so line, what if we did it this way? John listened to what Paul said, thought a bit, and said, 'Yeah, that's it.' And they headed to the studio" (Davies, 1968a, p. xxxv).

How would we chart the lines of authority for this decision? You could say Lennon made the call to refuse the recording session, then reversed himself, the band following him both times. But it was actually Paul who shaped the course the band took. His move to avoid a direct confrontation, to let John stay nominally in control, only underscores his operational strength.

Just as shorter people are more aware of height, Paul seems to have noticed the power dynamic more acutely. In a 1967 conversation about the band's Hamburg days, Lennon said that Paul had just recently told him about fights they had over who led the band. "I can't remember them," Lennon said. "It had stopped mattering by then. I wasn't so determined to be the leader at all costs" (Davies, 1968b, p. 79). This is crucial. *He* had decided he did not need to be the leader at all costs— itself a leadership claim. As the band rocketed to success, Lennon would increasingly acquiesce to Paul's ideas, much as a king in tumultuous times will defer to his counsel. But he never gave up the idea that he could, when he wanted, return straight to his throne.

*   *   *

"The tension between the two of them made for the bond," their producer George Martin astutely noted (Hertsgaard, 1995, p. 111). To the public, Lennon and McCartney famously declared themselves a fused pair. As soon as they began to write together, they decided to share credit regardless of individual contribution. At the top of their music sheets, they would write, "Another Lennon/McCartney original". They collapsed the space between them—not even an "and" would divide their names, just a slash. But the joint credit also served as balm on the cuts of a constant, intense—though often joyful— competition. "Imagine two people pulling on a rope," said George Martin, "smiling at each other and pulling all the time with all their might. The tension between the two of them made for the bond" (Hertsgaard, 1995, p. 111).

Martin's image is perfect. John and Paul constantly pulled away from each other, and moved closer at the same time. Their competition actually enhanced their individual differences, even as it brought them into a relationship that was itself a third entity, the space where two circles overlap. Even in their early years, when, as John said, they wrote "nose to nose" and "eyeball to eyeball", Lennon/McCartney songs clearly bore the stamp of their primary creators, John usually dwelling on betrayal and loneliness ("Tell me why you cried / And why you lied to me") and Paul on devotion and connection ("There's really nothing else I'd rather do / 'Cause I'm happy just to dance with you").

At the same time, the songs clearly evolved through a shared vision—at first, for engaging, infectious, emotionally direct pop, later for more ambitious, far-reaching ideas and sounds. Their harmonies make the chemistry and connection palpable, along with an implicit communication that extended to the whole band: "just being able to sort of blink," Lennon said, "or make a certain noise and I know they'll all know where we are going" (Wenner, 2000, p. 47).

The nature of John and Paul's intimacy evolved over the years. In the early days, the partners were hardly ever apart. In Hamburg, the Beatles famously played for hours at a time (adding up, as Malcolm Gladwell has pointed out, to the famous 10,000 hours of "deliberate practice" that Anders Ericsson has determined leads to true mastery). Paul and John essentially lived together on the road; even on days off, they got together to write.

After August 1966, when they stopped touring, their lives were more separate. John lived in a mansion in the suburbs of London with his wife and son. Paul lived in London, first with his girlfriend Jane Asher's family, and then in a townhouse not far from the EMI studios on Abbey Road.

In part because each man grew as an artist, in part because they marinated in wild, innovative scenes, in part because they turned so much of their ferocious energy into a meticulous, relentless, and inventive use of studio technology, the songs, beginning with the album *Revolver*, began to take on new colour and oddity and elegance. Lennon wrote the lyrics for "Tomorrow Never Knows" after reading *The Psychedelic Experience* and following its instructions on an LSD trip: "Turn off your mind, relax and float downstream". When it came time to record the song, he told George Martin that he wanted the sound of a hundred chanting Tibetan monks. He also suggested that he be suspended from a rope, get a good push, and sing while spinning around the mike.

McCartney, meanwhile, edged into an almost operatic narrative style with "Eleanor Rigby", and his infectious pop developed new layers, as with "Got To Get You Into My Life".

According to the conventional wisdom, their drift apart had begun. But the increased distance sometimes functioned like the space between boxers in a ring, giving more room for a powerful shot. "He'd write 'Strawberry fields,' I'd go away and write 'Penny Lane,' " McCartney said. "If I'd write 'I'm Down,' he'd go away and write something similar to that. To compete with each other. But it was very friendly competition because we were both going to share in the rewards anyway" (Hertsgaard, 1995, p. 111).

Friendly, yes, but with a sharp edge. "I would bring in a song and you could sort of see John stiffen a bit," Paul said. "Next day he'd bring in a song and I'd sort of stiffen. And it was like, 'Oh, you're going to do that, are you? Right. You wait till I come up with something tomorrow'" (Schrier, 2001, p. 79). The favourite back-and-forth—who was the *real* genius in the pair?—seeks to set one on a pedestal. But when we look closely at the back and forth, that debate's most cherished assumptions come into question—for example, that John charged ahead with the musical *avant-garde* while Paul nurtured traditional elements of melody and symmetry. It is true that John tended to stick his finger in the audience's eye while Paul usually preferred to coo to them. John's "Revolution 9" might be the oddest, most dissonant thing ever laid down on a big pop album and Paul's "Let It Be" and "Hey Jude" set a standard for sweetness and formal perfection.

But in some ways, it was Paul who forged the frontier and John who raced to catch and exceed him. From 1966 to 1968, John lived a weird, sleepy, deeply interior life. He spent days on end dropping acid and watching television. Paul, meanwhile, threw himself into the London art world and its "happenings", performances that blurred the boundary between artist and audience. In 1965, their music publisher Dick James gave them each a Brenell Mark 5 tape recorder. While John used his to record rough demos, Paul, immersed in the experimental work of composers like John Cage and Karlheinz Stockhausen, jiggered the machine to disable the erase head and make tape loops of layered sounds. He brought these to the Beatles sessions to create the sound for "Tomorrow Never Knows", the famous "John" song.

"I lived a very urbane life in London," McCartney remembered. "John used to come in from Weybridge . . . and I'd tell him what I'd been doing: 'Last night I saw a Bertolucci film and I went down the Open

Space, they're doing a new play there.'" Paul said John would reply: "God man, I really envy you" (Lewisohn & McCartney, 1990, p. 15).

In 1966, a far-out artist named Yoko Ono moved to London from New York City. Paul not only met her first, he had helped create the Indica Gallery where she and Lennon met. Although it took several years to ripen, Lennon eventually threw himself into the relationship—he literally asked people to consider them JohnandYoko. (Yoko made for the third person, following Pete Shotton and Paul McCartney, with whom he collapsed his name.) Joined with her, John left no doubt who would be master of the *avant-garde*. Where Paul had merely attended happenings, John and Yoko staged them. Where Paul used his tape loops to extend the pop form and kept his wildest, most experimental recordings in the can, John insisted that "Revolution 9" go on a Beatles record.

The point here is not to identify whether John or Paul was the "real" edge, but to underscore how keenly they watched each other. Indeed, Paul's dive into the London art scene might itself have been a reaction to his image as the "cute" Beatle, compared with John, the "smart" one. This constant give and take took a decisive shift in August 1967, when the band's manager, Brian Epstein, died. For some time, Epstein had been more figurehead than real leader, and it is telling that, by the mid-1960s at least, he deferred to Paul far more than to the others. But in a tenuous democracy led in strange fashion by two principals, he gave cover, the way even a weak parent will for squabbling boys.

Paul had asserted control before Epstein's death, when he conceived of *Sgt. Pepper's Lonely Hearts Club Band* and dominated the sessions. With Brian gone, Paul's role as a *de facto* manager became far more obvious—and far more threatening to John's own sense of control. "Paul had a tendency to come along and say well he's written these ten songs, let's record now" (Wenner, 2000, p. 54), John said, claiming that he and George became "side men for Paul" (Wenner, 2000, p. 49). But this bitter language came later, and for a long while, he acquiesced. He was too checked out to do much of anything else.

The traditional story is that John withdrew from the band even further when he took up with Yoko. She is cast as usurper, provoking rifts that led to the band's demise. But on closer examination, we have to ask whether John actually used her to assert his dominance, to claim his rightful, incontestable leadership. To the others, John's insistence that Yoko be treated as an equal seemed preposterous. But for John, however aware of his audaciousness, it all still fitted: it was *his* band. He could bring in new members the same way he had brought in Pete Shotton, the way he replaced Bill Smith with Len Garry, the way he brought in Paul. As strange as it might sound, even John's dramatic break with the band can be seen as a power move, a backhanded form of engagement. In September 1969, as Paul urged that the Beatles get back to their roots and play live shows, John shot back, in the account given by biographer Bob Spitz, "I think you're daft. I wasn't going to tell you, but I'm breaking the group up" (Spitz, 2005, p. 805).

The language is key. John's leaving the band would mean its dissolution. He later made the claim explicit: "I started the band. I disbanded it. It's as simple as that" (The Beatles, 2000, p. 348). But the break was hardly simple. It is not even clear that Lennon wanted a final break. For all his bluster in the band meeting, he never made his decision public—which is to say, he never made it real. To the contrary, just months after he told Paul he wanted a "divorce", he talked publicly about the band recording again and even touring. "It'll probably be a rebirth, you know, for all of us" (Carlin, 2009, p. 201), he said. Perhaps John needed to believe he could end the band in order to stick with it.

At first, Paul showed signs that he would step back and let John get what he needed. He saw the choice, he said later, to accept Yoko or to lose John, and he chose the former: "When you find yourself in times of trouble . . . let it be". But now, at a moment of great turmoil, two new factors came into play. For years, George Harrison had been the "quiet Beatle" at the side. Literally, as John and Paul faced the crowd side-to-side in performance, he stood far off facing them. But as he grew into his own, writing songs such as "Something" and "Here Comes the Sun", he bristled at Paul's bossiness and grew positively indignant at taking instructions from John's wife. At one point, according to George Martin, he and Lennon even came to blows. His energy made the tenuous balance between John and Paul much less stable.

Meanwhile, the Beatles, as a business, were in such a freefall that John predicted they could go completely broke. Someone needed to take control at Apple Corps, a wildly ambitious holding company that had turned to chaos. Paul wanted his new bride Linda's father and brother, Lee and John Eastman, to run Apple, but in another impetu-ous power move, John summarily signed with Allen Klein, a brash manager with a reputation for bullying record companies for higher royalties. (Klein was also a questionable character; he basically stole ownership of the Rolling Stones' catalogue and later went to jail for tax fraud.)

George and Ringo followed John and signed with Klein. Paul held out. But for all his defiance, his vulnerability came strongly into play as well. He had never yielded his essential devotion to John, and the rejections devastated him. "John's in love with Yoko," he said. "He's no longer in love with us" (Miles, 1998, p. 556). As Paul wrote in "Let It Be", the light always shone on him, even on cloudy nights. But now, as a storm raged, he fell into a profound depression. He stayed in bed and drank through the day. "Boy, you're going to carry that weight a long time"—this grew out of his despair, he said. But he also wrote, in what seems a plea to his partner, "You and I have memories, longer than the road that stretches up ahead".

In the spring of 1970, with tensions among the four Beatles still at a fever pitch, Paul released a solo album and included a short Q&A that he authored with his publicist. It included this exchange.

Q: Are you planning a new album or single with the Beatles?

PAUL: No.

Q: Is this album a rest away from the Beatles or the start of a solo career?

PAUL: Time will tell. Being a solo means it's "the start of a solo career . . ." and not being done with the Beatles means it's just a rest. So it's both really. (Carlin, 2009, p. 204)

Like John, Paul hardly said the band had broken up for good. "It's just a rest," he said.

But newspapers seized on the first public acknowledgment of the band's rumoured troubles. "McCartney Breaks Off With Beatles", ran the *New York Times* headline on April 11, 1970. This loss of face—the public acknowledgment of a coup—was more than John could stand. "I was cursing," he said, "because I hadn't done it. I wanted to do it, I should have done it. Ah, damn, shit, what a fool I was" (Wenner, 2000, p. 137). The time had long passed when he could just take a washboard and break it over a mate's head. The fight between these two partners now had the whole world in thrall. They would never work together again. But the history of their partnership was just beginning to be written. Hardly a straightforward account, it would be another winding road on their path together.

*   *   *

"It's like there was me, then the Beatles phase, and now I'm me again", Paul commented as he reflected on the trajectory of his relationship with John and the band (Meryman, 1971, p. 58). It is supremely odd how history would play the collaboration between John Lennon and Paul McCartney. The result of one of the most intertwined partnerships in music history, their work would consistently be reduced to static roles. It is almost as if, faced with the bound pair, a culture obsessed with individualism found a way to cleave them in two. Take, for example, the relentless focus on "John" songs *vs.* "Paul" songs, or sections of songs, or single lines, as though that is the skeleton key to the Beatles' inner workings.

Actually, this tradition has an impeccable source: John and Paul themselves. The irony is that the way they came to tell their own story, after their split, might speak less to the way they separated and more to the way that they remained connected.

First, consider the usual take. "Now your songs were co-credited, you know, in the Beatles era," Terry Gross said to Paul in a 2001 interview. "My understanding is, correct me if I'm wrong, that many of the songs were written by one of you or the other, although the other would do some editing on the song, but that few of the songs were actually true collaborations." "Is that right?" she asked. "Is that accurate?"

In response, Paul gave what has become a kind of official history: in the early days, he said, he and John were constantly in each other's presence, and

> everything was co-written; we hardly ever wrote things separate. Then, after a few years, as we got a bit of success with the Beatles and didn't actually live together or weren't just always on the road together sharing hotel rooms, then we had the luxury of writing things separately. So John would write something like 'Nowhere Man,' sort

of separately in his house outside London, and I would write something like 'Yesterday' quite separately on my own, and as you say we
would come together and check 'em out against each other. Sometimes we would edit a line of each other's. More often, we'd just sort
of say, 'Yeah, that's great'. (Gross, 2001, television Interview)

This bit—clear, ordered, and apparently airtight—is typical of
McCartney. Lennon delivered basically the same message in a 1970
interview with Jann Wenner and, typical for *him*, he both far over-
stated the case and then doubled around to underscore its true ambiguity. "When did your songwriting partnership with Paul end?"
Wenner asked.

"That ended," Lennon jumped in quickly, and then he paused for
several seconds. "I don't know, around 1962, or something." He
laughed, and it sounds like a nervous laugh, or maybe he was
announcing a joke: 1962 is when Paul and John first began laying their
compositions down on studio tape for George Martin at EMI. "I don't
know," Lennon went on,

> I mean, if you give me the albums I can tell you exactly who wrote
> what, you know, and which line. I mean, we sometimes wrote together
> and sometimes didn't but all our best work—apart from the early days,
> like 'I Want To Hold Your Hand' we wrote together and things like
> that—we wrote apart always, you know. (Wenner, 2000, p. 54)

Then he returned to the question and contradicted himself. "We
always wrote separately," he said, "but we wrote together because
. . . because we enjoyed it a lot sometimes, and also because they'd say,
'Well, you're going to make an album?' We'd get together and knock
off a few songs, you know, just like a job." John's statement sounds
like nonsense: "We always wrote separately but we wrote together"
(Wenner, 2000, p. 55). It is impossible to straighten into a literal meaning. But it actually captures the reality of their collaboration quite
well.

Sometimes, it is true, songs tumbled out of their creators in whole.
It is telling that McCartney seized the two clearest examples—
"Yesterday" and "Nowhere Man"—when he described the collaboration to Terry Gross. On waking one morning, Paul sat down and
practically transcribed the music for "Yesterday" on piano, using
nonsense lyrics at first—"Scrambled egg . . .". "Nowhere Man" has a

parallel story. After five hours trying to write a song, and failing, John gave up in frustration. "Then," he told *Playboy* in 1980, "'Nowhere Man' came, words and music, the whole damn thing as I lay down" (Sheff, 1981).

Neither experience was typical. For one thing, even when John and Paul were apart, they were constantly in touch, according to Cynthia Lennon's account of John's process. (She had a first-hand view through mid-1968.) John had a studio in their attic and he went there at all odd times. "Then," Cynthia wrote, "there would be phone calls back and forth to Paul, as they played and sang to each other over the phone" (Lennon, 2000, p. 168).

John and Paul also met frequently to work. In 1967, the journalist Hunter Davies sat in on several of those sessions. One priceless account shows the slow, ambling course of discovery on the way towards "A Little Help From My Friends". They started around 2.00 p.m. in Paul's workroom, a narrow, rectangular space full of instruments and amps and modern art. The previous afternoon, they had got the tune for the song. Now they were trying to polish the melody and write lyrics. John took up his guitar and Paul banged at the piano. "Each seemed to be in a trance," Davies wrote, "until the other came up with something good, then he would pluck it out of a mass of noises and try it himself" (Davies, 1968a, p. 263).

"Are you afraid when you turn out the light?" John offered. Paul repeated the line, agreeing it was good. John said they could begin each of the verses with a question. He offered another one. "Do you believe in love at first sight?" "No," he interrupted himself. "It hasn't got the right number of syllables." He tried singing the line breaking it in two between "believe" and "in love". "How about 'Do you believe in *a* love at first sight?'" Paul offered. John sang that, and instantly added another line. "Yes, I'm certain that it happens all the time." They repeated these three lines over and over again. It was now five o'clock. Some others came by, and as they bantered about, Paul started doodling on the piano before breaking out into "Can't Buy Me Love". John joined in, shouting and laughing. Then they both shouted out "Tequila" (Davies, 1968b, p. 62).

"Remember in Germany?" John said. "We used to shout out every-thing." They did the song again, with John throwing in words in every pause—"Knickers" and "Duke of Edinburgh" and "Hitler". "Then, as suddenly as it had started," Davies wrote, "they both went back to the work at hand". John sang a slight modification of the line they had agreed on. "What do you see when you turn out the light?" Then he answered the question: "I can't tell you, but I know it's mine". Paul said that would do and wrote the four lines on a piece of exercise paper propped up on the piano. Then they broke for cake (Davies, 1968b, p. 62).

Had Jann Wenner picked up *Sgt. Pepper's Lonely Hearts Club Band*, pointed to the second track, and took Lennon up on his offer to say "exactly who wrote what, you know, and which line", could Lennon have said honestly he had written that day's material? Sure. The only explicit edit of Paul's was the indefinite article "a". Yet, looking for concrete divisions in their labour, though not irrelevant, can certainly seem myopic. It feels, from Davies' account, as though the two men were bound by a thousand invisible strings (Wenner, 2000, p. 55).

Davies looked on at the partners before Yoko, before *The White Album*—"the tension album", Paul said. But tension had always been key to their work. The strings connecting them hardly dissolved, even in the times when the collaboration was adversarial, the kind of exchange that Andre Agassi described when he said that if he hadn't faced Pete Sampras, he would have a better record, "but I'd be less". Picking up on that incisive line, Kimmelman wrote in his review of Agassi's book, *Open*, that "rivalry . . . [is] the heart of sports, and, for athletes, no matter how bitter or fierce, something strangely akin to love: two vulnerable protagonists for a time lifted up not despite their differences but because of them" (Kimmelman, 2010, p. 8).

But even in the hardest times, it is hardly true that John and Paul stopped working together. In what was, ostensibly, the nadir of their partnership in January 1969, their concert on the Apple rooftop shows the two men in profound sympathy. At one point, John forgot a verse to "Don't Let Me Down". He and Paul proceeded in perfect synchronisation as John sang nonsense lyrics, then returned to the top of the verse as if nothing had happened. You can see on the film how John shoots Paul a look of pure boyish glee. Several months later, when John wrote "The Ballad of John and Yoko", he rushed to Paul's doorstep. With George and Ringo out of town, he insisted they go straight to the studio. They cut the song in one long day, John taking the guitars and lead vocal, Paul on bass, drums, piano, maracas—and coming in with breathtaking harmonies.

We typically look back on a broken partnership and assume it suffered from distance and alienation. But, as Arthur and Elaine Aron have shown (1996), relationships can suffer just as much from too *much* closeness and the consequent loss of control or identity. People describing these kinds of relationships use words like *suffocating, smothering, overwhelming*. They have lost too much of their individual distinction into a shared whole.

There is good reason to believe this happened with John and Paul. To understand why, we need to consider the reality of the early 1970s. Today, with Wikipedia and mountains of Beatles books, we have fantastic detail on the minutiae of their individual contributions. But when they worked together and when they split, they were, as writers, just as they appeared in their credits: Lennon/McCartney. When John took tea at the Plaza Hotel in the 1970s, the pianist would serenade him with "Yesterday". On a television show, the band played "Michelle" during a break. "At least I wrote the middle eight on that one", John said (Mike Douglas Show, 1972).

It was as though the partners had deposited every asset of reputation and identity into a joint bank account. After their split, they stood in line, day after day, to take the maximum withdrawal. Of course, there were literal bank accounts, immense financial and practical complications of their divorce. But what is interesting here is their self-conception, their desperate need to individuate. One of their most common words after the split was *me*. From Paul's self-questionnaire in April 1970:

Q: Did you enjoy working as a solo?

PAUL: Very much. I only had me to ask for a decision, and I generally agreed with me. (McCartney, 1970, Album liner notes)

The next year, John told Jann Wenner that his first solo album was the "best thing I've ever done". "Now I wrote all about me and that's why I like it," he said. "It's me! And nobody else. That's why I like it" (Wenner, 2000, p. 29). Paul got to the identity question even more directly in an interview with *Life* magazine. "It's like there was me, then the Beatles phase, and now I'm me again" (Meryman, 1971, p. 58).

As they gave their history, John and Paul became relentless in dissecting their own work. This formed the bedrock of the history of their collaboration. Asked about the songs, they often used the possessive: "That's John's," Paul would say, or "That's mine." John would do the same. It is telling that two men with notoriously poor memories—neither knew how many times they had been to Hamburg, for example—left in doubt the authorship of only a single melody in a single song ("In My Life").

Of course, they did make many distinct and identifiable contributions. But with the ferocity of their claims for singular ownership, did they protest too much? Even their bitterness after the split speaks to connection. After Paul's press release, and his public shot at his ex-partner's exhibitions ("too many people preaching practices"), Lennon wrote a song called "How Do You Sleep" with the lines "Those freaks was right when they said you was dead" and "The only thing you done was Yesterday" and "The sound you make is Muzak to my ears".

This is nasty stuff. But the opposite of intimacy is not conflict; it is indifference. The relationship between Paul and John had always been a tug of war, and that hardly stopped when they ceased to collaborate directly. Asked what he thought Paul would make of his first solo album, Lennon said, "I think it'll probably scare him into doing something decent, and then he'll scare me into doing something decent, like that" (Wenner, 2000, p. 122).

Predictably, Paul took a mostly sunny air in interviews after the breakup, and he returned to an admiring view of John that would grow over the years. He even thanked his ex-partner for ushering in a new and vital phase of life. "I sort of picked up on his lead," Paul said in 1971. "John had said, 'Look, I don't want to be that anymore. I'm going to be this.' And I thought, 'That's great.' I liked the fact he'd done it, and so I'll do it with my thing. He's given the okay" (Meryman, 1971, p. 56).

With John, the basic ambiguity came through—his loving Paul, and needing to stay separate. On *The Mike Douglas Show* in 1972, a young man in the audience asked John if "How Do You Sleep" was "vicious". John at first denied it, saying he had just had dinner with Paul who was laughing and smiling. "If I can't have a fight with my best friend," he said, "I don't know who I can have a fight with." Douglas was just moderating, but it seems he couldn't resist this striking declaration. He turned to Lennon. "Is he your best friend, Paul?" "I guess in the male sex, he," John stammered, ". . . he was. I don't know about now, because I don't see much of him, you know" (Krauss, 1972).

Two years later, John would mix up his tenses when describing Paul in an even more revealing way. It was Thanksgiving night in 1974, when he joined Elton John at a sold-out show at Madison Square Garden. Lennon wore a black silk shirt, a black jacket, and a necklace that dangled a flower over his chest. He had on his usual "granny" glasses with dark lenses. His thin, brown hair fell down past his shoulders. After storming through "Whatever Gets You Through the Night" and "Lucy in the Sky With Diamonds", Lennon came to the microphone to round out the set.

"I'd like to thank Elton and the boys for having me on tonight," he said. "We tried to think of a number to finish off with so I can get out of here and be sick, and we thought we'd do a number of an old, estranged fiancé of mine, called Paul. This is one I never sang. It's an old Beatle number and we just about know it." The song was "I Saw Her Standing There".

Although he lived another six years, John Lennon never took the stage for a major show again. His strange words have a peculiar and lasting echo. By then, Paul and John had been the most famous exes in the world for four years. But somehow, they were still "fiancés" — *prospective* spouses. As much as had passed, the energy between them was always in front of them—always, somehow, in the future.

References

Aron, A., & Aron, E. (1996). Self and self-expansion in relationships. In: G. Fletcher & J Fitness (Eds.), *Knowledge Structures in Close Relationships: A Social Psychological Approach* (pp. 325–344). London: Taylor & Francis.

Badman, K. (2000). *The Beatles Off the Record*. London: Omnibus.

Brafman, O., & Brafman, R. (2011). *Click: The Forces Behind How We Fully Engage with People, Work, and Everything We Do*. New York: Crown Business.

Carlin, P. (2009). *Paul McCartney: A Life*. New York: Touchstone.

Davies, H. (1968a). *The Beatles*. New York: McGraw-Hill.

Davies, H. (1968b). The Beatles. *Life Magazine*, 65(12): 61–62, 71–82.

Gladwell, M. (2000). *The Tipping Point: How Little Things Can Make a Big Difference*. New York: Little, Brown.

Gross, T. (Executive Producer) (2001). *Fresh Air* (television broadcast). WHYY, 30 April.

Hertsgaard, M. (1995). *A Day in the Life: The Music and Artistry of the Beatles*. New York: Delacorte Press.

Kimmelman, M. (2010). Deuce! *New York Review of Books, 57*(11): 8.

Krauss, M. (Producer) (1972). *The Mike Douglas Show* (television broadcast). KYW-TV, February.

Lennon, C. (2005). *John*. New York: Crown.

Lewisohn, M., & McCartney, P. (1990). *The Beatles: Recording Sessions: The Official Abbey Road Session Notes, 1962–1970*. New York: Harmony Books.

McCartney, P. (1970). Liner notes. On McCartney (record). London: Apple.

Meryman, R. (1971). I felt the split was coming. *Life Magazine, 70*(14): 52–58.

Miles, B. (1998). *Paul McCartney: Many Years From Now*. New York: Henry Holt.

Murray, S. (1999). The quest for conviction: motivated cognition in romantic relationships. *Psychological Inquiry, 10*(1): 23–34.

Schrier, E. (2001). Paul McCartney: getting better all the time. *Readers Digest*, November.

Sheff, D. (1981). Playboy interview. *Playboy Magazine, 28*: 1.

Spitz, B. (2005). *The Beatles: The Biography*. Boston, MA: Little, Brown.

The Beatles (2000). *The Beatles Anthology*. San Francisco, CA: Chronicle Books.

Wenner, J. (1995). The Rolling Stone Interview: Jagger Remembers. *Rolling Stone*: 723.

Wenner, J. (2000). *Lennon Remembers: The Full Rolling Stone Interviews From 1970*. London: Verso.

Finding voice, lifting voices — creativity and oppression: the 2011 Creativity Seminar

D uring the summer of 2011, the "Lift Ev'ry Voice" Festival celebrated the Berkshires' rich African-American heritage with partnerships between many cultural institutions throughout the county. The Festival was officially announced at the Second Congregational Church in Pittsfield, from which pulpit the Reverend Samuel Harrison took his leave to become chaplain of the Massachusetts 54th Regiment in the Civil War, one of the first all-Black units of the Union Army. After an all too brief honeymoon in Lenox, the commander of that unit, Colonel Robert Gould Shaw, would fall near Charleston in 1863, he and his men later to be memorialised in the movie *Glory*.

Around that same time and in that same place, the mother of DuBose Heyward was born. Some years later, this young white woman would take her son with her to sing Gullah songs, and out of this musical encounter came eventually the novel, play, then opera, *Porgy and Bess*, which was performed at Tanglewood during the "Summertime" of 2011. The world's most acclaimed Bess participated in that year's Creativity Seminar.

Just a few years after Heyward's birth and just a few miles south, another musical mother gave birth to a son, who, in 1900, on Lincoln's birthday, organised 500 of his young students to recite his poem, "Lift Every Voice," to visiting dignitary, Booker T. Washington. Later set to music by James Weldon Johnson's brother, "Lift Every Voice" was officially adopted by the NAACP as the Negro National Anthem in 1919. Ninety years later, Reverend Joseph Lowery quoted its third stanza in his benediction at President Barack Obama's first inauguration.

"Lift Ev'ry Voice" returned to Berkshire County with a summer-long celebration. It invited those of us interested in the creative process not only to remember the historical pain, courageous struggles, and amazing contributions of Black America, but also to wonder about the relationship between oppression and creativity, perhaps especially the role of collective voices in creating through oppression. For those of us in the mental health field, the theme reminded us that some voices are oppressed from the inside, so to speak-the oppression of inhibition. Tanglewood also provided a powerful example of that; when the young Brahms had his early work compared to that of Beethoven, he lost his compositional voice for years.

Helping a troubled person find his or her voice is at the heart of the work at Riggs, in both psychotherapy and, broadly speaking, in the creative work of the activities department. Bringing collective voices together and working from cacophony towards harmony is at the heart of the work in the therapeutic community programme and the theatre. But this process is a fraught one, for both the individual and the group, full of encounters with oppression, both internal and external.

How do we understand this struggle to find one's creative voice in the face of external or internal oppression? How do we understand the power of joining with other voices to accomplish this task? In the following chapter, the artist Rochleigh Wholfe takes up these questions in her own work and in the life of a young woman who inspired her.

Oppression, healing, and Delia's story

Rochleigh Z. Wholfe

In the summer of 2011, I was one of four artists invited to present at the Austen Riggs-Erikson Institute's Creativity Seminar: *Finding Voice, Lifting Voices: Oppression and Creativity*. The seminar was part of the first "Lift Ev'ry Voice" Festival, celebrating a rich African American heritage and its cultural contributions throughout the Berkshires. I was delighted and honoured to be a part of this historic event and to share my perspectives as a woman, African American, and visual artist.

We received a synopsis several weeks before the seminar inviting us to consider several questions: the interrelationship between oppression and creativity, inhibition as a form of oppression, and the role of others—the collective voice—in the creative process. In this chapter, I discuss these themes, utilising my own personal, cultural, spiritual, and artistic experiences. I also reference other artists, activists, and leaders who were social reformers and whose work was pivotal in both effecting social change and inspiring my creativity.

Oppression and creativity

Webster's Dictionary offers one definition of *oppression* as "the exercise of authority or power in a burdensome, cruel or unjust manner", and *creativity* as "marked by the ability or power to create, to bring something new into existence, to invest with new form, and to produce through imaginative skill". This suggests that oppression and creativity are both expressive acts of power. The key is intent, resulting either in empowerment or bondage, freedom or subjugation. I believe we are created to be free, to express our unique individuality, as long as it does not infringe upon the rights of others. That right is extended to all people regardless of race, gender, creed, or sexual orientation, as stated in the United Nation's Universal Declaration of Human Rights Article 1, "All human beings are born free and equal in dignity and rights. They are endowed with reason and conscience and should act towards one another in a spirit of brotherhood", and Article 19, "Everyone has the right to freedom of opinion and expression; this right includes freedom to hold opinions without interference and to seek, receive and impart information and ideas through any media and regardless of frontiers".

However, we know that these Articles are based on an idealistic theory, which the global community continues to strive towards, rather than on what is actually being practised. Throughout history/ herstory, human beings have endured tremendous pain and suffering through religious/political persecution, racism, cultural traditions/ beliefs, slavery, apartheid, genocide, homophobia, sexism, femicide, human trafficking: oppressive practices that deny basic human rights. The imposition of these dehumanising injustices breeds debilitating mental, spiritual, physical, emotional imbalances and dis-eases, which affect us all, whether we are conscious of it or not. These dis-eases oppress and inhibit.

My experience growing up as an African-American woman here in the USA is filled with painful memories as well as loving ones, and with courageous victories, past and present. Fighting against social injustice has been a continuous challenge for people of colour. Growing up in the metropolitan St Louis area in the 1960s, I witnessed a unified bold uprising against social injustices. Black leaders such as Dr Martin Luther King and Malcom X became common household names. A movement was born, which emerged from under the rock of racism. A call to arms beckoned to a people who themselves called forth the spirit of the ancestors to rise and walk with us as they had before, during the days of slavery. A new bodacious awareness of our identity as a people of African descent led to an explosion of creative expression in the1960s and 1970s through the arts—music, dance, theatre, visual art, and written works—never seen before in the black community. Even though we had to battle with the demon of racism again, this time it was done in the open with love and support from the Village, a combination of the Ancestors and the African-American community.

We survived, just as our ancestors did, through secret codes and messages hidden in our music, art, and language. The black church has been, and remains to this day, a crucial aspect of African-American life and culture. Daily prayer, meditation, sharing, and forgiveness are encouraged in order to have a joyful and prosperous life. Also, there is the idea of "each one teach one", taking under your wing youth who do not have a strong family foundation, offering mentoring and respect for the elders. The Village consists of family, elders, educators, spiritual leaders, friends, and so forth. Without having some type of support system available as a child and an adult, it is extremely difficult to navigate through life's journey.

My parents, who grew up in Mississippi and Alabama, were community activists closely involved with the Civil Rights Movement. They were role models who provided me with a strong foundation, which helped me in developing my own self-identity. As a child, I studied African dance and ballet, played the clarinet, and was a member of the thespian and drama clubs at school. My artistic talents were recognised when I was very young, so I was encouraged to pursue my interest in the arts. My grandmother lived with us and was a quilt-maker who taught me how to sew, cook, and create handmade crafts. She would always find something creative for me to do when I was feeling sad. She would say, "Let's go make some tea cakes" or "You want to help me make this quilt?" This always sparked my interest, and soon I would forget about whatever was ailing me.

We owned one of the first black bookstores in the St Louis metro-politan area. I had the opportunity not only to work and develop job skills as a teenager but also was able to read about the accomplish-ments of black leaders, inventors, scientists, doctors, and artists who were not in the books at the private, predominately white schools I attended. The education I received at these schools was top-rated and wonderful in many ways. However, as was the case with most schools in the 1950s and 1960s, private or public, Black History was not taught, especially the information available to me through the books in our bookstore. It opened up a portal into a brand new world of culturally relevant information and knowledge, revealing to me the character and tenacity of the African-American spirit. Through the bookstore, many civil rights leaders/activists such as Stokely Carmichael, Dick Gregory, and Reverend Jesse Jackson were invited into our home and community for gatherings and speaking engagements.

My mother, Mrs Ethele Evon Cook Scott, walked with Dr King in Selma, Alabama, and went to New York to the rallies of Malcolm X. She worked on John F. Kennedy's campaign, received numerous community and state awards for her outstanding service and leadership. She earned two Bachelor Degrees, two Masters Degrees and a PhD, and accomplished all of this while raising three children. My father, Mr Andrew A. Scott, was a fireman who worked his way up the ranks over the years to become the Fire Chief. He was so inspired by my mother that he went back to college in his forties and earned an Associate Degree. As a black man growing up in the segregated South, he obviously had many humiliating chapters in his life but chose not to allow them to make him bitter and always encouraged me and my siblings to enjoy life, get a good college education, give back to the community, and become viable citizens and positive assets to society.

Having such a wonderful childhood and upbringing did not shield me from the challenges a person of colour faces when she steps outside that Village. But it gave me the foundation necessary to persevere in the face of those challenges and have the courage to stand steady in the face of the racism. The point is that my parents knew what I would encounter, being born a black child. So, early on, they prepared me by exposing me to the arts as a creative outlet through which I have filtered my frustrations and disappointments ever since. Throughout my entire life, I have continued utilising the arts to find my way back to sanity and peace. My Village demonstrated through their actions how to handle injustices without mirroring the very behaviour that feeds the systemic beast. Discovering and implementing creative solutions to solve conflict within myself in the face of life's challenges is crucial to surviving and overcoming negativity.

Is oppression a catalyst for creative expression? Yes, without a doubt. It is an agitator that commands itself into action. In 1857, Frederick Douglass, the great social reformer and orator, who escaped from slavery and went on to become the leader of the abolitionist movement in the USA, said,

If there is no struggle, there is no progress. Those who profess to favor freedom, and yet depreciate agitation, are men who want crops without plowing up the ground. They want rain without thunder and lightning. They want the ocean without the awful roar of its many waters. This struggle may be a moral one; or it may be a physical one; or it may be both moral and physical; but it must be a struggle. (Marable, McMillian, & Frazier, 2003, p. 216)

Sometimes the struggle is an internal or interpersonal one where self-worth and acceptance have been damaged. Change happens one person at a time, motivated by the intensity of the desire for freedom, and by the recognition that some of the most significant achievements of mankind have come out of adversity. Brave hearts have continuously dared to stand up to their oppressors, seen or unseen, shouting, "Enough!" Fear could no longer hold hostage their need to speak their truth and stand in their power, which is in itself an act of powerful creative expression. Paraphrasing Dr King and Malcolm X, it is about *Making A Way Out of No Way, Any Means Necessary Way and like the song says, Ain't Gonna Let Nobody Turn Me Around ,Way*. It is about setting your spirit free so you can fly on freedom's wings. Change happens when, as Fannie Lou Hammer, the famous civil rights activist, stated, "You get sick and tired of being sick and tired" (Ware & Braukman, 2005, p. 269). It takes courage, will, determination, and patience with yourself and the process.

Influences

I am very much influenced in my own creative life by the work and philosophy of the German sculptor, art theorist, and art pedagogue, Joseph Beuys, one of the most influential artists in the first half of the twentieth century. His innovative concepts about art and artists had a major impact on both the American and European art scenes. His philosophy of art was radical: that each human life was a work of art and, as such, could transform society. Because every action has artistic value, every decision—even about the most everyday things—merits consideration, and because every artistic act contributes to societal change, each person is part of something larger.

We are all connected and the actions of the individual affect the whole community. Beuys understood that the process of making art in any form opens the door to higher states of consciousness, giving access to levels of awareness beyond ordinary perception. Indeed, he was aware of the sacredness of his work and of his role as teacher, reformer, and even shaman.

Art matters in every way and aspect of our lives. It is a powerful impetus for lasting revolutionary change within individuals and nations. Another powerful example of artistic influence on society is the work of the Mexican muralists Diego Rivera, Jose Clemente Orozco, and David Alfaro Siqueiros. These three artists, from the 1920s into the 1970s, created large murals with nationalistic, social, and political messages on public buildings in Mexico. They understood the plight of their fellow citizens, and created a visual dialogue through the murals, which helped the common people awaken from oppression and called them to action. In the process, a mural renaissance was begun.

Where do we start this call to action in our own lives and artistic work? We start where we are and with what we have. We utilise our natural skills, talents, knowledge, and wisdom received through life experiences, education, and training to help each other wake up. My own life work is focused on the empowerment and healing of women and children. Throughout my adult life, I have employed my knowledge and skills as a professional visual/performance artist, educator, mental health counsellor, personal development consultant/trainer, and ordained minister to assist me in working toward the change I want to see. This is an ongoing process of growth, observation, and action.

My personal belief is that God, the Divine Source, or whatever one relates to as Supreme Creator, is both male and female. While working on my MA in a Women's Spirituality programme at New College of California, I was shocked and amazed at how little is known, perhaps even what has been hidden, about the feminine aspect of God. We studied a fascinating, scholarly literature, which became tremendously helpful for me in my current work. It provided me with an academic foundation to support my personal, spiritual, and professional work and unveiled truths hidden in women's herstory. We worked on art projects where we created maps of our own bodies, which told stories relevant to each student's life experience as a woman. We shared thoughts and feelings about how art made by women and about women's lives can shift attitudes about how women see themselves and society in general.

One of my classmates who described herself as an artivist (a portmanteau word meaning artist and activist) invited the entire art class to participate in her installation piece based on the femicide of the women/girls of Juarez, Mexico. Part of the annual *Día de los Muertos* (Day of the Dead) Exhibit at SomArts Gallery in San Francisco, this dynamic graphic installation was in memory of the hundreds of women and teenage girls brutally raped, tortured, then murdered in Ciudad Juarez, Mexico. My contribution was a clay sculpture titled, *Holy of Holies*, which represented the sacredness of the female body/womb.

This project fuelled my further investigation of these sadistic crimes against women just below the USA's border and of other crimes against women now gaining attention throughout the world. In so many places, violence against women continues as a part of a culture of historic oppression. There seems now to be the beginning of a worldwide movement in which women, and many men, are organising and fighting back against abusive regimes, customs, and traditions, moving forward without violence but with faith and determination to stop this dehumanisation of the feminine. Women also realise that the very men abusing them are also loved ones, husbands, sons, fathers, uncles, themselves oppressed and dehumanised. And they realise they must find creative solutions that will not only free themselves but also help the men in their communities and families evolve toward mutual love and respect. As Rilke states,

> If we arrange our lives in accordance with the principle that tells us that we must always trust in the difficult, then what now appears to us as alien will become our most intimate and trusted experience . . . Perhaps everything that frightens us is, in its deepest essence, something helpless that wants our love. (Rilke, 1986, p. 92)

The collective voice

I shared earlier how critical the collective voice of the Village was to my own personal and artistic development. The collective voice can hold a position for a person until she has found the strength, courage, and confidence to take on the responsibility of her voice herself. A person's voice might be silent for a while, but it can never be replaced, because the individual voice is an integral part of the collective voice. Some traditions within African thought believe that the individual self is a composite of many selves, including ancestral spirits, present selves, and selves to be born: a human being as a community of selves. These voices join the collective voice and add to the collective consciousness, an idea that suggests we are interdependent beings whose lives are intertwined in the fabric of our collective existence.

In reflecting on the role of others in the creative process, we might consider the artist as a medium tapping into the collective consciousness of the collective voice, then communicating and translating her findings into an artistic dialogue for interpretation. Roland May said, "It is the passion of the artist . . . to communicate what he experiences as the subconscious and unconscious significance of his relation to the world" (May, 2007, p. 324). Picasso expands this thought:

> The artist is a receptacle of emotions that come from all over the place: from the sky, from the earth, from a scrap of paper, from a passing shape, from a spider's web. That is why we must not discriminate between things. Where things are concerned, there are no class distinctions. (Ashton, 1988, p. 10)

An artist brings a special gift to both the individual and the collective voice/community/village. Working as an artist has allowed me to experience other realities where spirits reach out across time and space with a request to share, heal, or teach through my artwork. This is a natural process where I allow spirit to work with and through me.

I see my artwork as a catalyst for personal, social, and spiritual transformation. The intent is to invoke critical thinking. Creative expressions are birthed from deep-rooted social, cultural, spiritual, and personal experiences. Each artistic venture teaches me lessons in respect, love, integrity, courage, and holding power for myself as well as for silent voices. I am a Griot, telling stories through art of the challenges and triumphs of the human spirit, especially of women and children. When I work with paints, coloured pencils, textiles, gourds, found objects, and clay, I am transported to a realm where I create from soul knowledge and heart wisdom. Spirit guides me to create that which I need to birth for myself and for others. My motto is, "I offer the gifts of my hands and talents on the altar of human service".

Delia's story

Delia was an adolescent slave girl who lived in Columbia, South Carolina in the1850s. In 2004, while working on my MFA in San Francisco, I purchased the book, edited by Dorothy Sterling, *We Are Your Sisters: Black Women in the Nineteenth Century*. I was preparing a chautauqua for my thesis presentation on Harriet Tubman, Harriet Jacobs, and Harriet Powers, called "My name is Harriet: three faces of courage, integrity and grace". Since Sterling's book was written about black women during that period, I utilised it to write my thesis. After I graduated in 2004, I packed the book away and did not pull it out again until I decided to enter an art exhibit, *Women of the African Diaspora*, in New York City at Pen and Brush Gallery. Founded 119 years ago, Pen and Brush is the oldest women's gallery on the east coast. Its exclusive membership at one time included First Lady Eleanor Roosevelt and Pearl S. Buck.

I was not sure what medium I wanted to work in or what I wanted to submit. The theme for the exhibit was broad, and I contemplated it for a few weeks. With only a month left before the submission deadline, I knew I had to move quickly. I sat down in meditation and asked for assistance. I browsed through several books on black women, but found myself repeatedly being directed back to *We Are Your Sisters*. Suddenly, I became aware that each time I opened the book, it automatically opened to the page on Delia's story. This happened at least five times. The daguerreotype photograph taken of Delia in March 1850, finally captured my full attention. My eyes locked into her eyes and I could see and feel the sadness, pain, and humiliation this young woman had endured.

As I stared into her eyes, what she communicated back to me was, "Please help me restore my dignity." My heart became overwhelmed with these feelings and knew that I had received my answer and my mission. As I continued to read on, I saw that her picture was right under Chapter Three's topic, "Seduction, rape, concubinage", and was the only photograph in that chapter. Delia was owned by B. F. Taylor and was ordered by him to pose for the famous Harvard naturalist Louis Agassiz's (1807–1873) scientific studies.

Dorothy Sterling, the book's editor, states, "Surely the experience was humiliating, yet she seems innocently unaware of any sexual interest she was arousing" (Sterling, 1997, p. 19). I disagree with

Sterling's observation. I believe that Delia was very aware of what was happening to her, though she may not have been thinking about someone's sexual interest in her nude body. Ordered by her owner to strip and pose for some strange man, her thoughts might have been more concerned with being sold, removed from her family, sexually abused, or all the above, and perhaps with the terrible fact that she had no choice. The look on her face implies humiliation, feeling disrespected, and fear of what might follow.

This original photograph of Delia is now the property of the Peabody Museum of Archeology and Ethnology at Harvard University, Cambridge, Massachusetts. It was discovered in the attic of the museum in 1976, after 100 years, along with seven other photographs of black slaves. The photographs were originally taken by J. T. Zealy, a respected photographer in Columbia, South Carolina in the 1850s. Apparently, they are the oldest documented photos of identifiable slaves. Delia was born enslaved in South Carolina and was the daughter of Renty, a slave brought to the USA from the Congo. Her father and sister are also subjects in this series of photographs. Molly Rogers placed the photo of Delia on the cover of her book, *Delia's Tears: Race, Science, and Photography in Nineteenth-Century America* (Rogers & Blight, 2010). She comments in this book that Agassiz had planned to use the photographs to support his theory of black people's inferiority to the other races.

After reading Delia's story, I felt that I received creative directives about how to proceed with the artwork. I decided on a mixed media textile wall hanging, to which I gave the title, "The transformation of Delia: a slave girl". From that point on, everything came together: from the concept I wanted to convey to the materials I would use in the construction. My intention was to transform Delia's experience of an oppressed slave girl into that of a powerful African princess/priestess. A dear friend who owned an international art and gift shop in St Louis gave me ancient clay beads from an excavation in Mali. She also gave me huge discounts on African mud cloth, or bogolan, from Mali, Kuba cloth from Zaire, Nigerian hand-woven panels, and cowrie shells.

"The transformation of Delia" is a story of healing, victory, and the restoration of dignity. The artwork depicts the healing and empowerment of this young adolescent girl who had been abused, dishonoured, and desecrated during her lifetime. It shows her moving from powerlessness to regality, beauty, and empowerment. Through the strength, blessings, love, and power of the Ancestors and the collective voices holding her place across time, Delia was emancipated and ascended like the phoenix. I used two acrylic canvas sheets to paint portraits of her before and after images. Then I surrounded both paintings with antique ritual Kuba cloth, cloth actually used in Shoowa tribal women's rites. Nigerian woven panels and mud cloth were then used to frame the images and create a pleasing contrast. The purple tie-dye cloth was chosen to represent regality and spiritual adeptness. Antique clay beads, thousands of years old, from an excavation in Mali, are strategically sewn around the top of each image. Cowrie shells, dragonflies, crystals, and feathers are used to represent the support of the natural elements and the Divine Feminine to assist in her healing. The figure in the centre is the spirit of the female Goddess Ancestor who performs the healing ritual. There are many

"The transformation of Delia: a slave girl", 2005, by Rochleigh Z Wholfe.

other hidden meanings in the piece that I leave to the observer to discover.

After more than forty hours of work, I submitted the image of Delia, along with other selected images requested in the call for the proposal, then waited to find out if my artwork, and my first submission to a New York gallery, would be accepted. I prayed that of the five images, Delia would be the one chosen. A month passed with no correspondence from New York, and I involved myself with work on another show for the St Joseph (Missouri) Museum. As I was driving to St Joseph, I decided to let go of my anxieties about the New York project. Later that evening, on my way to the reception, I received a call from the director of Pen and Brush telling me that Delia and two other works had been accepted into the show. I was elated. After the reception, on the way back to St Louis, I received a second call. This time the director informed me that "The transformation of Delia" had been awarded third prize in the Pen and Brush exhibition. I was absolutely ecstatic, and I felt that I had come through for Delia.

When I arrived at the gallery for the reception in New York, I was impressed with the elegant brownstone and the beauty of the surrounding environment. As I made my way to the room where Delia was displayed, tears came to my eyes. She was hanging over a fireplace in a room with huge windows overlooking a sculpture garden. She took her place in this prestigious historical building, where many highly respected and famous women writers and artists, such as First Lady Eleanor Roosevelt and Pearl Buck, had sat drinking tea and discussing the issues of the day. Delia was framed on either side by another artist's mud cloth dolls. She looked so regal on that wall. "We did it, Delia! We did it," I quietly whispered to her. This time when I looked into those eyes, I saw pride, joy, and dignity, and a faint voice said back to me, "Thank you!" It is never to late to heal and transform our lives, even after 156 years.

I am grateful to all the women who were involved in this process of helping Delia reclaim her voice and dignity. They might not have been consciously aware of their involvement, but they are indeed part of the collective consciousness. Ase! May your soul rest in peace, Delia!

References

Ashton, D. (Ed.) (1988). *Picasso on Art: A Selection of Views*. Cambridge, MA: Da Capo Press.

Marable, M., McMillian, J., & Frazier, N. (Eds.) (2003). *Freedom on My Mind: The Columbia Documentary History of the African American Experience*. New York: Columbia University Press.

May, R. (2007). *Love & Will*. New York: W. W. Norton.

Rilke, R. M. (1986). *Letters to a Young Poet*. New York: Knopf Doubleday.

Rogers, M., & Blight, D. (2010). *Delia's Tears: Race, Science, and Photography in Nineteenth-Century America*. New Haven, CT: Yale University Press.

Sterling, D. (Ed.) (1997). *We Are Your Sisters: Black Women in the Nineteenth Century*. New York: W. W. Norton.

Ware, S., & Braukman, S. (Eds.) (2005). *Notable American Women: A Biographical Dictionary, Volume 5: Completing the Twentieth Century*. Cambridge, MA: Harvard University Press.

The brightening glance — creativity and childhood: the 2012 Creativity Seminar

F or decades now, the Riggs Activities Department has included a Nursery School, in which local children receive care, guidance, and education from a Montessori-trained teacher *and* Center patients, who have chosen to learn the role of assistant teacher. This extraordinary programme has launched hundreds of children into their educational lives and quite a few former patients into their careers as well. Central to the Nursery School's success is the deeply creative intermix of people from quite different life circumstances and an environment co-constructed for both holding and imagination.

Paula Meade directed the Nursery School for forty years, retiring this past June. She arrived in 1971, a young, beautiful, inspired, and inspiring teacher. The comment most often made about Paula, besides how easy, engaging, and loving she was with the children, was: how did she work with a dozen children, indoors and outdoors for three hours, and not get a single mark or wrinkle on her white linen outfit? Perhaps the 2012 seminar would discover the answer to that question, along with the riddle of creativity itself!

Generations of children, parents, assistant teachers, and staff are deeply grateful for Paula's devotion and touch, and we could find no better occasion for the 2012 Creativity Seminar than to honour her work by exploring the links between childhood, creativity, and the "brightening glance" she brought to her students every day.

That lovely phrase belongs to William Butler Yeats and serves as the title of one of our speaker's, Erikson Scholar Ellen Handler Spitz's, many books. In the chapter that follows, Professor Spitz explores the emergence and shaping of imagination in the childhoods of two prominent artists and one scientist. In so doing, she illuminates something about the nature of childhood creativity—including its links to trauma—and what it might tell us about the creative process more broadly.

Snapshots of childhood creativity in science, music, and art: Richard Feynman, Clara Schumann, and René Magritte

Ellen Handler Spitz

T his chapter is prompted, in part, by a spate of alarmist articles in the media over the past several years concerning what journalists have called "the creativity crisis" (Bronson & Merryman, 2010), articles claiming, in other words, that American creativity is in decline. A corresponding call has arisen to seek remedies and determine how creativity might be fostered in the lives of children so as to stem the tide of this (alleged) decline. While taking these dramatic concerns and pronouncements *cum grano salis*, this chapter responds nevertheless by extracting a set of themes drawn from the childhoods of three individuals whose remarkable contributions to the disparate fields of science, classical music, and visual art are beyond question: Nobel prize-winning physicist Richard Feynman (1918–1988), virtuoso pianist and composer Clara Schumann (1819–1896), and the surrealist painter René Magritte (1898–1967). Highly variable and not always salubrious, the diverse milieus in which these individuals' childhood creativity flourished demonstrates by default how the topic itself has had an unfortunate tendency to bog down in sentimental rhetoric.

To reflect on themes highlighted in this chapter will be to take a sober stance. Setting aside well-worn shibboleths of "divergent" and "convergent" thinking, we shall bare some surprising contributions to childhood creativity: danger, extreme risk, extraordinary patience, occasionally harsh discipline, appropriation, and childhood trauma. To do this means confronting the unwelcome truth that highly diverse and not always apparently favourable conditions might foster as well as hinder creativity in children. High prices must sometimes be paid. We have no formulas for sure-fire success. My purpose is to stimulate and spark the creativity of my readers by offering these three examples in encapsulated form. Another aim in this chapter is to take the risk of juxtaposing a budding scientist, musician, and painter, for, in fact, no one knows in advance the precise direction in which a child's curiosity and gifts will lead. Too often, the arts and the sciences, as well as music and visual art, are unwholesomely segregated from one another. I bring them together here and also speak unashamedly of lives that occurred decades and miles apart: in the USA, Germany, and Belgium respectively. Moreover, while it is undoubtedly fair to acknowledge the superior endowments of the three individuals, the themes that played key roles in determining their future achievements are pertinent to the lives of many ordinary children (if, indeed, any child can be called ordinary). It goes without saying that my purpose in what follows is not to advocate exposing young children unnecessarily to poverty, peril, cruelty, or parental death! Yet these are all part of our story.

Richard Feynman

When the brilliant Nobel-prize-winning physicist Richard Feynman died in Los Angeles in 1988, these words were found chalked on his blackboard: "What I cannot create I do not understand". Let us begin with this arresting sentence and parse it: *I need to experience things in my own way, with my own words, symbols, sensibility, and invented imagery in order to feel I can grasp them and take them in.* Feynman, in an excellent illustration of this maxim, was, in his early teens, working out some equations in his head one day when he recalled a trigonometry book he had borrowed at about eleven years of age. He started drawing triangles and calculating sines, cosines, and tangents. Later on, when he took a high school trigonometry class, he found not only that his own demonstrations differed occasionally from what was in the textbook, but also that he was unhappy with the standard symbols for sine, cosine, and tangent; thereupon, he invented his own (Feynman, 1985, pp. 23–24).

His maxim ("what I cannot create I do not understand") actually sounds—rather excitingly—like the description of what every child does from the start of his or her life, a notion offered and explained by several renowned cognitive developmental psychologists, such as Jerome S. Bruner (1987) and Jean Piaget (1929) before him, who have called it "constructing the world". One of our failings perhaps, as educators and parents, is that we frequently get in the way of this fundamental creative process: we try to construct it for them. All children are creative in the sense Feynman articulates. If only we would let them be so!

Shifting for a brief aside into the domain of psychoanalysis, what would happen if we took Feynman's sentence ("What I cannot create I do not understand") and placed it alongside a quote from Winnicott, the noted psychoanalyst and paediatrician, who profoundly understood children and who wrote voluminously and with great insight about them. Winnicott, in a paper titled "Advising parents", offers several examples of inappropriate advice doctors and therapists give to parents: "All my professional life," he writes, "I have avoided giving advice" (1965, p. 114). He advocates, apropos the task of the therapist, the value of listening closely to what the patient says in each therapy session. He writes,

> Those [therapists] who . . . *suffer . . . for limited periods of time the agonies of the case,* need not know much [else]. But they will learn; they will be taught by their clients. It is my belief that the more they learn in this way the richer they will become. (1965, p. 120, my italics)

In other words, like the physicist Richard Feynman, the psychoanalyst Donald Winnicott believes that mental experience—imaginative, intuitive, empathic, and creative—is crucial for understanding: the therapist (and the patient, too, by the way) both need to create and to re-create in order to understand. Physicist and psychoanalyst come together in this joint *aperçu*.

Suppose we time-travel now all the way back to ancient Greece, to Aeschylus and the tragic drama (Lattimore, 1969). Let us pretend that we are on stage with the elders of Argos during a performance of

Agamemnon. The Trojan War has ended, and the chorus, in the presence of their queen, Clytemnestra, is describing how her husband, Agamemnon, brutally sacrificed their daughter, Iphigenia, to make the winds blow favourably so that Greek sailing vessels and triremes could put forth for Troy. Aeschylus gives us the scene in heart-rending detail, word by word: how the girl's eyes beseeched and accused like arrows as she was held aloft because they had stopped her mouth lest she cry out a curse upon the men. "Wisdom," chants the chorus, "comes through suffering" (Lattimore, 1969, line 179). Sashaying back and forth, vocalising, the chorus of Argive elders intones the well-known tale of bloody forfeiture, and the audience—upwards of 16,000 souls—sits silently on rows of stone built into the immense open-air theatre dedicated to Dionysus. What are they doing, these people, as they watch and listen? Surely, they are thinking hard: surely they are imagining and creating for themselves, each in his own mind's eye, the scene of the girl's death at her father's hand: *creating it in order to understand*.

Richard Feynman was born in New York, in 1918 (Feynman, 1985, p. 11). Times were hard, and his immigrant Jewish father, Melville, fascinated by science, had no chance to study formally. With great delight, he encouraged his curious first-born son. Feynman recalls sitting on his father's lap with the *Encyclopedia Britannica*. When they read an entry, such as the name and the dimensions of a particular dinosaur, his father would say, "What does that mean?" He would explain to his son, "If this dinosaur were standing in our front yard, its head would be just high enough to reach the window but too wide to go through the window without breaking the glass." In this way, the child learnt the difference between knowing *about* something and actually knowing something. (His father, by re-creating what was in the book, enabled his son to create it anew in his own terms.) Let us focus on three aspects of Feynman's childhood: first, risk-taking and danger; second, time and patience requisite for complex mental processes to occur; third, playfulness and a sense of humour.

Curiosity, which sparks creativity, can lead a child out of safety and into danger (of many kinds, both psychical and mental). This is one reason why adults suppress it. The world, however, needs to be explored: each newborn child must test limits and push against boundaries. Children, moreover, often take risks unknowingly, so that even awareness of risk constitutes an element of the creative process. But how far do you let a child go? If harm threatens, safety trumps all. How do you make the best call? Over-anxious adults might swiftly derail a child's or an adolescent's process of discovery.

The little boy, whom nobody knew would grow up to be among the ten top theoretical physicists of all time, played with electricity (Feynman, 1985, p. 15). He set up a primitive lab with a wooden crate, made his own fuses out of tin foil wrapped around old burnt out fuses, used sweet wrappers and a five-watt bulb to create glow effects, invented a burglar alarm, which—one night when his parents innocently tiptoed into his room to turn off his headphones—suddenly went off with an ear-splitting racket. "It worked! It worked!" he shrieked, jumping out of bed, adding to what must have been their shock (1985, p. 16). He loved to find old broken radios at jumble sales and tried to figure out how to get them to work.

He played with a spark coil from a car, and one day, punching holes with its sparks, the piece of paper he was holding caught fire. When it burned too close to his fingers, he dropped it into a wire wastebasket filled with newspapers. Newspapers, he learnt, burn fast! As the blaze reared up, he shut the door so that his mother, who was playing bridge with friends, would not know there was a fire in his room. He tried smothering the fire by putting a magazine on the wastebasket. It went out, but now the room filled with smoke. Since the metal wastebasket was too hot, he took a pair of pliers and carried it across the room, where he held it outside the window for the smoke to blow away. A strong wind came and rekindled the fire; now the magazine was no longer nearby. He pulled the flaming basket back inside the room, but, as he did so, he noticed how close the curtains were: the danger suddenly felt real. He put the magazine back on the basket. The fire died again. This time, keeping the magazine near, he carried the basket to the window and tossed burning coals down to the street. After this, carefully closing the door, Feynman told his mother he was going out to play, and the smoke wafted gradually out the open window.

Is there a parent or a teacher of young children who would not cringe at this story? Suppose the child had caught on fire, or the house had burned down! Yet, what a stunning recital of a child's step-by-step thinking process: what ingenuity, resourcefulness, and creativity! One move at a time. He never calls for help. He never panics. He trusts himself and uses his own mind to solve each unanticipated problem as it arises. *Pace* the genius of Richard Feynman, every human child is born with the capacity to react to the world in this manner: that is, to meet unexpected events with thoughtful, purposeful action, to take one step at a time, to judge the effectiveness of each move and to proceed accordingly. Psychoanalysts would speak here of ego functions: of perception, memory, and judgement.

What we often do is forestall this functioning in children. We intervene, well in advance of a real need to do so. Internalised anxiety and dependency, however, can block high levels of ego functioning, which are essential for creativity. Perhaps we should reflect on our monitoring, programming, and protecting; are we presenting children with too many ready-made solutions, trivial choices that lack meaning, and virtual situations that entail no true consequences? If trial and error are central to the creative process, why do we refuse to let children fail?

Please understand that I am not advocating unsupervised play with electricity. Richard Feynman's early life experience, however, poses challenging questions for our topic. Imagine that something similar was going on in *your* presence: a child is confronting a risky situation and obviously trying to figure out what to do. You stand by. At what point do you intervene? How long do you let the child try to come up with a solution? It is very tempting to short-circuit the process and, no doubt, it is a lot easier that way—in the short run. But the long-term costs, the losses in terms of fostering childhood creativity, could be high.

Second, by the time Feynman had turned eleven, it was the Depression, and, in spite of being a little boy, he had acquired a local reputation for fixing radios. One day, a poor down-and-out fellow asks him to come over to his place to fix a broken specimen that roars and wobbles when you turn it on, but that, a minute or two later, sounds fine. The eleven-year-old goes over to the man's house in a disreputable part of town, looks at the radio, and thinks: gosh, how can *that* be? So, he starts pacing up and down, and we can readily picture him in our mind's eye—small, slender, wearing a newsboy cap, perhaps. The owner of the radio watches him for a few minutes and gets annoyed: "Hey!" he complains, "I thought you were going to fix my radio. All you're doing is walking around!" "*I'm thinking,*" answers the child (Feynman, 1985, pp. 19–20). Gradually, the young Feynman reasons that if he takes out all the tubes and puts them back in a different order the noise might go away. It works. "This kid," the owner tells everybody, "he fixes radios by thinking." Feynman comments years later, "The whole idea of thinking, to fix a radio—a little boy stops and thinks, and figures out how to do it—[and that guy] he never thought that was possible" (1985, p. 20).

How is this relevant to our topic, and what are we doing today that is obstructive? For one thing, we rush children. We propel them from one activity to another. We give them no time to look around, to notice things, to wonder about them, to ask questions and ponder the possible answers. One day, Feynman told his dad he noticed something: when he pulled his wagon forward, the ball inside the wagon moved to the back, but when he stopped the wagon, it rolled forward, and he wanted to know why. This precipitated a discussion of inertia. How many children, by contrast, have you seen recently just quietly thinking? We not only rush them but we also stuff their minds as if they were French geese in the Périgord, being force-fed and fattened up for *foie gras*. We do not allow them the time they need to come up with things on their own: to create in order to understand.

Third, in nearly all the surviving photographs of Feynman, pictures taken from all stages of his life, including snapshots and candids, he seems relaxed. No tense, furrowed brow, no stodginess, no pathos marks his face. His joy in using his mind is ever-present and infectious. This attitude, which illuminates the pages of his memoir as well (a book remarkably free of cant and pretention and delightful for its light-hearted humour and self-deprecation), is not a special gift but available to every child. A child who learns to trust in and use his own mental processes can derive enormous pleasure from doing so. Such a child stands to grow into a creative individual. Such a child rarely experiences boredom. There is always a puzzle to solve, an oddity to observe, something beautiful to capture, an idea to try out, a melody to note down.

Clara Schumann

Clara Wieck Schumann was one of the great piano virtuosos of nineteenth century Europe. In addition to being a lifelong performer (sixty years of performing in concerts), she was a composer whose piano and choral works are still highly regarded and performed (May, 1912;

Reich, 2001). Before the age of twenty, when she married composer Robert Schumann, which she did defiantly after anguished hesitation and enforced separation because her father adamantly opposed the union and at one point threatened to shoot the composer if their love persisted, Clara Schumann had been a *Wunderkind*, a child prodigy. The small, delicate daughter of Friedrich Wieck of Leipzig performed for the crowned heads of Europe. She played for Goethe twice in Weimar; she played in Paris, where she met Paganini and Meyerbeer; she even played for the reigning Emperor and Empress in Vienna. Her concerts were the rage of the day, invariably sold out and universally applauded by critics.

From the age of five, Clara was taught piano and made to practise daily (three hours by age seven, one expressly for her lesson and two for practice); her entire life was regulated, regimented, and managed by her father. It is hard to imagine a more despotic parent than Friedrich Wieck and, simultaneously, one who so clearly loved his daughter that he spared nothing for her musical education (by seven, Clara had been taken to every opera staged in Leipzig and been prepared for them by having studied their scores at the piano with her father).

Not a gifted musician himself, or from a musical family, and lacking formal training, Wieck's goal was to turn his daughter into the virtuoso he was not and could never be. We might observe a parallel here with Feynman's father, who, lacking opportunity himself, fostered it in his son, albeit with gentleness, whimsy, and *laissez-aller*. Musicologists have expressed amazement at Wieck's success as a teacher, both of Clara and of others, for this self-taught man made his living selling pianos and giving lessons. A stubborn, opinionated individual with a violent temper, he demanded unquestioning obedience, and his marriage to Clara's mother, Marianne Tromlitz, a gifted soprano, erupted into scenes that proved unendurable for her. Resorting to a rare course of action for a middle-class German woman of 1824, Marianne left him in the ninth year of their marriage and returned with Clara to her father's home. Up to this point, the little girl had shown no signs of the genius that lay ahead. She was, in fact, totally mute and did not speak a single word until after her fourth birthday, silenced perhaps by all the anger that surrounded her (Reich, 2001, p. 14). She was a quiet, solitary child.

According to the laws of Saxony, children were their fathers' property, and Marianne was forced to give Clara up when she turned five.

It is heart-breaking to imagine the scene: although Marianne begged Wieck to allow the little girl to be at least delivered "from my hand to yours", her humane plea was ignored, and a maid was sent to pick Clara up, like a parcel, from a town halfway between Plauen, where her mother's family lived, and her father's home in Leipzig (Reich, 2001, p. 11). After this, Clara's relations with her mother were attenuated for decades.

From the moment she was returned to her father, Clara was placed under a rigorous regime and primed for her future. Music quickly became her life, and playing the piano became equated in her mind with love. If she resisted her father, which was rare, Wieck controlled her by withholding what she loved best, her favourite piano pieces: an especially cruel deprivation. Most shocking, perhaps, is that, when she was seven, Wieck gave her a diary and, until she was eighteen, every entry in this diary was either supervised by her father or actually *written* by him, who wrote under Clara's very name! When she was eleven, we have the following words in Wieck's handwriting: "From now on, I will write in my diary myself, whenever I have the time" (Reich, 2001, p. 18). Clara Schumann's biographer, Nancy Reich, calls it a veritable theft of identity (2001, p. 20). In Weimar, a prominent government official's wife chided Wieck for making Clara perform so much and not letting her play with other children. Wieck was incensed and replied that he lived only for the education of his daughter: he had been thinking about education for twenty-five years; he needed no advice from anyone and declined to accept any (Reich, 2001, pp. 28–33).

What might come to mind while reflecting on Clara Schumann's childhood is a widely circulated book by Alice Miller (1979) titled *The Drama of the Gifted Child*, also published under the title, *Prisoners of Childhood* (1981). This book argues that many parents exhibit tendencies to exploit their gifted and creative children. Parents tend to treat these children as narcissistic projections and to live vicariously through them. In return, duty-bound and aware of the great sacrifices made on their behalf, the children so treated often revere, defend, and strive to please these very parents. Along the way, grave psychic damage might occur. Miller frames her argument with power, and, surely, Clara Schumann's father fits the bill. Yet, his daughter's long life reveals that, even in this extreme case, damage was by no means the whole story. Despite his tyranny, Wieck gave his daughter the wherewithal to develop and blossom artistically, he encouraged her to strive toward the outer limits of her musical potential, and Clara grew up to be a woman of strength, with lasting confidence in herself and her art. With grace and competence, she managed not only a dazzling career performing and composing, but seven children, and the care of her beloved genius husband, Robert Schumann, who soon fell mentally ill and died, leaving her a widow at thirty-six, when their youngest child was barely two years old—this in a period when women were not expected to combine careers with wife- and motherhood.

An example of Clara's mettle occurred during the violent May uprising of 1849 in Dresden; she was thirty (Reich, 2001, p. 104). Seven months pregnant, already mother of four small children, she hid her husband away so that he would not have to fight; she fled with him through the back door of their home, then, in the middle of the night, she returned to Dresden, crossing open fields, facing squadrons of armed men, in order to retrieve little Ludwig, Julie, Elise, and Marie, aged one and a half to six, so as to bring them to safety outside the city. Father Wieck had instilled in her indomitable determination and the spirit of resistance. Indeed, Clara was finally able to stand up to him, although not without pain. It was he who had given her the reason for needing to do so, and it was he who showed her how.

How is Clara Schumann relevant for our topic? Her childhood differs, certainly, from that of Richard Feynman. Their fathers, both living vicariously to some extent through their offspring, practised dissimilar educational methods. Yet, not entirely, and we must distinguish style from content. Rigour, discipline, practice, the perfecting of skills are significant ego functions, and without musical technique, counterpoint, improvisation, constant exposure to beautiful music—the stuff of Clara Schumann's regimented childhood—she could not have expressed herself musically. She wrote, at age nineteen,

> Art is a beautiful gift. What is more beautiful than to clothe one's feelings in sounds, what a comfort in sad hours, what a pleasure, what a wonderful feeling, to provide an hour of happiness to others. And what a sublime feeling to pursue art so that one gives one's life for it. (Reich, 2001, p. 58)

In mulling over her childhood, we might ask ourselves whether discipline *per se* might need to play a greater role in children's lives today, and, if so, to ponder the forms it might take. Not cruelty, punishment, or exploitation, but discipline, rather, as drawn from its Latin root, *disciplina*, meaning "instruction" — discipline as education that builds wisely, level upon level, and that delivers an increasing competence out of which the highest forms of creativity can emerge. In this sense, I offer Clara Schumann's childhood to you for contemplation.

René Magritte

With René Magritte, the Belgian Surrealist painter, born in 1898, we meet another theme entirely, clear but never simple: that of childhood exposure to trauma, in this case, the abiding horror of maternal suicide. How could such a dreadful experience generate creativity? Once again, I am not advocating a childhood laden with catastrophe. However, I must insist that trauma need not be an implacable foe of creativity. Magritte, as a child, grew up with a depressed, suicidal mother, Regina Bertinchamp, who, after making several attempts on her life, was locked up by her husband at night (Spitz, 1984). Nevertheless, she managed to escape and, in early March 1912, her youngest son, Raymond, woke up and found her missing from the bedroom. He alerted the rest of the family — his older brothers, Paul and René, and their father — who followed footprints and discovered that she had drowned by throwing herself from a nearby bridge into the cold waters of the River Sambre, near Charleroi in Belgium, where they lived. Magritte, thirteen at the time, reported the events this way to his friend, later biographer, Louis Scutenaire. He added wryly that he then acquired some local notoriety among the village children as *the son of the drowned woman*. Suicide, however, in Catholic Belgium, was a mortal sin that carried a terrible stigma, and was, hence, a source of deep shame for the family.

Magritte's account includes one detail that seemed to imprint itself on his mind: when the dead mother was found, her white nightgown, he said, was washed up over her face, the implication being that her naked body was exposed. This story, long accepted by scholars as true and never, to my knowledge, either corroborated or denied by the younger brothers, was challenged by a newspaper article, discovered decades after Magritte's 1967 death, which reported that the body was actually recovered a fortnight later, which, if true, would invalidate the artist's version. Magritte stood by his story. On some level, it seems to have represented a deep psychic truth, and it formed a spur to his lifelong creativity. Studying his art, we cannot deny the ever-present effects of this childhood trauma. What did he make of the untimely death of his mother?

When we look at paintings he created over the course of his lifetime, starting in his twenties, although he actually began earlier, we note that Magritte painted numerous versions of an image, sometimes titled *The Empire of Lights*, in which we see a house set in a time–space that simultaneously suggests both daytime and night-time. (Although Magritte, dwelling his entire life in francophone Belgium, gave his pictures French titles, often containing important puns and allusions, I am nevertheless, for the limited purposes of this short chapter, giving them in English translation only. Also, Magritte's paintings are widely reproduced. Many of the works referred to in this essay can be seen in the pages of Spitz (1984).) This image, following our theme, conveys the lasting shock of being awakened in the dark and finding your mother dead: light floods the darkness, the confusion and horror are palpable; nothing is as it should be, ever again. Another related picture, *Thoughts of a Man Walking Alone*, seems to evoke the river, the bridge, and the naked body of the mother, except that here a floating immobile figure conveys an unmistakable aura of androgyny, as though the artist himself were identifying with his dead mother. *Pandora's Box*, painted when Magritte was over fifty, recalls the bridge and the never-to-be-forgotten scene: a man wearing a bowler hat, the artist's well-known insignia, is seen from the back, and a large white rose nearby on the right might evoke his lost mother, her gown, and her sweetness, albeit not without thorns.

A large theatrical canvas, *The Menaced Assassin*, now in the permanent collection of New York's Museum of Modern Art, was painted when Magritte was twenty-nine, and its strange scenario includes a window through which three young men with expressionless faces are peering. They might remind us, in keeping with our theme, of the three boys who were abandoned when their mother killed herself that night in the artist's childhood. Inside the boxlike room with its barren walls, into which they stare, a nude woman lies bleeding from the mouth on a chaise longue, her white nightgown thrown up to expose her body, while on either side, behind or in front of walls, depending on your perspective, stand two bowler-hatted men, one with a fishing net and the other with a club that resembles an eerily distorted human limb. The testimony of violence in the picture—both past and deferred—evokes fantasies of mysterious aggression that often plague the troubled minds of survivors after the suicide of a loved one.

Notoriously a joker and determined to preserve a veil of mystery concerning his art, Magritte was both cavalier and careless about dating his pictures, so that we do not always know when a particular work was made. Themes derived from his mother's suicide, however, may be detected for decades in his art. One strange image, *When the Hour Will Strike*, presents a decapitated female torso beside an expanse of water. The figure is neither living nor dead, as might be the case with a mother who died violently by her own hand while the artist was a child but who cannot be exorcised and who, therefore, lives on eternally in the mind. Perhaps she is headless because the nightgown had covered it that night. The painting's title seems to hint that the future is unknowable, or that time might be reversible, as it is in the minds of young children who have not lived sufficiently long to have grasped the irreversibility of death. Let us place Magritte's picture in our minds next to one of the most famous icons of western art, the *Venus de Milo*, who is armless only, but who is also disabled and vulnerable. Doing so might help us to see how brilliantly the mature artist, carrying his childhood within, melds his deeply private feelings with the roots of traditional art, public and accessible, but to which his private anguish lends a new edge of pain.

Motherhood was what Magritte first called an unforgettable picture, now in London's Tate Gallery; later, he changed its title to *The Spirit of Geometry*. He paints a mother and child couple but transposes the baby's and mother's heads. In so doing, he uncannily reverses the usual direction of dependency, and we can only imagine what his mother's helplessness and misery must have felt like to him as a child. Belgium is not only a Catholic country, of course, but one that generated centuries of glorious religious art, including numerous images of the Madonna and Child. Let us mentally juxtapose this Magritte picture with, say, Raphael's *Madonna of the Granduca*, obviously not Belgian, but an image undoubtedly known to the artist. The contrast between the two speaks volumes about the artist's suffering and about the creative flow that kept emerging from him pursuant to childhood loss.

In *Discovery*, a nude woman turns into the wood of her own coffin, so that boundaries are breached, and she is neither living nor dead, neither animal nor vegetable. *The Red Model* is a canvas that refers directly to the story of maternal suicide by portraying breasts that protrude grotesquely from the white nightgown that was meant to hide, but did not hide, the mother's body, against the wood of a coffin, perhaps, and a pair of high-heeled ladies' shoes that are morphing into feet or the other way around. We are queasily confronted with the child's confusion that night: my mother *was* alive, but suddenly, she was not alive. How can that be? The puzzlement. However, unlike many of the puzzles that challenged Richard Feynman, *these* riddles, weighted down with emotional freight, seem endlessly insoluble. Magritte invents image after image, trying to come to terms with what cannot be banished from his childhood.

Rage, too, accompanies suicide and abandonment. *Collective Invention*, which is the ugly image of a reversed mermaid, asks angrily how a human mother could have been so stupid as to think she could breathe underwater like a fish. The degrading picture reveals still-smouldering bitterness in this once-abandoned child. Besides, what can an artist do, anyway? Although Magritte admired the French painter Jacques Louis David's portrait, *Mme Récamier*, of 1800, he ridiculed it and revealed that, in fact, the portrait is merely a testament to the fact that its sitter is dead. Repainting the picture, he calls his new work *Perspective: Mme Récamier of David*. The lovely young woman who was lounging in a white Empire gown has metamorphosed into a bent coffin, placed on the same couch, and a few folds of white fabric steal out from under its wood.

In *Perspicacity*, the young Magritte paints himself painting at an easel. Is he performing his magic? On the table rests an unhatched egg, but the canvas presents a bird in flight: which comes first, the bird or the egg, and how can we ever know? We cannot know, Magritte argues, because of *The Treachery of Images*, as he calls his most famous picture, the pipe under which are written the words: *This Is Not a Pipe*. Even though we call the pictured pipe a "pipe", we cannot smoke it. What kind of enjoyment does it give us? What relation has a picture to our *idea* of a pipe, or to our *word* for pipe? What relation, in fact, has art to life, or a living mother to a dead one, and how can a needed mother die, anyway? *Maybe I don't really know what I think I know.*

Just like Richard Feynman, René Magritte is creating in order to understand. In *The Human Condition*, he paints a canvas set up in front of a window so that the painting both represents and occludes the scene behind it. What do we see when we look out at the world? Do we see what is there, or do we see what we *want* to see, what we *need* to see, what we *think* we see, what we have the capacity to see, what we are permitted to see? *My mother was there, but my mother was not there. I saw her, but she was gone.*

In a beautifully lush painting in Washington's National Gallery titled *The Blank Signature*, an equestrian rides among the trees in a forest: the mother partially appears, and disappears, then reappears. Elegantly, she trots through the artist's life, never abandoning him. And in another painting, *The Waterfall*, Magritte sets up his wooden easel to paint some shrubbery. But the subject of his picture, the greenery, refuses to stay in the background. It comes forward, like the childhood trauma itself; it pushes its way into the forefront of his art, while he, with skill, craft, patience, and imagination, keeps painting — making imagery out of his unhealing wound.

With regard to many children, trauma, unfortunately, only derails and damages them; it prompts little if any creativity. Magritte was both damaged and creative, as I think we must say also for Clara Schumann, who, in a far less irrevocable way, also suffered, as a child, the loss of her mother. Feynman alone of the three managed to escape into a world of problems that took him both out of, as well as very deeply into, his own mind and that thus protected him, while, of course, in other emotional ways, it perhaps limited him. It is important to aver that Clara Schumann also used her music this way, as did Magritte his art. All three began to learn how to do this in childhood.

The three snapshots of creativity in childhood I have offered are presented in the hope that they may prove helpful as we consider the best ways to foster creativity in children today. They remind us of the need to allow risk-taking, the need for plenty of patience so as to allow mental processes to unfold, the need to cherish the role of pleasure in creative activity, mental and otherwise, the need for discipline, practice, and skill, and, finally, the need for a better understanding of the ways in which even devastating major trauma in childhood can serve as a spur for "creating in order to try to understand".

References

Bronson, P., & Merryman, A. (2010). The creativity crisis. *Daily Beast*, 10 July.

Bruner, J. S. (1987). *Making Sense: A Child's Construction of the World*. London: Methuen.

Feynman, R. (1985). *Surely You're Joking, Mr. Feynman! Adventures of a Curious Character*. New York: W. W. Norton.

Lattimore, R. (Trans.) (1969). *Aeschylus I: Oresteia*. Chicago, IL: University of Chicago Press.

May, F. (1912). *The Girlhood of Clara Schumann: Clara Wieck and her Time*. London: Edward Arnold.

Miller, A. (1979). *The Drama of the Gifted Child*, R. Ward (Trans.). New York: Basic Books.

Piaget, J. (1929). *The Child's Conception of the World*. London: Routledge & Kegan Paul.

Reich, N. B. (2001). *Clara Schumann: The Artist and the Woman*. Ithaca, NY: Cornell University Press.

Spitz, E. H. (1984). *Museums of the Mind: Magritte's Labyrinth and Other Essays*. New Haven, CT: Yale University Press.

Winnicott, D. W. (1965). Advising parents. In: *The Family and Individual Development* (pp. 114–120). New York: Basic Books.

Tell me a story —
creativity and storytelling:
the 2013 Creativity Seminar

"Tell me a story!" What parent has not heard this exuberant request, this happy insistence, this mournful plea, a thousand times? What parent's heart has not quickened at the thrill in those words or has not sunk as fatigue overtakes the adult even more than the child? Which of us has not relished entering into a good story, or wept at its heart-breaking moments, or felt the reassurance of a familiar ending before sending ourselves — or our children — off to that evening's dreams? Some researchers tell us that American creativity is declining, even as others report that childhood creativity is three times more important to lifetime creative achievement than childhood IQ. Might this wonderful invitation to "tell me a story" open a path towards understanding essential creative processes?

Perhaps creativity is critical to a child's development in other ways as well. Some data suggest that when a culture revives interest in its stories and language, collective health improves. Children naturally play out the emotional stories they are processing from family life. Eventually, how they tell each story, how it evolves, how it opens up with flexibility and resonance, is a measure of that child's accruing health. Even for adults, psychotherapy can be seen as an intimate — though, to be sure, embattled — request to "tell me *my* story, as I unconsciously tell it or live it out with you". In the Lacanian psycho-analytic tradition, analysts in training are actually authorised by the authenticity with which the story of their own analyses can be told.

The psychoanalyst Adam Phillips once remarked, "people are only ever as mad as other people are deaf" (1996, p. 34). The Austen Riggs Center, which is home to the Erikson Institute and the Creativity Seminar, can be seen as an archive of the stories that need to be told but were not previously able be heard, and, because not able to be heard, could not be told—except in symptoms, nightmares, and actions. From this angle, psychopathology is suppressed creativity, and psychological growth is about storytelling and story listening. But how do we enable this essential creative process? What might a child's "tell me a story" teach us about that process? Which stories work and which do not, and why? How does storytelling deepen our under-standing of creativity more broadly?

As this telling of the story of the Creativity Seminar comes to a close, the Seminar itself continues, and such are the questions we hope to take up a few months from now. Perhaps the tellings and listenings in this book have also addressed some of these questions, as we have moved back and forth—sometimes in playful leaps and sometimes risky jumps—between the work, the play, and the spirit that impels both creativity and psychoanalysis.

Reference

Phillips, A. (1996). *Terrors and Experts*. Cambridge, MA: Harvard University Press.

INDEX